Gay Fathers, Their Children, and the Making of Kinship

Gay Fathers, Their Children, and the Making of Kinship

Aaron Goodfellow

Fordham University Press | New York   2015

Fordham University Press has no responsibility for the persistence or accuracy of URLs for external or third-party Internet websites referred to in this publication and does not guarantee that any content on such websites is, or will remain, accurate or appropriate.

Fordham University Press also publishes its books in a variety of electronic formats. Some content that appears in print may not be available in electronic books.

Visit us online at www.fordhampress.com.

Library of Congress Cataloging-in-Publication Data

Goodfellow, Aaron.
   Gay fathers, their children, and the making of kinship / Aaron Goodfellow.
      pages cm
   Includes bibliographical references and index.
   ISBN 978-0-8232-6603-6 (hardback) — ISBN 978-0-8232-6604-3 (paper)
   1. Gay fathers. 2. Gay fathers—Family relationships. 3. Children of gay parents.
4. Parenting. I. Title.
   HQ76.13.G66 2015
   306.874′208664—dc23

                                                                    2015002956

Printed in the United States of America
17 16 15   5 4 3 2 1
First edition

Contents

Gay Fathers, Their Children, and the Making of Kinship

Introduction: Uncanny Kinship

From late 1999 to the beginning of 2002, I worked as an ethnographer with men who identify as gay and have formed families with children. I wanted to understand the different ways people build and maintain kinship and conceptualize family relations when the symbolic logic of heterosexual reproduction, the law, and biological notions of descent and affiliation are neither readily available nor immediately applicable to them. As I show in the pages that follow, the families of gay men are among the most important sites we can engage to understand how the law and biology are simultaneously made manifest in everyday relations and questioned in daily life. The families of gay men with children draw into sharp relief the skepticism that accompanies legal and biological regimes that foreground kinship in everyday life and relations.

My research took place in the urban centers, suburbs, small towns, and rural areas of Maryland, Massachusetts, New Hampshire, New Jersey, New York, Pennsylvania, Rhode Island, and Vermont, as well as in Washington, D.C. The arguments I develop in this book are based on the time I spent in the close company of thirty-two families and on the interviews and conversations I held with various professionals and the members of organizations, agencies, and institutions that either provide support for, facilitate, or work against the formation of queer families.

In this book, I explore the institutional and intimate landscapes across which the desire for kinship unfolds and the family lives of gay men with children take form. I understand the multiple sites—family residences, vacation homes, restaurants, cafés, churches, seminar rooms, public "pride" celebrations, private commitment ceremonies, and offices of adoption agencies, lawyers, advocates, state officials, and therapists—to operate as individual points that, together, suggest the features, however incomplete, of the larger assemblages that constitute the conditions of possibility for gay men to build families and live in kinship with children.

The picture of queer family life I present here is the result of my efforts to place the insights and experiences of my interlocutors in conversation with the broadly construed field of kinship studies within the discipline of anthropology. I am not concerned with whether gay men are fit to be parents. I neither address nor care to address whether same-sex couples should be allowed to legally form families. Rather, I focus on the challenges the lives of gay men with children pose and the opportunities they offer to anthropologists and other scholars interested in the kinds of family and kinship arrangements found in the United States today. What desires, ethics, forms of freedom and constraint, and regulatory apparatuses are at work in making and maintaining family and kinship at the beginning of the twenty-first century?

When setting out to define the parameters of my study, I had a very limited idea of the lives and relations that would become the subject and object of my study. I was neither unfamiliar with nor naive about the intricacies and complexities of queer kinship, but, like many, I had a sense that the increasingly public presence of gay men with children in the United States indicated something new and emergent. Looking back, I took it for granted that, in this country, queer families were challenging many of the established ideas informing the origins of kin relations (Butler 2002; Lewin 2009; Schneider 1997; Strathern 2005; Weston 1991). It seemed obvious to me that gay men who were building families and staking a claim to living in kinship with children displayed a clear commitment to the long-term diffuse forms of solidarity recognized to lie at the heart of Euro-American kinship (Fox 1983; Needham 1971; Schneider 1968), but in ways that were challenging the gendered divisions of labor and biological notions of being related that are thought to be central to making family and determining who counts as kin in the U.S. (Borneman 1996; Richman 2010; Schneider 1968, 1972, 1997; Weston 1991, 1999; Yanagisako & Collier 1994; Yanagisako & Delaney 1995). I believed, again, like many, that the capacity of gay men to form and live openly in family relations with children lay in changing ideas about accepted norms and, thus, the place of sexuality in citizenship and the wider political and public spheres (Povinelli 2002a, 2002b; Warner 2002). If homosexuality were no longer seen as inherently abnormal and abhorrent, and thus a threat to children, the idea of same-sex erotic relations as counterposed to family relations would eventually become obsolete. In this light, the increasingly public presence of queer families could be understood as the result of the loosening of state-based restrictions and the legal and institutional administration of sexuality in the family.

My preconceptions proved incorrect. I quickly had to incorporate into my thinking the fact that gay men have been living in family and kin arrangements that include children for as long as there have been gay men

(Newton 1995) and that, when building and maintaining family relations, gay men draw on and use the very biological, legal, and theological concepts often thought hostile to the emergence of viable queer forms of social life (Carrington 1999; Lewin 2009; Viefhues-Bailey 2010). The reliance on biological notions of kinship, religious images of fatherhood, and established legal definitions of the family by the men I came to know made it difficult, if not impossible, to determine what is new and emergent, as opposed to a reconfiguration or repetition, in the family lives and kinship of men with children.[1]

I argue that the difficulty of determining what is new or emergent in queer family relations resides in the ambiguous place of sex and sexuality in kinship and in the uncertainty that haunts paternity—even in the most normative settings—when being related is configured as biological. The difficulty of conclusively determining paternity and of settling questions concerning the relationship between kinship and sexuality is well known to anthropologists. In fact, one could argue that the very predicaments associated with determining the relationship between sex and kinship launched the discipline of anthropology. One need only recall the importance that such figures as Johann Jakob Bachofen, Henry James Sumner Maine, Lewis Henry Morgan, John Ferguson McLennan, and W. H. R. Rivers placed on knowledge of biological paternity in their early efforts to describe the evolutionary precedents of the Euro-American social order and formulate anthropology as a science (Kuper 1988; Povinelli 2002a, 2002b).

The long-standing uncertainty about the place of sex and sexuality in kinship makes it difficult to derive criteria that can be used to establish the family relations of gay men with children as a distinct and stable object of inquiry (Lewin 2009; Povinelli 2002a; Schneider 1997). This uncertainty calls for taking into consideration the alignments, alongside the disparities, between gay men and others who desire to build families that include children. Rather than focus on differences, it is perhaps more productive to think about how gay men's experiences of family and kinship overlap with the experiences of those whose families come into being through assisted reproductive technologies or those whose kin relations exist in tension with the law, such as recent or illegal immigrants, biracial couples, religious po-

---

[1] Kimberly Richman (2010) makes a similar claim when discussing the indeterminacy of such concepts as paternity and family in the law. Richman demonstrates that the transformations that have enabled same-sex families to gain increased legal standing and protection in the United States rests on legal responses to uncertainties about such things as the place of biology in the making of family for heterosexual couples.

lygamists, or those who espouse and live in accordance to "threatening" political ideologies. When similarity is taken into consideration alongside difference, the analytic frame shifts from questions concerning the effects of sexual identity—as if such a thing is ever clearly separable from notions of kinship—to the more general epistemological problem of coming to know how and if one is related to another as kin. By approaching the place of sexuality in kinship as an open question, as is common to many generations of anthropologists, I bring into view other, often overlooked, agencies at work in making kinship and family relations—such as pleasure, suffering, and participation in discursive formations (Asad 2003; Warner 2002). As I demonstrate ethnographically, the need to address the threat posed by uncertainty and skepticism to the creation and maintenance of kin relations configures the daily life of family and the meaning of kinship for the men with whom I worked. My interlocutors' words suggest that it is perhaps the need to consciously derive and fortify the meaning and existence of family, when the force of biological notions of relatedness continually threatens to turn one's family relations into fictions, that most powerfully distinguishes gay men's experience of family from that of heterosexual couples. William and David's experience demonstrates this need.

As will be seen, the manuscript moves through many sites where kinship is made and unmade. Each chapter focuses on the everyday experience of a single family or man as they perform the tasks necessary to build and maintain kin relations. My focus on the specificities found in individual lives to reveal more general movements within the social draws on a minor but established tradition in anthropology demonstrated in the work of such scholars as João Biehl (2005), Vincent Crapanzano (1980), Veena Das (2000), Robert Desjairlais (2003), Sidney Mintz (1960), and others. Each chapter addresses a specific aspect of making and living in kin relations for one or two people so as to illuminate the circumstances in and through which individual actors are constituted as subjects (Humphrey 2008). When read together, I hope, they provide a wider, but still partial view of the dispersed desires, sites and space, as well as the institutional operations that comprise the making of kinship for gay men with children.

William and David

I met William and David in the summer of 2000. They were sitting on the front porch of the apartment they rented in a large Victorian home located on the outskirts of a quaint village in central Vermont when I first saw them, taking turns cradling, rocking, and feeding their twin African American girls. My arrival interrupted a lively conversation about their future. As I was to learn, William and David were relatively new parents, having taken custody of the four-month-old twins at the time of their birth. The future had become an increasingly pressing and important topic of conversation since the children were placed in their care.

Two days before we met, William had returned from a job interview in Baton Rouge, Louisiana, and it looked as though he would be offered the position. While William was in Louisiana, David had approached his boss with the proposal that he continue working in his current capacity but as an independent contractor from home. He thought his boss had been amenable to the idea.

The couple was quite excited, and they eagerly began telling me that they were on the brink of achieving their idea of the perfect family life. After four years of hardship and struggle, it appeared they would finally be able to return to their home state of Louisiana and raise their children in close proximity to both their biological families. If William were offered the job in Louisiana, and if David could begin telecommuting to work, their dream would come true.

The hope William and David expressed for a shared future filled with happiness lay in sharp contrast to the sadness that had infused their previous intimate relationships. Together, and in separate conversations, they told me that, until meeting one another, they had imagined their desire for fatherhood to be foreclosed by their sexuality. They recalled in great detail the sorrow that had pervaded their earlier relationships—the result of what they saw as a conflict between their desire for a family life with children and their desire for exclusively intimate and erotic relations with men.

David attributed his sadness to a particular notion of homosociality that counterposes gay relationships to the reproductive future promised by bringing children into one's life. He said,

> There just aren't a lot of young gay men out there looking to get knocked up, and the younger you are the harder it is to find one. Most young gay men don't really want to think about the future of a relationship anyway, especially if that future includes kids. Maybe there are more men thinking about kids and families than you would first guess, but it's hard enough to find a relationship that works even marginally well when you're young and figuring out how to deal with yourself and your sexuality, let alone one that might be stable enough to include kids in the mix.

The sadness and melancholia that infused William's sexual relationships with both men and women prior to meeting David led him to believe his union with David was truly special, unique, and something to be deeply cherished and nurtured.

William had once been engaged to a woman. He felt compelled to end the engagement because of the pressures his sexual attraction to men exerted on the relationship. He described his reasons for ending it:

I was reasonably happy, or at least not deeply unhappy—just awkward, slightly uncomfortable, and feeling completely incompetent [when it came to having sex with a woman and planning for married life]. About a month before the ceremony, it just became too much. I realized I had to be a man, step up, and break things off. I had to be an adult and end things with my fiancée and get down to the messy business of coming out. I wanted to prevent the big disaster I knew we were headed for if I didn't do anything. It was really the first step I had to take in changing my life. Wow, it was hard, but I had to tell her, "Look, I love you, I love being with you and everything we've done, but I can't be with you in the ways you need me to be because I like men." It was unbelievably hard, but the idea of asking the woman I was engaged to—the woman who was planning on having my children—to be second in my sex life with men just wasn't fair. She kind of knew about my thing for men. We had talked about it a couple of times—joked about it, even—but we did what most people do and buried our heads. We just plowed on as if it didn't really matter, or was something we could deal with later—as if there is a right time for such a thing, ever. But the pressure got to be too much, and I did what I knew deep down I had to do, or at least what seemed less wrong, and I called the whole thing off. When I think about it, I still get really sad—depressed even. I still miss her at times and I wish things didn't have to go the way they did. I mostly wish I hadn't dragged her through what I did, but in the end it really was the right thing to do, no matter the pain. But, you know, one of the hardest things for me to let go of, and one of the things that kept me in the relationship longer then I should have stayed, was imagining myself as a father. Here I was with this beautiful woman who was planning on having my children, happily, and I had to let it go. I could have easily gotten married and become a father that way, but I had to let that whole idea go along with the marriage. That was one of the toughest things I had to face when I was coming out, letting go of that image I had of myself as a father next to my beautiful wife, and me as a good upright family man.

David, unlike William, had always been exclusively involved with men, and he described his sadness prior to meeting William as related to his partners' surprise that he would want to bring children into a homosexual relationship and their feeling that such a desire was a little odd.

> I was sad, but not generally. I would just get sad, but it was the type of sad that comes on when you realize a relationship just isn't working out. You say to yourself, "Well, now I know where I can and can't go with this person, and it's time to move on. Time to have something different." When you're young you really wish you could just have everything right away, but when you want kids, you have to be patient and do some thinking and planning. At a certain point you have to make it a priority or it will never happen. It's not like there is ever a right time to do it, but there are certainly times that are more wrong then others. And, I was finding myself in the wrong situations more and more often. "So, we've been together for a while now, and you don't want kids? You think it's weird and strange that I do? Well, okay. You and this relationship are no longer my priority." That's the way it would work. Almost like natural selection.

William and David's words illuminate how kinship fits alongside other forms of relating and how the desire for kinship with children forecloses certain forms of being in relationship while opening the possibility of others. How modes of relating become foreclosed, and are even mourned, when the desire for kinship and a family life with children asserts itself demonstrates how queer family life is partially incommensurate both with accepted notions of gay sociality and with idealized figurations of heterosexual kinship. In William's and David's descriptions of the sadness they endured for the sake of forming a family with children, we hear about the cost of kinship and family life and about how the actions of two sexually involved men, each pursuing the desire for a family with children, rendered neither heterosexual kinship nor more commonly imagined ideas about queer sociality illegible. Rather, their stories convey the image of fatherhood and the desire for a life with children as objects on a horizon toward which some relations are capable of moving and others are not. Questioning what futures are available to certain relationships and what futures are not does not necessarily bring a relationship to an end. Rather, it brings the issue of the capacity of different types of relations to endure such things as dependency into discussion (Povinelli 2006). When these ideas are brought into focus, the idea that kinship and its form might be a matter of choice evaporates.

When William and David discovered they shared the desire to have children, and to live in a future framed by the needs of caring for children, each felt as though he had found something "rare and precious" in the other and that he could not live without the other. They revealed their mutual desire for kids and a family life on their first date. A month later, William was planning to move from New Orleans, where the two then lived, to Vermont. He had accepted a job at a prestigious research hospital and was relocating to take up the position. William said he impulsively invited David to join him, even though they had only known each other for a few weeks, and he was immensely relieved when David jumped at the offer. When I met the pair, they had been living together for four years, and the only hurdle that seemed to remain between them and their dream of family was packing their belongings and driving to Louisiana with the twins.

Familiar Movements

The move to Louisiana was essential to William and David's vision of family life. Both felt that living in close proximity to their extended biological families was crucial if they were to properly raise and provide for their kids. They had each grown up in rural Louisiana, and their parents and siblings still lived in the areas where they had been raised. For William and David, living close to family would allow their children a type of immersion in kinship that helps create a strong sense of belonging in the world of civil society. William and David thought society's future was jeopardized by children who grew into adulthood without being properly cared for, and that kin were the central actors who should provide that care. In other words, William and David felt compelled to move because building caring family relations entailed immersion in extended family networks—as defined by blood and law. To be good fathers, and to raise children who would one day become responsible citizens, meant living in Louisiana.

William and David certainly had access to other visions of family and other versions of living in kinship. Two year before adopting the twins, they had performed an informal commitment ceremony that was presided over by the minister of the Congregationalist church they attended. The ceremony had been witnessed by their families, friends, and fellow parishioners, and, afterward, on their honeymoon in Hawaii, the couple had had matching tattoos inked into the skin on their left calves to signify and display the lifelong commitment they had made to each other. The tattoo was an interpretive design built around the fleur-de-lis, and they conceived it as a type of family crest that symbolized their common Cajun ancestry, the family they had made together, and the future life they hoped to build and to pass on to their children. In 1999, when Vermont passed legislation recognizing same-sex civil unions, William and David had their previous informal commitment legalized.

It is important to note that the legalization of same-sex unions and same-sex marriage does not provide a stable footing for the kinship of gay men with children. As quickly as legislation is passed to legalize same-sex unions, it is challenged and often over turned. The continuing contest over the legalization of same-sex marriage demonstrates how homophobia persists in the arena of kinship and family, perhaps being underwritten by these very figurations, and the different ways politics, professional resources, and collective affects continue to make claims on the construction of kinship. While William and David, as well as the other men with whom I worked, were attempting to project themselves into a stable future defined by normative configurations of kinship, the meaning and status of gay kinship in the present from which these projections were being articulated was indeterminate.

Suffering as Method

When William and David recounted the details of their experience of becoming fathers through adoption, they provided a more complicated explanation for their decision to return to Louisiana. In their more extended narrative, the move emerged as a response to an emotionally difficult and challenging series of events and as an opportunity to heal injuries they had suffered from a succession of punishing institutional encounters experienced during their efforts to become parents. In the more extended narrative, the company of biological relatives held the promise of healing very deep wounds of the kind suffered by many who enter into the adoption market. William told me that attending to the trauma they suffered was crucial, since he and David imagined their children's future to depend on it. And, if they knowingly put their children's future at stake, they would be unable to imagine themselves as good parents.

The appearance of the word *trauma* in William and David's narrative is not casual. Rather, the word indexes both William's professional training as a clinical psychologist and the more general place of clinical discourses, such as psychoanalysis and clinical psychology, in U.S. notions of family. The ease with which the vocabulary of the psychological sciences and clinical concepts are utilized and applied in the description of family relations in the United States, and graphed to their meaning, registers the ways medical and other institutional knowledges are folded into, and become the terms of, the intimacy built by gay men with children (Biehl et al. 2001; Chatterji, Chattoo, & Das 1998). The intimacy of family relations positions clinical knowledge and therapeutic discourses, as well as suffering, as constitutive of kinship and its making (Asad 2003; Povinelli 2006). I have tried to elaborate the ways clinical and legal discourses circulate in and through kinship since these discourses, in many ways, have become the material of relatedness itself and the modality of subjectification born of desiring to live in familial relations (Foucault 1978, 1997).

William and David began their journey to parenthood two years before we met. They initially contacted an adoption agency in New York City that was nationally known for placing children, both foreign-born and not, in the homes of lesbian and gay families. For a year everything proceeded smoothly, and William and David thought they would become fathers without the usual delays and distress endured by many prospective adoptive parents, both gay and straight. They believed the ease with which the adoption was taking place was attributable to the advice they had received from a highly regarded lawyer, who had urged them to conduct a single-parent international adoption. William and David had initially expressed the desire to adopt a U.S.-born child who possessed physical features similar to one of them. Their lawyer told them it was nearly impossible for prospective parents, especially gay men, to be selective when adopting, and that the "next best thing" was to adopt a child from either Russia or one of the former Soviet-bloc countries. The lawyer implied that a child born in Russia or Eastern Europe "would most likely have northern European physical features," that is, would be white and, thus, would generally appear physically similar to both William and David.

David recounted how the lawyer had strongly advised against a domestic adoption, drawing on his expert knowledge and professional experience to convince them that the most expeditious way for same-sex couples to bring a child into their lives was by not being overly discerning about the child's physical appearance. To be selective was to risk being selected against by the placing agencies. The lawyer also advised that either David or William enter the international adoption market as a single prospective parent, to avoid any institutional chauvinism that might exist toward gay men outside the United States. In this way, the question of the couple's sexuality could be sidestepped when the decision was made to place a child in their care.

After William or David had successfully adopted a child, a second parent adoption would be performed and the family made complete. The couple decided William should begin the adoption proceedings, because he could more easily show long-term financial stability. Once the adoption was finalized—meaning William had completed the mandatory probation period and his parental status was formalized by the state of Vermont—David would then adopt William's child and become the child's second parent. Upon completion of the second-parent adoption, David would hold the same legal relationship to the child that William did. The couple followed the lawyer's counsel and did their best to shield William's homosexuality from the eyes of adoption officials in Russia.

The arrangement William and David made would not result in their own relationship becoming legally recognized and sponsored by the state, as would have been the case had they adopted a child jointly as an openly gay couple or been married. Rather, William and David would be independently bound to a common child and individually obliged to protect the child's best interests; they would not be bound to each other and their relation would not be recognized or sanctioned by the state. At the time, civil unions were not yet available in Vermont, and gay marriage was not yet legal anywhere, but children were routinely being placed in the care of same-sex couples by U.S. adoption agencies, including those in Vermont.

By refusing to acknowledge William and David as a couple, the law solidified the existence of "actual" relationships of descent, outside the virtual relationships created by its own operations. The existence, in the eyes of the state, of actual life-giving family relationships distinct from the one lived by William and David with their children indexed commitments to cultural models that configure adoptive families as imperfect or as potentially problematic and, thus, in need of constant monitoring, even though the state is perfectly aware of the heterosexual nuclear family's capacity to fail (Richman 2010). As Jacques Donzelot (1979) has argued, it is precisely because the adoptive family is always viewed as an imperfect solution to the state's own recognized failure to provide for its citizens that adoptive families come to be continually policed.

The indeterminate status of same-sex couples in the eyes of the law should not be seen as a failure on the part of the state to organize social relationships, nor should it be seen as indicating a limit to the law's ability to regulate the social field. Rather, I believe such indeterminacy should be viewed as productive of a type of citizenship characterized by the presence of administrative institutions and institutional figures in daily life (Das & Poole 2004; Richman 2010). The continuous monitoring of the relationships in same-sex families by officers of the court and members of the therapeutic "helping professions" indexes the web of juridical and legal power that enables such a form of citizenship to emerge (Foucault 1978, 2009). Tracing the presence and inclusion of lawyers and therapists in the family provides insight into the use of the law as a reproductive technology, just as it challenges commonly held assumptions about the precultural operation of anatomical bodies in the creation of recognizable forms of life, relationships, and citizens (Das 2006; Franklin & McKinnon 2001; Leach 1966a). Ethnographic detail allows one to trace the intricate networks and webs of affect born through the interweaving of legal and therapeutic discourses into the process of making kin.

Russia

The events precipitating the move to Louisiana began after William had completed the legal work necessary to bring a Russian infant into the United States and after he had traveled twice to an orphanage in Russia—trips that entailed accumulating significant amounts of debt. While in Russia, William had attended parenting classes and spent supervised time holding and feeding the baby boy he was led to believe would one day become his son.

On his third trip to Russia, when he believed he would be returning home with "his baby boy," things took an unexpected turn. Over a period of ten days, William slowly came to realize that the adoption was not going to take place. Through the course of the trip, he was denied access to "his" child for increasing periods. After ten days, William was no longer allowed to see, let alone feed or hold, "his" son. All access had been cut off.

In response, William attempted to enlist the services of his lawyer, who contacted Russian adoption officials and eventually the U.S. consulate but to no avail. Adoption is not a right before the law, and the subjective nature of the judicial decisions ending in an adoption are very well known (Richman 2010), so William had no legal grounds on which to pressure Russian or U.S. officials. After three frustrating weeks, he returned to Vermont heartbroken, having received no adequate explanation for what had happened and having been unable to say goodbye to the baby.

A framed photograph of the infant in a red hat, blue pajamas, and pink swaddling cloth sat on William and David's mantelpiece, marking his absence—and continued presence—in the family's life. For both William and David, the picture was a reminder of a relationship that could have been but was lost, and it marked the grief, mourning, anger, and pain they had come to associate with what they called a "legal miscarriage." It was the pain brought about by the law and its miscarriages that the couple hoped to contain by moving to Louisiana.

William and David initiated a lawsuit against the lawyer they had consulted and contacted a second adoption agency shortly after William returned from Russia. The second agency insisted that they work together as a couple and that they give preferential treatment to children born in the United States. Eight months after filling out the paperwork, undergoing a second home study, and putting together their "home book," William and David drove to a small town in central Pennsylvania during a snowstorm to attend the birth of the twin African American girls who are now their daughters.[2]   UNCERTAINTY

William and David believed the events they endured to become parents instilled in them a sense that their status as fathers was uncertain and somewhat uncanny. They repeatedly told me that they found themselves startled when confronted by their own image as fathers and that neither felt as though their daily life reflected an assured or known set of relations (Freud 1919; Cavell 1994). The "uncanniness" that accompanied William and David's sense of themselves as fathers speaks to a wider experience of family formation and its meaning for many who chose to adopt where the condition of being related often entails enduring repeated episodes of violence that take place within the law and established institutional procedure.

It is very tempting to configure William and David's treatment at the hands of the lawyer and the adoption officials in Russia as exceptional—as based on the discovery of the facts of William's sexuality. Yet, William and David shied away from such a conclusion. Instead, they seemed to favor uncertainty and indeterminacy over certainty and determinacy when trying to establish the place of sexuality in their experience of becoming parents and the trauma they suffered. Their concern was not with the suffering inflicted on gay men and their families by a chauvinist society but with the different, often unintended, ways the law and other institutions inflict pain on those who wish to bring children into their lives through adoption. William and David acknowledged the pain they suffered as partly responsible for the significance they attributed to their biological kin ties, and they were deeply concerned about how their own experiences might deform their children's futures and their ideal image of family relations.

In William and David's narrative, we hear how the future subjectivity of the child causes parents a great deal of anxiety. Both men were concerned that the pain they experienced while becoming parents could take hold and come to life in their children. The idea and possibility that their own pain might take root and shape their children's future disrupted their imaginations of themselves as good parents. For William and David, there was no easy correlation between the pain they suffered while trying to adopt and

---

[2] A "home book" is a small book assembled by prospective parents to describe their life and relationship to women who are placing their children up for adoption. It generally comprises a short narrative about the prospective parent's life and a series of photographs documenting how and where a child will come to live.

their sexuality. In fact, they remained deeply uncertain as to the place, if any, of their homosexuality in the ordeal. After a significant amount of research, William and David believed the Russian adoption officials remained unaware of William's sexuality. The explanation they more readily offered to me and to others attributed "the miscarriage" to their having worked with a bad lawyer and to their own failure to seriously consider other possibilities when choosing the best course to adoption.

William and David's story stands in contrast to scholarly analyses that express concern over the place of trauma in the emergence of queer forms of sociality (Butler 1993; Sedgwick 1993; Weston 1999). Scholars have examined the violent ways in which gender norms and forms of power greet the appearance of homosexuality within the nuclear family (Butler 2000; Sullivan 2004). In these analyses, the injuries caused by violently rendering homosexuality as abject within the family are understood to stunt the emergence of viable queer forms of life (Borneman 1997, 2013). Scholars have argued that viable queer forms of subjectivity are unable to emerge and to flourish because of the exceptional pain and suffering inflicted through kinship norms themselves on those who seek to live under the sign "gay" (Butler 2000; Sedgwick 1993; Sullivan 2004). Others have argued that knowingly subjecting children to this violence of kinship justifies preventing queer subjects from engaging in family life with children (Lerner & Nagai 2001).

For William and David, it was not just possible but also likely that the emotional injuries they suffered during the adoption process would come to limit their ability to nurture the development and satisfy the needs of their twins. The move to Louisiana was an effort to contain the past and prevent these injuries from overwhelming their children's future. For both William and David, the most appropriate and appealing way of attending to this task was to seek out care from and to share their experience of having suffered with the members of their extended biological families, or those whom they shared a "mutuality of being," to quote the recent work of Sahlins (2014). David summarized their thoughts:

> It would be terrible if Eudora and Eulalie were not able to be all that they might be because of the crap we went through. Once in Louisiana, we can put all the mess [from the past] behind us, and not worry that the girls' future will be mucked up by all our pain. Of course we're pissed off at the lawyer and the people in New York, so a little more distance isn't going to hurt. And, of course the kids are going to need therapy, God knows everybody ends up on the couch at some point in their life—at least they should—but this way it might not be for life.

When William and David expressed the need to protect their children's future from the legacy of their own suffering, they embraced a modern notion of memory in which the symptoms of past injuries can be passed from one generation to the next through the unconscious communication of pain (Bersani 1996; Laplanche & Mehlman 1976; Leys 2000). The idea that William and David's past suffering could stunt their children's developing and future subjectivity is informed by psychological discourses and the practice of viewing one's daily life through the lens provided by psychoanalysis and public notions of trauma (Fassin, Rechtman, & Gomme 2009; Leys 2000). Discourses of trauma could be said to pervade William and David's relationship, because each had training in the psychological sciences and William worked as a clinical social worker.

The professional knowledge held by William and David provided each with a theoretical apparatus for articulating the ways queer forms of sociality and queer forms of identity are stigmatized. This same professional knowledge participates in wider cultural circulations in which the "poison" associated with stigma and the capacity of the stigmatized to spoil the identity of others, particularly those in close association gains salience (Goffman 1963). It is often argued that the communicability of stigma and its pains demonstrates the inability of gay men to effectively care for and raise children, since protecting the best interest of a child does not include knowingly and actively causing that child to suffer (Richman 2013).

William and David's experience demonstrates how kinship, the law, and suffering are always already woven into family relations in ways that configure pain as a modality that brings relationships into being, whether queer or straight. When the place of pain in the making of kin relations is considered, suffering can no longer be seen as an external force or exceptional influence that might be eliminated from family relations through something like the application of clinical procedure or alterations in the law and institutional process (Asad 2003; Das 2000).

William and David undertook the move to Louisiana partly in the hope that their suffering could be shared, collectively remembered, and thus domesticated through its absorption into an ongoing and larger set of caring relations. The desire to domesticate their pain by sharing it with family members, and thereby turn its agency toward relationship building, as opposed to corruption and negation, reflects cultural ideals about what constitutes appropriate and inappropriate forms of remembering and about those with whom pain can be shared in an effort to find relief (Carsten 2007; Das 2000). For William and David, the biological nuclear family was a site of confession, and thus of self-formation, where the revelation of truth about the self was offered as the basis both for healing the injuries inflicted by an impersonal public sphere and for building an ideal image of caring paternal relations (Carsten 2000b).

In the context of James Faubion's (2001a) discussion of ethics and kinship, William and David's experience demonstrates how the desire for an idealized form of kinship, and the effort extended to make paternal relations, simultaneously limits the possibility of the self to be in relation with others and enables the self to cultivate and explore different forms of relating. It is the freedom of reflexivity, the freedom to work on the self and undergo the necessary pedagogical training to become a certain kind of subject, that establishes William and David's efforts to build paternal relations and to live in kinship with children as an ethical concern.

As the move to Louisiana indicates, the ethical concerns informing William and David's pursuit of paternity were not about cultivating a set of practices or acquiring a necessary set of skills so as to become expert at completing the tasks associated with being a good parent. William and David did not imagine becoming a father, and raising children, especially in the case of adoption, as a purely mechanical and instrumental process. Rather, they teach us that becoming a father, or pursuing kinship, entails reflection and training to become a certain type of ethical subject. Because it is necessary to undertake an educative process, or to undergo training, when becoming a father, paternity might best be understood as a type of *doing* as opposed to acquiring a practical set of skills or set of legally backed credentials.

As a form of doing, paternity involves performance and, thus, engaging in a poesis of self-making (Faubion 2001b). And, as Michel Foucault (1997) reminds us, cultivating such a relation to self and to others is an ethical action, and working through and performing the training necessary to become a specific type of ethical subject has little or nothing to do with choice. Rather, it implies coming to embody and to exercise the forms of freedom and constraint that Foucault names "governmentality." Foucault makes this clear when he describes governmentality as a concept that covers "the relationship of the self to itself" and as "the whole range of practices that constitute, define, organize, and instrumentalize the strategies that individuals in their freedom can use in dealing with each other" (1997:300). William and David experienced such freedom and constraint as they learned to come to terms with themselves and with others as parents.

The "Uncanniness" of Paternity

William and David's story shows that the meaning of being a relative, or a member of a sexual community, is neither pregiven nor preformed. For

William and David, being a relative entailed taking part in the mimetic performance of a cultural ideal in which the relation is understood as a continual form of becoming that is inseparable from the contingency of the events defining everyday life (Deleuze 1987; Connolly 2010). They advanced a performative notion of the family, in which an image—in their case, the ideal father—was brought to life in the subject through conscious and unconscious movements, gestures, and forms of emulation. The mimetic and performative aspect of making kinship and family challenges the idea that kinship can be understood exclusively through the symbols or grammatical arrangement of categories, as David Schneider claimed of American kinship in 1968 and of queer kinship specifically in 1997. When being a father is thought of in terms of becoming, and as an ethical form and a performance, paternity, sexuality, and the relationship between the two can never be definitively known. Rather, each is achieved temporarily through the flows and vicissitudes of daily life and the active work of projecting one's self and one's relations into the future, or striving to transfigure the virtual into the actual.

The need to expand our thinking about queer forms of kinship rests on the growing awareness of the performative force of kin terms within emerging biosocial forms of modernity (Butler 1993; Franklin 2013; Franklin & McKinnon 2001; Haraway 1991). Just as the law, technology, and biology must be considered to understand the actors responsible for making kinship, the circulation of images and the capacity of words to bring about (or to undo) relationships cannot be separated from the experience of belonging in family (Borneman 2013; Povinelli 2006).

The importance of images and their circulation was reflected in William and David's desire to move to Louisiana. They did not have to live in close proximity to their extended biological families to be fathers. It would be more accurate to say that they did not wish to produce or participate in an image of fatherhood that did not include close proximity and full immersion in the lives of their extended biological kin. Working through the uncertainty associated with building a family life without the support that comes from close relations with one's biological kin would have been an emotional and intellectual strain for William and David, one they wanted to avoid.

William and David's sense that they might not actually be fathers unless they overtly participated in known family arrangements is congruent with the perspective of the state. At the time of our conversations, they had yet to complete the probationary period mandated by the state of Vermont before a person's status as a parent is made permanent. The state's ultimate

decision would be based on a clinical social worker's evaluation of the relationships William and David were forming with their children and the
material care they were providing them. The social worker's decision would
draw on the objective criteria found in clinical and legal discourses to determine how closely William and David's family relations were aligned with
state-sanctioned images of paternity. In this context, William and David's
feeling that they were not truly fathers is understandable.

Yet the uncertainty the two men experienced exceeded the legal standing of their paternity, flooding their sense of self. The uncertainty William
and David experienced indexes cultural notions about the biological family
and ideas about similarity and difference that enable certain relationships
to be recognized as familial and others not (Howell & Marre 2006; Povinelli
2006). William and David's haunting suspicion that they were not truly fathers resided partly in the capacity of another's gaze to void one's own sense
of being a relative. Not only did others mark William and David as racially
different from their children, which meant the true biological parents of
the children existed elsewhere, but, in addition, two men together caring
for children did not necessarily register as a family in the eyes of others.
It is the potential for such (mis)recognition that speaks to the capacity of
biological kinship to undo other state-sanctioned forms of relatedness by
stripping the subjective and legal meaning of family relations away from
the subject of kinship itself.

David revealed the terrains across which such skepticism could and
did travel when he recounted the following experience: He and William
were sitting in their car waiting for a traffic light to change a couple of
months after the twins arrived. In the car next to them was a woman with
a child roughly the same age as the twins. David exchanged glances with
the woman, and the two mutually acknowledged and silently admired each
other's children. The encounter initially left him feeling proud, but then a
profound sense of disbelief and anxiety overwhelmed him. For David, ex-
changing glances with the woman called his status as a parent into question,
and the sensation proved so powerful that he was temporarily paralyzed
by emotion. When the light turned green, he pulled to the side of the road,
got out of the car, opened the back door, and stared at the two sleeping little
girls in their car seats until he felt reassured that his family life was neither
fraudulent or a mirage. David described the scene:

> After pulling away from the intersection, I had to stop and stare and stare and
> stare until all my nerves calmed down and my senses returned. I just couldn't
> believe these two little girls were really mine, and that we really were fathers.

It took a long time for me to figure out it really wasn't all a dream, and that I wasn't some fraud trying to pass myself off as a father, and that that woman looking at me could see that we were dads. That woman probably just looked into our car and didn't even question whether or not we were a family, even though it was two gay white men with two black baby girls in the back of a jeep. All she probably saw was a family, and smiled. Maybe all she saw was me and didn't even notice William, or she saw William and didn't notice me—who knows? What I do know is she didn't even react. She didn't seem to question anything, but it sure threw me for a loop. Who knows what she was thinking and seeing, but it really rattled my bones. William freaked out and kind of fell apart as well. He had no idea what was going on, or why I was crying, but when I finally tried to explain he burst into tears as well. So there we were on the side of the road, crying and crying, but crying together as a family.

EPISODE OF UNCERTAINTY

Sigmund Freud famously linked the uncanny to eyesight and to the possibility of being robbed of the ability to see, which he argues is a substitute for the dread of castration (Freud 1919). Freud goes on to say that visual stimulation instantiates intellectual uncertainty as to an object being animate or not, or the feeling that an inanimate object is too lifelike, which awakens the sense of the uncanny. The uncertainty surrounding animate (living and life) and inanimate (mechanical and dead) objects has its origins in the child's primary narcissism and the child's projection of multiple selves into the world. The subject attempts to preserve against extinction and achieve immortality by splitting or "doubling" and bringing inanimate objects to life. Examples include children projecting life into their dolls and stuffed animals or the animism projected on the world by "primitives". The "double," which carries the traces of the psyche's futile repetitive efforts to preserve against demise (life's own repetition, death), transforms from "an assurance of immortality" "to a ghastly harbinger of death" after the primary narcissism of the child has been worked through (Freud 1919:235). Encountering the double is "uncanny" because it tests the material reality of a phenomenon while expressing and reactivating the most primitive aspects of mind. Freud describes this aspect of mind in "Beyond the Pleasure Principle" as superseding the pleasure principle and orienting the organism towards its own demise (Freud 1922).

Stanley Cavell (1994) takes Freud to task for his insistent denial that the uncanny concerns the distinction between the animate and the inanimate, arguing that Freud overstates his claim about the fear of castration and unresolved aspects of the Oedipal complex giving rise to the uncanny.

According to Cavell, by Freud's own logic it is only after the resolution of the Oedipal complex under the threat of castration that one can make a clear distinction between the animate and inanimate, or see "others as other, know and acknowledge their (separate, animate, opposed) human existence" (Cavell 1994:87). Cavell proposes that the capacity to see others as other, or to distinguish the animate from the inanimate, is thus a gift (or curse) of the father, and that the issue of the uncanny is one of distinguishing difference, say between the waking world and dreams or between natural and mechanical things. It is the inability to arrive at criteria establishing the features in which such difference exists and the pressing need to decide, if one is to go on living, that founds vision as a form of death-dealing skepticism. It is the horrifying capacity of the world to vanish all at once with the thought that one might be dreaming, or the horror of seeing the self and other in their unremarkable ordinariness, and thus instantaneously loosing the distinction between the animate (composed of flesh and blood, separate, alive) and inanimate (automaton performing life's repetitions, dead), that defines the uncanny for Cavell (Cavell 1994:101).

It is Cavell's sense of the uncanny as "a difference in which everything and nothing differs," a condition born from the inability to discern and distinguish the inanimate machine-like repetitions of daily life from the animate creative and improvisational aspects of living, that I feel best characterizes uncanniness of paternity described by the men with whom I worked. I offer Cavell's reworking of Freud's original description of the uncanny to step out of the diagnostic logic of psychoanalysis which risks reducing the experience of the men with whom I worked, as well as my own, to unresolved aspects of the oedipal complex and the fear of castration. Through Cavell I hope to retain the philosophical insights offered by both Freud's work and that of my interlocutors to the ethnographic encounter.

William saw the episode as emblematic of his and David's overall sense of the simultaneous frailty and strength of the kinship they were creating and of the symptoms born of their encounters with the law and its institutions. From this incident, we learn how the subjective and legal meaning of one's kinship can be abducted by the gaze of another. For William and David, the multiple meanings, possible interpretations, and suspicions about the existence of a kin relation collided when, as a couple, they became the object of another's gaze. The collision dissolved the subjective and legal formulations of their kin relations until their sense of paternity was reconstituted by time and shared tears. That the meaning of one's kinship can be dissolved by the gaze of another indicates how living in viable family relations entails formulating ways to address one's own and others' skepticism while it also begs questions concerning the different ways kinship operates to make the subject and subjectivity legible or illegible and even incommensurate.

The Power of Intimacy

Western political discourse configures participation in kinship and the family as central to membership in society and to citizenship (Donzelot 1997; Elshtain 1982; Giddens 1992; Hobbes 1998 [1651]; Locke 1982 [1690]; Rousseau 2002 [1762]). As with all adoptive parents, William and David were granted access to the state's sponsored forms of belonging by actively constructing family relationships that mirror those forms (Borneman 2013; Butler 2002; Lewin 2009). As a result, the overtly subversive implications of two gay men forming a family with children become complicit in the silent operations of power that infuse the family in Western liberal democracy (Butler 2005; Chambers 2009; Donzelot 1979). In exchange for bringing state-sponsored forms of sociality to life, William and David were able to stake a claim to living a normal family life.

William and David's pursuit of happiness was transformed into a political engagement with the continuing efforts of conservatives to (re)define family as the exclusive domain of heterosexual couples (Butler 2004, 2006; Richman 2010; Viefhues-Bailey 2010). The continuing legacy of the HIV/AIDS epidemic and the ongoing politically motivated attempt to establish the origins of family relations and human life at the moment of biological conception position life and death at the center of kinship (Borneman 1996; Franklin & Roberts 2006; Franklin 2013; Haraway 2003; Harding 1986). The close relationship between life, death, and kinship was reiterated by many of the men with whom I worked when they traced links between commitments to family relations and children and surviving the initial onslaught of the HIV/AIDS epidemic. For instance, David made the relationship between family and survival strikingly clear when he speculated that he "would ... most likely have moved to California, contracted HIV, and died, like so many of my friends, if I had not met William." Here, the imagination of kinship and the future it provides posits a type of immortality that recapitulates many normative notions about the social and its means of reproduction through heterosexual sex and biological notions of kinship (Marx 1906; Engels 1942; Pateman 1988; Rosaldo 1980; Stacy & Thorne 1985; Strathern 1987)

The imagination of paternity as holding power over life, the power to "make live," positions family life as an always already political form of living (Agamben 2000; Borneman 1996; Das 2006; Foucault 1978; Hobbes 1998

[1651]; Pateman 1988). We can understand the politics of family as being actualized in U.S. public policy, in which the family is envisioned as the primary vehicle for transforming the subject into a citizen and, thus, giving an embodied life to the wider political culture (Carp 2000; Das 2006; Legendre 1997). Forming a family with children, then, is not a simple matter of finding and founding intimacy, either for heterosexual couples or for gay men.

The public controversy over the figure of the gay father, in the absence of empirical research into what it means to be both gay and a father, resonates with the deeply seated contest over the place of paternity in contemporary society. The contest is well known to political philosophers, anthropologists, and historians of liberalism, among whom debates over the figure of the father and his place in maintaining the social order are not only long-standing but also seen as crucial to the emergence of contemporary representative forms of governance (Elshtain 1982; Kuper 1988; Maine 1861; McLennan 1885; Mehta 1999; Morgan 1870; Pateman 1988; Tylor 1889). I am not suggesting that the entire history of Western liberal philosophy or anthropology has been a long debate over the meaning of paternity and kinship, but, in Western political thought, the need to secure the meaning of paternity and thus the figure of paternal authority is seen as essential to determining the future of the social order itself (Donzelot 1979; Foucault 1978; Hegel 2008; Hobbes 1998 [1651]; Kant 2002 [1821]; Locke 1982 [1690]). The Defense of Marriage Act signed into law by Bill Clinton in 1996 and recent efforts by the state of California, Michigan, Utah, Virginia, and other states to overturn the right of same-sex couples to marry illustrates the political sense that the heterosexual nuclear family is fragile, indeterminate, and in need of legal defense if the social order is to be maintained.

It is difficult to imagine the men I worked with as posing a threat to civil society and the social order. Virtually every family I came to know embraced the ideals associated with bourgeois imaginations of the nuclear family and its value as the primary site for building responsible citizens and securing the future of civil society. In fact, many described how building and strengthening family bonds were crucial to healing the larger ills of a needlessly divided—whether along sexual, ethnic, or racial lines—and, thus, violent society. At the same time, the men with whom I worked were acutely aware that their family relationships were viewed with skepticism because of their perceived difference. Such skepticism, which challenges the existence and quality of paternal relationships that do not arise through heterosexual reproduction, makes gay fathers vulnerable to social forms of regulation that are not experienced by others (Donzelot 1979; Povinelli 2002b, 2006).

The Law and Ambiguity

When William and David decided to follow the advice of their second law-yer, they knew it was perfectly legal for same-sex couples to adopt children in the state of Vermont and that their relationship was sanctioned by the state and the community in which they were living. Their decision reflects the conflicting and often ambivalent attitude gay men display toward the state's involvement in their lives, particularly when men wish to become parents or kin (Borneman 2013). The ambivalence points to the need to think about legitimacy and how one comes to know if, in fact, one is a parent within a legal environment that is unpredictable and hostile but simultaneously holds the promise of happiness and, thus, offers hope. The majority of scholarship devoted to understanding homosexuality and queer forms of sociality has concentrated on difference and the need to protect, respect, and value the presence of diverse sexualities within and across public and private spheres. Yet, when listening to William and David, we learn how assimilation and recognition do not always provide protection against societal violence.

U.S. adoption laws vary widely from state to state, and prominent gay advocacy groups describe the legal environment in which gay adoption takes place as being in continual flux and a state of indeterminacy due to the subjective nature of the judicial process that brings adoptive families into being (Richman 2010, 2013). The sense of the law as yielding uncertain outcomes creates an environment in which even legally recognized relation-ships are experienced as precarious (Richman 2010). The sense of the law as unpredictable, and as placing the families it creates on an uncertain footing, makes the original path to parenthood chosen by William and David as appealing as it was sensible. Single-parent international adoption seems to provide a means of sidestepping questions currently being debated in the United States concerning the appropriate place of sex and sexuality in the family and the place of sex in citizenship. Lesbian women and gay men who wish to bring children into their lives through adoption often feel that by stepping outside the regulatory environment of U.S. adoption agencies, they can avoid the question of sexuality in the making of family or postpone it until after a child has been placed in their care. We might think of William and David's efforts to work through an international adoption agency as a freedom exercised within the known constraints of the law, which simulta-neously restricts access to family relations while establishing the conditions of possibility for building and maintaining kinship.

The overarching sense that the law is unpredictable reflects its differen-tial operation across different bodies and relations, and the variable way it

→

establishes the milieu in which all family relations are lived and come to be experienced (Legendre 1997). It is the presence of the law in relationships, and the ways it simultaneously inflicts pain while holding out the promise of therapeutic address for the suffering it induces, that determines the experience—whether one is queer or not—of bringing a child into one's life through adoption.

Unlike analyses that fall under the headings of political science, legal studies, or queer theory, the experience of the law as it becomes manifest and embodied through the desire for familial relations is central to an ethnographic account of gay parenting (Das & Poole 2004). The experiential aspects of the law are quite different from abstract scholarly descriptions of the impact of the state on lived relations (Goodrich & Carlson 1998; Lehr 1999; Richman 2010, 2013; Robson 1998; Stychin 1995) or studies that view the law as the singular and all-encompassing force that shapes intersubjective relationships, subject formation, and, thus, life itself (Agamben 2002; Butler 2000). In this book, I offer an account of such experiences as I examine the different ways life is lived in the shadow of the law (Sarat & Kearns 1995) and the different ways the law is brought to life and held in lived relations (Cavell 2005; Das & Poole 2004; Legendre 1997).

I argue that the ambivalence arising from the unpredictability of the law is not amenable to address by either further legal pronouncements, clinical discourses, or publicly witnessed performances. Thus, the uncertainty experienced by William and David was not assuaged by their gaining legitimacy in the eyes of the state or garnering societal recognition for the family relations they built. This is because the law and clinical discourses operate as the very vehicles that configure certain kin relations as fictional and others as real and certain forms of suffering as exceptional and others as normal.

Unlike the anatomical pain understood to accompany the creation of maternal relations, the suffering that attends the emergence of paternity does not readily register in and on the flesh (Asad 2003). The pains accompanying the birth of fatherhood, while no less real than those accompanying the formation of a maternal relation, are strictly social in their origins and distribution. Because the suffering that accompanies becoming a father is dispersed across and through social networks and intersubjective relations, knowledge of paternity is established as a site of subjugated knowledge for gay men with children (Faubion 2001b; Foucault 1978).

The work of suffering, as a living presence and an active agent in the making of queer kinship, challenges many current depictions of the family lives of gay men with children (as well as other forms of family that fall in the category of "alternative"), in which acting on the desire for children is

duality of law [margin annotation]

seen as embodying a pioneering spirit of resistance and the heroic drive toward new and supposedly less painful and restricted forms of family relations (Borneman 1996; Stacey 1998; Sullivan 2004; Weston 1999). I argue that the willingness to endure the suffering that accompanies paternity challenges the idea that gay men who form families are necessarily engaged in acts of creativity and experimentation whereby they design and come to embody a living critique of established notions of filiation and reproduction, as much recent scholarship assumes (Borneman 1997; Carrington 1999; Lehr 1999; Sullivan 2004; Weeks, Heaphy, & Donovan 2001).

In the pages of this book, I look at the suffering entailed in the desire to lay claim to the status of a normal family when contemporary state-sanctioned notions of relatedness are not readily accessible. In so doing, I illuminate the different agencies and forms of knowledge at work in making relatives within the biopolitical assemblages of contemporary U.S. society and polity.

Traditional Family Values

When deciding to bring children into their life, William and David broke with many conventional images of queer sociality as well as with the idealized place of paternity and paternal authority in the nuclear family (Lewin 2009). In William and David's family, paternal authority does not rest in one individual. This break, while couched in the language of tradition, draws on the image of the family as an extended and enduring network of intimate and caring relations that track the genealogical grids brought into being through biological notions of kinship (Povinelli 2002a, 2002b). As William and David's family life shows, the couple envisioned fatherhood as a relational form that is always already embedded within an extended web of affective bonds. The image stands in opposition to other cultural figurations that also draw on genealogical notions of being related, in which the father is seen as an independent sovereign figure that stands apart from but in a contractual relationship to the state (Hobbes 1998 [1651]; Locke 1982 [1690]); Rousseau 2002 [1762]). Thus, William and David evoke a material form of masculine care that takes place under the sign "gay" but does so in the name of securing the future promised by enfolding one's relations in a supposedly traditional and stable form of family and law. While William and David were acutely aware of the pain inflicted by the law and the suffering exacted by the state for desiring to care for another as a father, they were also banking on the promise that legal acts and the performance of care would enable them to live as fathers without engaging in procreative sex or heterosexual marriage. David expressed the couple's relationship as faithful to the spirit of the law and saw their investment in the future as promised by juridical acts when he described how he and William had become near experts in family law in the wake of the mishaps that took place along their journey to parenthood. The expertise David and William developed expresses the types of freedom and knowledge that emerge from investing in the law's forms of care and it's promises. The application of such expertise demonstrates the possibilities for building relationships with the self and others that emerge from the uncertain status of same-sex families in the eyes of the state. David described how they developed their expertise:

> We got a complete crash course in family law as a result of everything we went through. William and I now know the ins and outs of family law better then many lawyers. Since we know so much [about the law]—and we have an excellent attorney now, by the way—I'm completely confident we can bring about whatever we want. Trusts, joint custody, godparents, children with blond hair and blue eyes—green skin and purple blood—whatever. No problem. In fact, we now know that we could have been far more choosy [about the children we brought into our lives]. Not that we're complaining— we would never change a thing—but those rumors that you have to settle for whatever child you can get when you adopt are all bullshit. You can and should get what you want, and nothing should stop you. But the only reason we know this now is because we had to learn the hard way about how to make the law and everybody else work for us. We had to figure out how and what we could and could not do by doing it, and this meant we had to go through a lot of things we never should have, but we did. We also happen to have access to a certain amount of cash, like a lot of other gay men, which gives us a bit more room to wiggle and maneuver than some. Being professional DINKS [Double Income, No Kids] for so long has its benefits. We now know how to get what we need and what we want, and we know how to make it permanent.

"Getting what you want" when adopting alludes to David and William's shared anger about the practices of adoption agencies. As David went on to describe, the efforts of adoption agencies to distance themselves from the idea that they are trafficking babies in a free market results in the sense that prospective parents cannot be overly discerning about the child they will adopt. Instead, the sense among prospective adoptive parents is that one must settle and be grateful for the first child that comes one's way, at the cost of personal preference and desire. In other words, adopt is supposed to unfold in accordance to the logic of the gift as opposed to the logic of the market place (Ragoné 1994).

As William and David's story bears out, the view that adoption is an altruistic act, limited by the moral position that one should be grateful for having been bestowed the gift of any child—particularly if one is gay—lends itself to the constitution of family as a site of suffering. I found that I myself subscribed to this moral position: I was aghast when a man described how he and his partner had decided at the very last minute not to adopt a child because of his looks. "The child simply wasn't beautiful enough, so we said no."

Upon reflection, I found I had absorbed the sentimental cultural ideal of family as a site that is resistant to the logic and aesthetics of free market capitalism and sovereignty that define the public sphere in liberal democracy. Yet one cannot help but wonder how William and David's experience of family is being defined and will continue to be defined by racial discourses. Did William and David freely choose to have the politics of race played out on the bodies of their children? Or have they settled for a less than ideal scenario? If so, where might this affect spill over, and how might it become salient to understanding their experience of relatedness?

A Different Picture of Relatedness

The picture of the relations and the future promised by William and David's efforts to become fathers by forming a legally recognized family is seen by conservative lawmakers and jurists as a dangerous and profound threat to civilization.[3] Conservatives see gay families as threatening to topple the central place of the heterosexual nuclear family in the United States and, in so doing, upend what is considered natural about the social order and its reproduction through procreative heterosexual sex.

The conservative rhetoric intensified in reaction to the 2003 U.S. Supreme Court decision to protect the right of same-sex couples to engage privately in consensual sex and the Supreme Court's 2013 decision to strike down the Defense of Marriage Act, which defined marriage as between a man and a woman for purposes of federal law. However, the anxiety in conservative declarations speaks to the complex entanglement of the law and politics in everyday life. It is this anxiety that fuels the ongoing effort of the political right to legally define marriage as a "religious, cultural, and nat-

---

[3] On April 12, 2013, the Republican National Committee resolved unanimously to oppose legalization of same-sex marriages because of the threat they see such unions as posing to the "natural" procreative order of one man and one woman, which provides the "solid foundations on which our society is built and in which children thrive." See Republican National Committee Resolution for Marriage and Children, April 12, 2013.

ural union between a man and a woman," as opposed to the "ever evolving paradigm of recognized intimacy" advanced by the Massachusetts Supreme Court, at the federal level, and the conservative effort to overturn state-based legislation that grants same-sex couples the right to marry.[4] The continued political mobilization around same-sex marriage in the United States and abroad demonstrates that the place of eroticism within the family remains contested within the political and public culture of liberal democracy (Povinelli 2006).

Bringing the questions that arise from everyday life and the daily tasks of maintaining family relations for gay men with children to bear on political processes pushes one to think outside the simple binary arrangement of terms such as *gay* and *straight* or *relative* and *friend* that arise from the commitment to biogenetic notions of kinship. It is necessary to think beyond such familiar binaries because everyday life and its meaning are not preformed, prefigured, or predetermined. Building kin relations, like everyday life, is an achievement. To develop an anthropological sensibility that might engage such phenomena entails being open to the possible, to what *might* be. Remaining open to what might be means postponement and embracing the idea that one does not and cannot know the meaning of such well-worn terms as *family, relative, parent, father, mother, gay, straight, queer,* or even *child,* outside the specificities of the relations and entanglements that animate these terms (Sahlins 2013). After all, what emerges when gay men form families and bring children into their lives might not be anything new at all (Schneider 1997).

In this book, I braid the experiences and narratives of gay men who have formed families with children with the operations of institutions and institutional actors to understand how gay families are positioned within cultural discourses of care and how, for these men, paternal relations arise alongside ethical figuration. Drawing from recent anthropological work, I show how fatherhood for gay men exceeds and transfigures, while remaining embedded within, the parameters of the law and the organizing grammars of the heterosexual family. By examining the intersection between knowledge and experience, my study reveals the struggles of gay men with children to formulate their relationships in ways that attempt to reduce the uncertainty and suffering entailed in having one's intimate relations defined as *different* while acknowledging the specificity of a relationship's origin and meaning.

---

[4] As this book goes to press, same-sex marriage was legally allowed in thirty-seven states, banned in thirteen states, and under legal review or appeal in six states.

How does the formation of family by subjects who identify as gay articulate with dominant images of being a relative? How does gay men's creation of families with children contest, dovetail, or overlap with accepted cultural notions about the origin of kin relations? What futures are open to gay men with children when societal recognition and acknowledgment of belonging are increasingly defined by the principles of biology, legislative acts, and legal pronouncements? This volume is an empirical exploration of these very questions.

1   Sensing Kinship

An anthropological study of queer kinship in the United States that does not draw on David Schneider's insights into American kinship is hard to imagine. Not only did Schneider (1997) specifically address the topic of gay and lesbian families in one of his final publications, but in his earlier work on kinship he also helped establish queer relations as a valid topic of anthropological inquiry (Carsten 2004; Dean 2009; Weston 1993). Yet Schneider's work remains problematic because of his basic assumption that the norms structuring family and kin relations in the United States are shared across all social sectors (McKinnon 1994; Yanagisako & Delany 1994). Whether they share generally accepted norms of relatedness and intimacy is not at issue for gay and lesbian families; what is of concern is whether the forms of intimacy and care found among gay families are actively stigmatized in political and public life (Borneman 1996; Butler 2000, 2002).

In this chapter, I ask how gay men who have formed families with children come to acknowledge their family members as kin, given that they must negotiate an environment in which their relationships fall under constant suspicion. The question of acknowledgment is particularly acute for gay men with children, as the experience of William and David shows. Gay men clearly endow terms such as "family," "marriage," "father," and "child" with personal meanings drawn from wider repertoires of affection, intimacy, and desire, yet they are denied the normality indexed by these terms through legal, political, and religious operations. Marilyn Strathern (1992b, 2005), Rayna Rapp and Faye Ginsburg (2001; see also Ginsburg & Rapp 1995), and Sarah Franklin (2001, 2013; see also Franklin & Roberts 2006) have argued that the taken-for-granted quality of kinship relations is constantly being redefined because of the increasing use of new reproductive technologies and the increasing visibility of alternative forms of family in the public sphere. For Strathern, clarification of who is a parent and who qualifies as kin comes to bear on emergent legal judgments and biological science. I argue that these questions are not simply matters decided in the courts of law, and neither are they only raised by the deployment and availability of new reproductive technologies. Rather, the affective qualities of kinship also invite one to consider how parents and children in gay families come to recognize and know each other as kin in the terrains of everyday life. It is in this context that I take up the question of uncertainty in kinship, but rather than turn to biotechnology and the courts for answers, I look at how uncertainties are mediated within everyday family life.

Signe Howell and Diana Marre (2006) argue that achieving a sense of certainty that a child belongs to a family when kin relations are not predicated on a model of shared biological substance entails sensory perception. The cultural assumption that relatives share biological material implies a certain physical resemblance between parents and children, which is a constant source of comment within families. Thus, when families are formed by such alternative means as transnational adoption, resemblance takes on greater salience than biological connection. Criteria such as personality and emotional traits, tendencies, personal interests, or a child's innate "gifts" define the child's resemblance and, thus, connection to a parent. This resemblance wards off the possibility that relationships formed outside biological conception and legal marriage are only "fictive" forms of kinship.

In what follows, I describe my encounters with Thomas, Jon, and Tim, three fathers who identify as gay. I trace the implications of a comment Thomas made about uncertainty and examine the importance he placed on conversation as a means of establishing connection, of learning about family relations. I then examine the implications of the anxiety he expressed about how others might receive his family relations, anxiety that resonates in Jon and Tim's recollections of *their* experience of founding a family. Thomas, the father of two teenage boys—Andrew and Todd—was a graphic designer and the head of a local gay fathers organization in Washington, D.C. Jon, his partner Tim, and their two children—Josh and Madeline—live outside Baltimore. Tim is a judge, and Jon works in the arts.

Wait and See

It was a warm spring evening in Washington, D.C., and I was sitting in a sidewalk café having dinner with Thomas. Earlier, after I had explained my research interests to him on the telephone, he had expressed an interest in meeting me and taking part in my study because he saw participation in academic research as a means to counter the negative images of same-sex parenting that circulate in public culture. He had already taken part in several academic studies, finding those that deal with the effects of gay parenting on the psychological development of children particularly relevant to his decidedly political goals. Academic research, for Thomas, was not something confined to the ivory towers of universities. It was a means of influencing public opinion and shaping public culture so that his life, his relationships, and his claims to normality might be more readily accepted.

After sitting down to dinner, Thomas asked me two questions: "Are you gay?" to which I answered, "No." Then, "Do you have kids?" I again said, "No," and I asked him in return, "Does it matter?" For a moment my question hung in the air. Then Thomas replied, "I'm not sure. You see, I knew I was a father when I was twenty-two and I saw my first child being born. But I didn't know that I was gay and a father until after I had my second child, was thirty-two, had left my wife, and was dating men. We'll just have to wait and see."

Thomas's words express hope that clarity as to the meaning of these words will arrive in the future and that the uncertainties defining the present as unstable will be transformed into certainties through time. The sentiment found in Thomas's words reflect the current legal and political status of gay families where the present in which these relations are made and lived is in flux, but the future into which the relations are projected is imagined to be stable. The discordance between the present in which the daily life of family for gay men with children unfolds, the institutional milieu in which gay kinship is made, and the future into which these relations are projected speaks to the untimely quality of kinship. This chapter is devoted to articulating the implications of having to "wait and see" before coming to know how one's relationships, sexual or otherwise, affect the formation of knowledge.

I took Thomas's response as an invitation to proceed with what, in my imagination, was an anthropological line of inquiry, steering the conversation away from my own biography and toward his experience of family and kinship. I now realize that my initial interpretation of his questions ignored the importance he placed on time and the difficulty of coming to know the present, or time we live in. It was not until much later, when writing about my research, that I was struck by Thomas's effort to make me cognizant of the relevance of sensory perception and time for understanding the place of sexuality in notions of fatherhood and the place of fatherhood in notions of sexuality.

His words signal the importance of patience and endurance when it comes to understanding relationships. It is as if we must wait so that the present in which we live and experience others can become the past, thereby allowing us to discern the character of our encounters.

Sensing Uncertainty

My exchange with Thomas evokes the troubling sense of uncertainty (and the importance of addressing its implications) that arises when attempting to understand how one's relationships might determine knowledge of the self and others. Thomas's words invite reflection on how questions concerning how we are and are not related shadow the anthropological and philosophical concern with what we can and cannot know about one another (Clifford & Marcus 1986; Geertz 1983). Might they also point to what can and cannot be known about the self?

I understand Thomas's sense of knowledge and its limits, as well as my own, as motivating our mutual search for biographical and experiential details. We each proceeded as if information about sexuality and kinship could provide us with anchoring points from which to develop a sense of what the other was capable of absorbing, what the other might take for granted, and how each of us might come to learn what the other had to tell.

As the preceding exchange of questions ("Are you gay?" "Do you have kids?" "Does it matter?") indicates, one's relationship to the words "gay" and "father" cannot be immediately known by another; it is not self-evident. Expression is needed and solicited to clarify the meaning of one's present relationships, just as words are needed to address how relationships in the present might be transformed in the future. Yet autobiographical statements such as "I am (not) gay" or "I am (not) a father" may not provide the clarity that is desired, especially when what is at stake is the potential that one's words might inadvertently cause injury. When Thomas sought these biographical details from me, the burden associated with determining the weight of paternity and sexuality—or, perhaps, the weight of kinship itself—in creating the conditions for knowing became overt and dispersed across the anthropological encounter. As the stories in this chapter demonstrate, words are not enough to generate this knowledge. (In Chapter 3 I address the conundrums that arise from living in kin relations whose meaning arises from the nomination and signatory events of others.)

If the knowledge one seeks and holds is tied to one's identity, as is assumed in certain forms of politics, then questions of disclosure in anthropological research become very interesting. If I am working with gay fathers, then my hiding my status as a father or hiding my sexual orientation—either of which can be done through declarative statements—might be construed by those men as intentionally misleading and a betrayal. I conducted this research while affiliated with Johns Hopkins University. The university committee overseeing human-subjects research requested that I disclose my sexual orientation to those with whom I worked, a request that marks the institutionalization of these very political and ethical concerns about regulating identity and risk.

The ethics committee did not seem to think that my parental status or my filiation held the same capacity to injure that my sexuality did. Yet, the shadowy presence of uncertainty haunts confessions about fatherhood just as it haunts disclosures about sexuality (Butler 1993; Cavell 1996; Peletz 2001). While it might not seem reasonable for me to be uncertain if I am a man or a woman, as Thomas's words indicate, the possibility always exists that somebody else might know more about my sex, sexuality, and paternity than I know about myself. It is the possibility that one's desires and the details of one's kinship might be hidden, from the public or from one's self, that permits both kinship and sexuality to function as "closets": revealing the truth about oneself and one's relations in these contexts of relating carries the potential to generate disruptive effects (Cavell 1996). It is the possibility of such hidden knowledge, and the multiple meanings attached to paternity, I claim, that makes one vulnerable to kinship. I think Thomas indexed this vulnerability when he said, "We'll have to wait and see."

Could the condition of possibility for living in families in which the creation of relatives is not linked to reproductive sexuality reside in developing modes of addressing such uncertainty? In posing this question, I am trying to imagine the implications of switching the perspective of kinship study in the United States from one in which anatomical birth is configured as the point of origin of subjects who give rise to voice and culture (Schneider 1968) to one in which *voice* is understood as giving birth to culture, as Veena Das (1995) has suggested in a different context. In considering this question, I focus on the place of the senses and of time in creating certainty about the relationships gay men form with their children. Such certainty is especially important given that forms of kinship created by means other then heterosexual conception are routinely greeted with skepticism and violence (Povinelli 2002b; Weston 1999; Yanagisako & Delaney 1995). Does such uncertainty and violence configure sensory knowledge as the most plausible route to belonging in the family? If so, we must recognize that becoming related, just like developing sensory knowledge, requires work and time, and thus endurance—hence, the importance of *waiting* within the mise-en-scène of *seeing*.

I am interested in exploring how sensory perception can solidify the meaning of being a relative when kinship is grounded not in a founding event of biology or the signing of a legal contract but in the day-to-day putting together of care through which a sense of belonging emerges (Das 2000). I am not arguing that such forms of caring make gay subjects immune to hurt. Images circulating in the wider culture that represent gay sexuality and gay parenting as pathological strongly influence the way relationships are constructed. I am arguing, rather, that there are productive ways to meet an accusatory gaze.

The Place of Vision

The place of vision in coming to know if one is a relative was made evident to me by my interlocutors' repeated use of visual tropes in their efforts to fix moments when they felt certain about what it meant to be gay and to be related to one's child as a father. For instance, Thomas described "knowing" that he had become a father when he gazed on his first child at birth. Yet the same certainty did not materialize in his relationship to the category "gay" until much later, after Thomas had become, and saw himself as being, sexually involved with men.

The strong association between seeing and certainty among the men with whom I worked speaks to how the senses, vision, in particular, are embedded in the creation of knowledge about kinship (Howell & Marre 2006; Seremetakis 1996). For example, Jon explained as we walked through the streets of Provincetown, Massachusetts, during Gay Family Week in August 2001 that he can always "spot other gay dads" because "they just have a look about them." Both Jon's and Thomas's descriptions of coming to know the character of another's relationships through vision articulates the particulars of a rapport that exists in the United States between language, the senses, and the world (Cavell 2005). The veracity of kin relations comes about through a combination of sensing, speaking, and reflecting, which together enable the meaning of a relationship to emerge in time. Because of the combination of processes involved, it is necessary to defer arriving at the meaning of biographical statements about sexuality and family until further perceptions can confer momentary certainty. Thomas clearly appreciated the importance of such deferral.

Late one afternoon, when Jon and Tim and I were heading from the beach toward the house the couple had rented, their two children in tow, Jon spoke about becoming aware of forms of belonging that do not participate in the logic of the heterosexual nuclear family.

I just love Provincetown in summer. God, I don't know when it was—it must have been like 1980. All I know is that it was when those Izod or Polo shirts—you know, those ones with short sleeves and the knit collars—were all the rage. My grandmother had rented a house out here for that entire summer. We would all drive up from the city and spend a couple of long weekends a month hanging out on the beach for that whole summer. I don't know what it really was, but I remember so clearly walking around at night, going for ice cream after spending the day on the beach, and seeing all these guys with their shirt collars turned up. I don't know why, but for some reason I really identified with those guys. I didn't even know I was gay then, I didn't even really know what it meant to be gay, or what being gay even was. I certainly had no clue about what all those guys were doing. All I knew was those guys were different, and I was attracted. I knew I was like them, and I knew I belonged with them, and I could see and feel it. So whenever we were out, I would try to catch their eye, and distance myself from whatever family member, grandma, grandpa, or whoever I was with, by wearing my shirt collar up. I would even walk a few paces behind everybody else just to put some space between me and my family. This was my little code I'd made up. It let those guys I saw know that I was one of them.

Here Jon recounts becoming aware of a specific form of relating and belonging—a form he later learned to name and recognize as gay—by seeing it. When he initially recognized himself in what he saw, Jon did not know what it meant to be gay or what it was he was looking at when he gazed on queer social life. All he sensed was affinity, that he was like, and thus belonged with, the men who wore their shirt collars up. He then developed a code to signal his likeness to them by creating a visual resemblance that distanced him from his biological family.

The meaning of affinity and difference, for Jon, surfaced at a later point in time, when he could draw an analogy between the intimacy he sensed with the men in Provincetown who were wearing their shirt collars up and what he has since learned about relationships from witnessing his biological family. While he sensed *difference* in the men, it was the similarity of the language of care and love he learned from his biological family that prepared him to recognize queer forms of sociality as also entailing relations of care, love, and sexuality (Weston 1999).

In Jon's reflection on discovering his belonging in a community of men, participation and visual resemblance are congruent and emulation equates with affinity. Jon identified with the men through sartorial display. As he recalled this moment in his youth from the vantage point of our conversation, Jon avoided more sophisticated descriptions and interpretations of his early sexual awakening and related that it was more important for him to identify and participate by crafting himself as visually similar to the men in Provincetown than it was to articulate the characteristics of the relationships with which he felt a sense of affinity and belonging.

Jon also described what it means to be gay in terms of a spatial relationship to his extended family of birth. To belong with the men who wore their shirt collars up entailed stepping away from the space of care he associated with the biological family and entering an alternate space within the more general public sphere. Jon's description asks us to imagine gay sociality as located at an almost geometrically defined distance from the referential codes of the normative family. Neither totally immersed within this sociality nor totally apart, with no clear split along the binary lines of gay/straight, Jon articulates his experience of learning that such signifiers of identity as family and sexuality are continually at play and unstable. The experience of such instability means neither set of signifiers provides shelter from skepticism when it comes to defining one's relationships as real and valuable. As we shall see, though, it is the image of the extended biological family from which he later separated that gives Jon the tools for securing and articulating the meaning of being both gay and a father.

Like Father, Like Son

The hybrid configuration of distancing and belonging Jon spoke of becomes more complex when the question of paternity arises in conjunction with the meaning of being gay. When I posed the question of paternity simultaneously with the question of homosexuality, Jon and Tim both added biographical details to the mimetic logic that Jon first used to define his close, yet measured distance from the men who wore their shirt collars up. Jon, for instance, described how his understanding of himself as gay *and* a father was informed by his own childhood experience of fathers and by the place of the father figure within the family as presented in dominant religious models.

We can begin to sense from such biographical details how the family and its meaning are assembled from dominant cultural images concerning affect, care, the meaning of caring and being cared for, and the origins of life, which then become animated in the subject's lived relations. Tracing Jon's insights into the meaning and origins of paternity enables us to track the emergence of the family and of relatedness when the origin of fatherhood is uncoupled from the biological reproduction.

Jon's understanding of what it means to become a father came across in a brief conversation we had while I was sitting in his kitchen chatting idly with him about sterilizing baby bottles and making organic yogurt. Our conversation turned toward religion when Jon said that, although it was a hassle, it was crucial to him that the ingredients in his yogurt and the process of its making be kosher. When I asked if he tries to keep his children on a kosher diet, he said he personally tried to adhere as closely to the rules of kosher living as he could but that he did not feel the need to maintain a completely kosher household or to live a life of religious orthodoxy. (Tim jokingly recounted how Jon had successfully seduced him when they were first dating by cooking a delicious pork loin.)

For Jon, eating kosher foods was a matter of common sense, derived from his experience of growing up in an Orthodox Jewish household and his belief that consuming mass-produced food was harmful to the health and well-being of growing children. When I pushed Jon to further explain how the principles of Judaism were folded into his life with Tim and his children, he responded exuberantly, saying, "Of course I'm raising my children Orthodox! My father was an Orthodox Jew, and I was raised in an Orthodox household. I only know how to be an Orthodox dad. It's just what I do."

Jon went on to say being an Orthodox father meant extending a type of Jewish fatherly love to the world at large and to his own children in particular.

> I was taught by my father that part of being Jewish is believing the world is broken and needs repair. If a child is crying and hungry, no matter whose it is, the world is broken. If you pick that child up, feed it, and put the child to bed under your roof, then you've begun to repair the world. That's a philosophy of fathering I believe in even if the ideas behind it are religious. Being a father is trying to repair the world wherever and however I can.

The ethical orientation toward the world Jon elaborated is well known and occupied by many within Judaism—men, women, parents, nonparents, queer, straight, orthodox and nonorthodox alike. Jon expresses his connection to tradition, lineage, and family through his elaboration of taking up and occupying a known image and position within a collective religious and political assemblage. Jon also describes how identifying with and occupying a known position within Jewish cosmology solidifies the meaning of kinship, in this case fatherhood. To be a father is to gaze on the world from the vantage point offered by Judaism and to act in accordance with its known truths about the world. Within this assemblage, quite specifically, paternity is not tied to a singular event, such as birth, or to biological notions of being related, and homosexuality does not exclude one from participation in religious forms of community and belonging.

Jon's description of how he inhabits the meaning of fatherhood he inherits demonstrates how queer forms of family draw meaning from dominant cultural images often associated with the exclusion of those who embody alternative sexualities, just as they emulate many of the figurations of family and childhood often thought to be oppressive to queer forms of sociality. The nonheterosexual family, as articulated by Jon and Tim, challenges the position of theorists such as John Borneman (1997), who see the families of gay men as possessing a completely different psychic and erotic structure than their straight counterparts.

Jon's configuration of fatherhood and its origins, however, also reveals a limit. Only a select set of gay men are allowed by law, economics, and forms of governmentality to be parents. The state actively formulates and regulates what constitutes a family relationship and the care of children, and if one's relationships cannot be contained within the law's defining frames, due to age, political commitments, race, or religion, institutional forces prevent one from forming families (Butler 2002; Carp 1998; Donzelot 1979). This is particularly important for gay parents, whose forms of parenting are institutionally treated with suspicion because of fear, both expressed and unexpressed, that gay sexuality is potentially predatory and that gay parents might impose their sexuality on children (Berlant & Warner 1998; Edelman 2004; Sedgwick 1993), a matter I explore at length in Chapter 3.

Nevertheless, Jon's self-conscious efforts to emulate and embody the image of a Jewish father troubles the idea that identifying oneself as gay and as a father entails reconfiguring the promise of contentment offered by the cultural ideal of the nuclear family. It also challenges the idea that the families built by same-sex parents are exempt from the costs, in terms of suffering, that accompany belonging within the heterosexual nuclear family. Jon bridges the distance between what are commonly thought to be two distinct domains of sociality, that of gay sexuality and that of the Orthodox father, by taking up and enacting an image of paternal care found in a Judaic cosmology.

Jon's introduction of an explicitly mimetic logic to describe the origins of paternity, in this context, denies the strict grammar of biogenetic kinship found in the United States, where the terms *gay* and *father* are assumed to be mutually exclusive because homosexual unions are pictured as inherently sterile.[1] Jon's words reveal how becoming a father involves enacting the fatherly forms of care found in the dominant cultural images that are handed down through a sensual and affective education.

---

[1] Following the mimetic logic introduced by Jon reveals a complex set of transferences in which Jon, as a gay man, is able to occupy a position within Orthodox Judaism by bringing to life a specific image of fatherhood. Simultaneously, Jon, as a gay man, is able to become a father and gain state sanction for his family relations by bringing to life the image of an Orthodox father.

According to Jon, it is the childhood experience of having one's own hurts soothed by being picked up and held that brings a particular image of fatherhood to life. It is participation in such repeated scenes of instruction, complete with their accompanying violence and tenderness, that allows a particular image of paternity to be passed on from one generation to the next. With the bringing of such an image to life, fatherhood becomes embodied and its meaning secured through the sense.

Jon's words paint a picture in which paternity is brought into being through sensual scenes of instruction. Here, rather than the gendered division of labor associated with the reproduction of biological bodies through marriage, procreative sex, and birth, it is learning and proliferating specific modes of care and feeling, through having been cared for oneself in particular ways, that makes one a father. Legitimacy comes through care, and as Jon's narrative emphasizes, it does not rely on the reproductive capacity of a relationship, the biological body, or the certainty promised by blood and the law in establishing the paternal relation. Rather, trust that one is a father resides in the expression of feelings and continuing to provide the very forms of care one has received oneself—has inherited from the past—and in performing that care and expressing those feelings in the public sphere. Yet how Jon knew he wanted to become a father, and thus become involved in the kind of instruction described, remains unaddressed.

Seeing Is Believing

Jon describes how and when both he and Tim knew they were ready to bring children into their lives:

> Having kids was something I always knew I wanted to do. I think it came from watching my father as a kid. In this culture of ours, being a parent is so much about being an adult. One really isn't seen as an adult until one has children. This is particularly true when you take my Jewish upbringing. You just become a parent when you grow up. That's what my brother did, and that's what my sister did. Anyway, I'm not sure when it was but I was browsing in a bookstore and I picked up this book called *Getting Simon*. It's a book about a gay couple who became dads through a "penny saver" ad. So I read it, and began talking about it with everyone I knew, and discovered that nearly everyone was really supportive of me becoming a father. At that time I didn't have a steady partner, so having a child wasn't really a criterion in my dating life or anything I really consciously discovered. I just began acting on something I always knew I wanted to do. I guess in a sense it happened along lines of natural selection. I would tell somebody that I wanted to have

children and they would either freak out and leave or hang around a bit. Now, when Tim came into the picture, we talked about it quite a bit. But you know how gay men are; we weren't really in a monogamous relationship or anything, but we were dating. That's one funny thing about gay kinship. There aren't any real points to mark the beginning of a relationship or anything. I mean no weddings or formal anniversaries. That will have to go into your thesis somewhere. So after a while I brought it up and was telling Tim children were a big deal to me, and that it was really an important part of how I wanted to live. He wasn't really too warm to the idea at first. He just wasn't sure about the whole thing. So, I just kept reading books and passing them on [to Tim], and he would read them and gradually warm up to the idea a little, but then he would always cool off again.

Then one night about four years ago after we'd been to the theater, Tim and I walked into the same bar we always went to. And, I remember sitting down with a group of friends who were there, as they always were, and looking around at what was going on. It was all so familiar, but for some reason it suddenly seemed sad. This sounds terrible, but it was the same old people doing the same old things, practically sitting on the same old bar stools. Seeing it all, I suddenly thought, you know, I don't want that to be me in ten years. It was then that I really pushed the baby issue with Tim, and he was just about in the same place. He just had to get used to the idea that we had to act if we were going to go through with it. And, pretty soon after that we did. We began by putting an ad in the paper, contacted an adoption agency, and began looking into surrogacy.

A visual and spatial perception accompanied Jon's realization that a shift had occurred in his knowledge of himself and of the future promised by his current relationships. As he relates it, visual cues provided him with a means to identify and recognize an objective change in his own inner state and thus to be certain about his desire to become a father. It was when he realized that his life and relationships no longer looked or felt as they once had that he claimed certainty about his desire to be a parent. With the arrival of certainty, the promises held by the kind of relationship Jon first discovered in Provincetown as a teenager were diminished and infused with sadness. In the place of the future and the pleasures represented by the men with the turned-up collars, an image of an alternate future emerged—that of being a father—which transfigured the meaning of the very social milieu that initially drew Jon away from familial forms of belonging.

If we follow Jon's description of acting on his desire to be a father, we arrive at an alternate way of coming to know if one is kin. Jon's account suggests knowledge of kinship is not based on a preexisting genealogical grid on which relationships are placed and then rendered legible (Povinelli 2002a). Rather, familial relationships become known and gain meaning through the senses and through affect (Desjarlais 2003).

Tim recounted a similar logic when describing his own discovery of wanting to have children. In his account, like Jon's, we hear of a sadness that infused his life prior to his becoming a father. Unlike Jon, Tim's desire to be a parent was shaped by the structure of time and the connections between generations that the image of the nuclear family evoked for him.

> I guess it really hit home that I was searching for something more in life when I was having these prolonged bouts of sadness. I really first became aware of it when I was sitting at my uncle's funeral and watching everyone in my family shuffle in and out of the church. It was when I was watching my family that I began to think about generations and the continuity of families. At that point Jon was really thinking about children and really pushing me towards the idea, but it never really hit home until I was sitting there looking at my brother and sister with their kids in that church, and looking at my cousins with theirs. I remember looking down that row of pews and seeing all the generations lined up and thinking that's what I want to have. That's what I want to be part of. You know, Jon and I had a totally rewarding and fulfilling gay life. We were never really all that wild or into that whole circuit party scene, but that's not the point. That just wasn't our crowd, but we had the typical gay lifestyle. We traveled, we went out to bars and clubs regularly, we had a collection of gay friends, but after a while I just felt that something was really lacking. It wasn't my relationship with Jon; that felt totally stable and satisfying and good. It was just that a sadness would sweep over me once in a while, and I think I can say "us" here. I would be sitting at a stoplight or something, and suddenly I would get sad and feel like crying. You know I'd be in a bar in the middle of a conversation and I'd just get hit by this feeling of "is this all there is?" "Is this all life has to offer?" Don't get me wrong, it's not that gay life wasn't rewarding. My life just happened to have a strange hollow place that was sad. So it was only after the funeral and seeing how families are about filling up the future that I decided kids was the way to go.

Like Jon, Tim linked his desire to have children to his sensory experience of the relationships of the heterosexual nuclear family—the family he gazed on at his uncle's funeral. It was in the church that Tim saw a connection between children and the possibility of addressing what increasingly felt like his own empty set of relationships and empty future. Tim's uncertainty about his life—"Is this all there is?"—and his unaccountable bouts of sadness were assuaged by the idea of participating in a family oriented toward a future filled by the demands of caring for children. This image of the family provided Tim with a means of rendering legible what he felt was lacking in his social relations and of addressing his sadness.[2]

By becoming a parent, neither Tim nor Jon seemed to feel he was inventing anything new. Instead, both felt they were developing a variation on a common cultural practice. Both referred to their inability to point to singular founding events in their life together, such as a wedding, but this did not mark their family as radically different from other families, including those of heterosexuals. Instead, their parenting practices and their inability to locate the origins of their family in a singular event made them like and aligned with others.

In the Eyes of the Other

Though Jon and Tim repeatedly drew attention to their family's similarity to others, for both of them, anxiety surfaced around questions of "if" and "how" their relationship to each other and their children would be acknowledged as *familial* by the outside world.

Recalling Jon's assertion that being a parent is about becoming an adult, I believe it safe to say that, for both Jon and Tim, denial of family status amounted to denial of full membership in society. Having children seemed to provide them with the hope of being acknowledged as full citizens, as mainstream middle-class Americans. Jon captured this sentiment when he said, "You know, we just aren't that different from any other middle-class family with two kids and two dogs. We just happen to have begun our

---

[2] The societal correlation between full adulthood, citizenship, and building family relations with children serves as Lee Edelman's (2004) point of departure for criticizing the societal investment in the figure of the child and the future promised by reproductive heterosexuality. In what has become known in queer theory as the "antisocial" critique, queer forms of sociality are positioned as negating the future promised by reproductive heterosexuality and thus offering a site for advancing an alternative ethics that does not partake in the temporality and obligations of heterosexuality and its multiple forms of reproduction. Perhaps obviously, Tim and Jon do not embrace the call to negate the future held in the iconic image of the child and have instead embraced the future promised by generation and its reproduction but from within a different relationship to heterosexuality. It is perhaps Foucault who describes the subversive and revolutionary aspects of two men living happily and tenderly together after having sex that best describes Jon and Tim and their commitment to a future filled with caring for children.

relationship like most gay men do, in a nonmonogamous dating pool. Just like a lot of heterosexuals I know."

When it came to solidifying the meaning of their family relations, Jon and Tim seemed to place trust in others' perceptions and in their own likeness to publicly circulating images of parent/child relationships rather than in the institutional signatures that authorize one's status as father or son. I see the idea that institutional signatures cannot secure a family relationship as guiding their decision to bring children into their life through surrogacy, rather than adoption, and as influencing their decision to have the same woman carry both of their children. Jon and Tim assumed that looking like a family was crucial to gaining recognition, especially by strangers in public places, where sensorial knowledge seemed more important than legal standing. And crafting recognizable physical similarity between family members was integral to this project.

Two men with children were much more likely to be "seen" as a family, and acknowledged as such, if they shared a degree of physical similarity (Howell & Marre 2006). By separately inseminating the same woman, Jon and Tim hoped to produce two children who resembled one another as well as their respective sperm donors. They were clearly drawing on cultural ideas about biogenetics and family relations, the idea that kin possess similar physical qualities because of their genetic similarity, to counter the skepticism that they felt their kids would face as the children of two gay fathers. We might understand the cultural commitment to biogenetic notions of kinship, and the accumulation of biocapital, as a condition of possibility for Jon and Tim to become fathers.[3] Tim explained why they chose artificial insemination over adoption:

> We decided to go with a surrogate because we felt it was just too much to
> ask of a kid to be both adopted and have gay parents. I mean, think about it,

[3] "Biocapital" is a term used to describe the confluence of biology, or the material of life, with the circulations of producing objects and value associated with capitalist exchange (Foucault 2010; Franklin 2003; Helmreich 2008; Lock 2003; Rajan 2006; Rose 2008). The majority of scholarly work devoted to elaborating the concept has focused in the transformation of biology into an informational science, and the melding of capitalist speculation with bench science in the production of living objects that are brought into being through market speculation, product making and profit taking. I am using to term to describe the accumulation of cultural capital enabled by the application of biological and social technologies to produce a desired "living" outcome—meaning family relations that express and align with a particular set of normative traits and characteristics.

a Vietnamese adopted kid living in America with two white gay dads, one of whom is Jewish. It's just asking an awful lot for a kid to bear all that. It's just way too much stigma, and Jon being Jewish makes me particularly sensitive to this. This way, when we walk down the street we at least seem like a normal family because we look alike. Now, I might not look like Madeline, and Josh might not look like Jon, but Madeline looks like Josh, and each of them looks like one of us, and that's important. That's what mattered to us.

Tim's words do not explicitly address ontological questions concerning the existence of the family. Rather, they reveal an anxiety about how others, especially strangers, might read the sight of two gay men with children and the available means by which this anxiety—particularly on Tim's part—might be assuaged. Both Tim and Jon are, in effect, anticipating and addressing doubt in the eyes of others by drawing on dominant conceptions in the United States of the biological basis of relatedness, the promise of the reproductive technologies available to them, and their access to capital (Ragoné 1994; Weston 1991; Yanagisako & Delaney 1995).

Tim described anticipating such doubt:

I always expect people to notice us more than they seem to. I think when people see us together they don't automatically assume that we are a couple even when we are both holding the children and passing diapers back and forth in the grocery store. Instead, they probably see a man and his uncle or even his father—I just look a lot older than Jon. They certainly don't seem to see two lovers. They might see a family, but not a nuclear one. They definitely see relatives, but not the actual relations between us.

Kinship studies have traditionally relied on linguistic terms and on systems of classification to delineate the meaning of the various relations in one's kin universe (Lévi-Strauss 1969; Malinowski 2001; Morgan 1870; Needham 1971; Radcliffe-Brown 1965; Schneider 1968, 1972). Jon and Tim, by contrast, seem to instruct us that it is not what one individual calls another that holds the key to understanding important aspects of kinship but, rather, that a whole repertoire of sensory knowledge is brought to bear on determining the meaning of particular enactments of care. For them, what it means to be "actually" related is drawn from the daily experiences of fathers, mothers, brothers, and sisters—it does not dwell in the binary relations of the heterosexual genealogical grid but in a network of scattered affects and in modes of perception (Herzfeld 2001; Povinelli 2002b; Seremetakis 1996). Returning to Tim's imagined scene in the grocery store, one can speculate that revealing his and Jon's sexual relationship would undo others' imagination of their familial status.

Tim's evocation of vision acknowledges uncertainty, whereas a commitment to kinship terminology presumes certainty. A girl calls a man "father," but the man does not look like he is the right age, or he is not the right color, or he does not have features that resemble the girl's, so can one trust that he is the father? Such anxiety is the stuff of daily life in gay families when the juridical and linguistic order of the family is known to be threatened by the gaze of others (Kaeser & Gillespie 1999; Lewin 1993; Sedgwick 1993). Such binary divisions as self/other, gay/straight, family/stranger, man/woman, masculine/feminine, or same/different—the foundations on which kinship studies have traditionally relied—are broken by the visceral entanglement of images and care that take place when caring for a child.[4]

Thus, Tim puts an enormous weight on the psychological burdens a child has to carry if he or she does not resemble either parent. Families, after all, are made not only in homes and courts of law but also in the world of parks, grocery stores, and encounters on the street. Children may be affirmed and made secure in their relationships or made to feel as if their family relations are always in question depending on whether familial resemblances register in the eyes of strangers. Tracking the place of resemblance in Jon and Tim's descriptions of family returns us to the question of how we can best know the existence of familial relationships, whether gay or straight.

The Image of Commitment

When I asked Jon about the place of sexuality in his experience of parenting, he responded,

> So, you want to hear about my gay lifestyle? Tomorrow I'll get up, make breakfast for Tim as he gets ready for work. Then I'll wake the little ones, make a second breakfast for them, get everybody ready to go for a walk in the park with the dogs, get to the park, hang out with all the straight moms with their kids, come home, clean bottles, make yogurt, go grocery shopping, probably do some laundry, pick up the nanny, take a nap once she gets here,

---

[4] The manifestation of these entanglements in everyday life and their gradual working through in language, the state's administrative apparatus, and the efforts of children to negotiate the place of their parents' sexuality in the public sphere are matters that orient the remaining chapters of the book.

and spend a couple hours working before Tim gets home. It's just about the same as today. It's no different then any other upper-middle-class household with kids. We just aren't that different. As Tim is fond of saying, "Rather than ending up with kids because of an accident involving a six-pack [of beer] and the backseat of a car, we went to a lawyer." Something hundreds of people do every day.

Jon's commitment to an image of gay family life that essentially follows the heterosexual norm is reinforced by his detailed description of the domestic routine he follows. Unlike heterosexual parents, however, he and Tim have to continually emphasize that their family relationships conform to the norm. Normalcy, it seems, cannot go without saying when two gay men raise children.

Jon articulates the experience of difference along lines of class and the performance of the labor needed to maintain domesticity rather than according to the markers of sexual difference (Carrington 1999). Seeing their family as conceived through a series of conscious choices and the agency of applied technologies, as opposed to the contingencies of an accident, is a way for Tim and Jon to align their experience with that of many other parents. Tim's description of going to a lawyer to bring children into their life (as opposed to accidentally ending up with a child as a result of getting drunk and having sex in the back of a car), ironically, prevents their familial bonds from being read as natural. Jon domesticates the radical implications of how they formed their family by suggesting they pursued the very ordinary legal path hundreds of people follow everyday.

In an exchange I overheard during an outing in Provincetown, Tim revealed the tensions inherent in viewing gay families and heterosexual families as the same. Jon and Tim and I had taken their kids to a dinner for families taking part in "Gay Family Week." After dinner we joined a small group of fathers at an ice-cream parlor. I was pushing Josh and Madeline in their stroller, enjoying an ice-cream cone and listening to the other men chat.

We passed a store window where a collection of photographic prints and drawings was on display. At the center of the display were photos of shirtless men in sexually provocative positions, framed drawings by Tom of Finland, and a series of black-and-white photographs of men having sex in the various cruising areas in and around Provincetown. Seeing the photographs evoked not only memories for Jon and Tim but reflections on the present as well.

TIM: Ah yes, the dunes of the cape, we'll have to tell you [meaning me] about that sometime.

JON: Oh look, there's underneath the pier; I remember those days. [The men in the group collectively chuckle.]

TIM: That's why I love coming to P-Town, you can enjoy the beach and get your dick sucked in the dunes.

JON: Yeah, but that was then. Look at us now. I mean we're pushing a stroller down the street. [The men laugh loudly.]

TIM: Well, maybe we can get our anthropologist to babysit a couple of nights and we can go out roaming. That would be great.

The alternative world of erotic pleasure displayed in the storefront, although an important part of the life Jon and Tim once led, was almost completely erased from the picture of relatedness composed by the men with whom I worked when they framed their self-presentation in terms of family. In fact, the images behind the store window represented what gay family is *not* about. In other words, the images on the storefront depicted a social life against which the family could be and was defined. The force of the movement away from the overtly sexual forms of gay sociality reflected in these images is reiterated in Jon and Tim's earlier reference to the sociality of bars and circuit parties and their description of how family life has removed them from these forms and modalities of building relationships.

Yet the public circulation of images like those in the display window indexes a supposedly "real" difference that troubles efforts to represent non-heterosexual family life as virtually the same as the heterosexual norm. What is being pushed aside in narratives of similarity is the potential for violence that arises in conjunction with the image of two erotically involved men performing the domestic duties of loving and caring for children in an aggressively heteronormative world (Bersani 1995; Bersani & Phillips 2008; Foucault 1983; Povinelli 2006).[5] As Tim intimates, being vulnerable to such violence is part of the everyday experience of family.

[5] Foucault (1983) has famously described how it is not the specter of two men having and enjoying sex that unsettles the social order. Rather, it is the specter of two men who have had sex living happily and tenderly ever after that proves unbearable. According to Leo Bersani, two gay men living together tenderly after sex is threatening to the existing political order because it demonstrates a type of "counterproductivity" in which same-sex relationships are not configured as "lifting the barriers to seething repressed

I don't dwell on this all the time, but I definitely have a very powerful imagination of an event that I just know, one day, will happen. The scenario is something like this: We are all out walking and somebody yells, "Hey, faggot," or something like that. Of course the kids are going to know that we're gay, that's obvious. But what I can't quite figure out is how to deal with that moment of shame when even though we are out completely, we are targeted by bigotry. When all that work we've done to show our kids that being gay is all right—that there is nothing wrong with being gay—will be undone by some son of a bitch driving by in a car. That's going to be a real challenge to me as a father, to everything we've built. I want to be able to say that I will gather all my gay positive strength and go over and knock the guy's teeth out, but in reality that's unlikely. In a way the guy isn't wrong. We are a couple of faggots with kids.

The imagination and anticipation of such violence, and the possibility that the meaning of one's relationships can be stripped away through another's words, makes "waiting and seeing" crucial to the meaning of relatedness in nonheterosexual families. In the wake of Tim's reflections, Jon's assertion that "we just aren't that different" must be understood in the context of an ever-present skepticism found in the self and others that draws on biological notions of being related in such a way that the meaning of one's relationships can be stripped away by an outsider's knowledge or insinuation (Cavell 1994; Schneider 1997). What Jon's statement gives voice to is the doubt that haunts the idea that investments in love, legal contracts, and the performances of care necessary for raising children make the existence of family factual, beyond the threat of reasonable doubt. Such uncertainty about how one is related can be transformed into the radical skepticism and excuse for violence Tim fears. Hence, despite all the efforts Jon and Tim have made to ensure that their children do not evoke suspicion in the eyes of a vaguely defined public, they remain anxious about a future moment when an unknown person utters the term *faggot*, and all those efforts come undone.

What Tim and Jon offer in response is an ethic of "waiting and seeing" that entails reflecting on one's feelings and experience of paternal, family,

---

drives, but of consciously, deliberately playing on the surfaces of our bodies with forms of intensities of pleasure not covered, so to speak, by the disciplinary classifications that have until now taught us what sex is" (Bersani 1996:81). Happy gay men are troubling because they are "trying out" subversive and revolutionary social arrangements that threaten to undo the existing social order.

and sexual relationships before arriving at the meaning of a kin relation. Such an ethic stands in direct opposition to efforts that seek to derive the meaning of belonging and intimacy within a family through the application of an overarching theory—such as biogenetic configurations or the symbolism of blood and law often situated at the center of U.S. forms of kinship (Schneider 1968, 1972). The difficulty of giving voice to forms of relatedness that cannot be readily described in any standardized language is expressed in Jon and Tim's comments about designing a birth announcement. Jon described the struggle:

> We're in such a quandary over this. I mean how do we include Jennifer [the woman who gestated their children]. She is definitely a part of all our lives, yet at the same time she doesn't really fit the usual profiles. Sure, we could just put "birth mother," or "surrogate mother," or "bio-mom," or just "born from" on the card. But all these are problematic because strictly speaking she is none of these. There ain't no moms here! She isn't a surrogate mother, which is how all the legal documents refer to her, because there is no mother here. She isn't standing in for anyone. At the same time, we want to recognize her part in the formation of our family and put her on the birth notice. Now, don't get me wrong. Madeline might play mommy and daddy with her friends, but the kids don't have a mommy. Instead of a mommy and a daddy, our kids have a daddy and an Abba—that's me [*Abba* is the Hebrew word for *father*]. Everybody here knows exactly what's going on and how it all works. We don't have an identity problem, we have a naming problem, and that's why the design of this card is so hard.

As Jon recalled the various strategies he and Tim had pondered while trying to adequately represent Jennifer's place in their lives, it became clear that the problem was not the inadequacy of existing terms but their overdetermined quality (see Borneman 1996; Carrington 1999; Lehr 1998; Sullivan 2004). For Jon, using terms associated with dominant notions of kinship was problematic because it reinforced the definition of biogenetic relations and those relatives brought into being through heterosexual reproduction as original and factual, leaving his and Tim's status and relationships to be seen as derivative and fictive (Carsten 2000). In other words, Jon and Tim seemed to be working against what they recognized as the excessive and overwhelming capacity of normative notions of kinship to simultaneously serve up both meaning and death-dealing doubt.

The solution Tim and Jon came up with was to draw two curved lines in the form of an elongated horizontal S across the bottom of the card.

Below—in the same style of calligraphy that appeared on the rest of the card—they simply wrote Jennifer's first and last name. By allowing Jennifer's name to stand independently and unqualified by a prenamed position in the family's life, Jon hoped to express the incompatibility between their family relationships and family relations defined in terms of birth and the law. The card was a graphic and textual experiment that expressed belonging in the family through modifications in the established genre of the birth announcement. It was by adapting an established expressive form that Jon and Tim hoped to provoke contemplation and solicit, through the reader's gaze, a modified understanding of family.

Of course, the design and distribution of the birth announcement does not render Jennifer a mother, and neither, strictly speaking, does it render Jon and Tim fathers; but it signifies inclusion in a family and kinship to a reading public. Tim explains, "Those who know where Jennifer fits in recognize her place in our lives. And, those who don't, well, they can guess and call her what they will. At a certain level, it's beyond our control, but we try."

Both Jon and Tim are perfectly aware that preexisting sets of meanings confront their family relations and that these meanings impose an order that is external to their own sense of being related. They are perfectly aware of the variety of vocabularies that can be and are hung on their relationships to make them intelligible across varying social fields and public spheres in different ways. They are also aware of the multiple readings to which their own words and graphic representations can and will be put and of the cost that these readings could exact in terms of their family's ability to exist together. Yet both remain committed to finding words and ways to represent their daily experience of family and belonging in kinship so that their relations would be received with their complexity intact. Tim made this very clear when he announced one evening, "You know, the thing about our family is that it's complex, but it's not complicated. Nobody here is confused about what's going on or where they belong."

Framed by Kinship

Tim and John's moment of reflection before the storefront window in Provincetown casts light on the complexity to which Tim refers. It invites consideration of the experience of being seen and the effects of having one's relationships become the surface for another's reflections on the meaning of being related, and it says something about the possibility of living outside kinship and the role of the closet and closeted knowledge in determining what can and cannot be known about gay parenting.

The storefront display led Jon to contrast the life he was living with Tim and his children with his old life—the one reflected in the images displayed behind the glass. In Jon's reflection, fatherhood became a principle solidifying each form of identity and unifying time. Jon attempts to encapsulate the meaning of being gazed at, and of gazing at others, by evoking a notion of time in which the meaning of one's present-day social relationships have a known past which provides for a clear present and the possibility for predicting the future. In so doing, he devises a means of distinguishing family life and paternity from its represented other. Through the "now" of fatherhood, Jon reworks the meaning of difference in such a way that one's care of children marks the separation between the "us" in front of the glass from the "them" behind it. With Jon's words in mind, and the frame they provide for understanding the encounter between different social worlds, I propose reversing the equation and thinking about what, in a sense, the men in the pictures behind the glass see.

For the men in the images, the words "look at us now" take on a different meaning from that intended by Jon. With the phrase "look at us now," Jon brings the distinguishing characteristics of difference associated with the terms *father, anthropologist, child, gay,* and *straight* into a historical consciousness. He juxtaposes the known characteristics of the present with those of the alternate social world of his and Tim's past—a past they are separated from by the play of light across reflective surfaces and the distance granted by evoking the ironic mode.

As I "look at us now" from the vantage point of writing after the fact, the emergence of difference that accompanies this moment of (mis)recognition illuminates the series of mimetic transfers that define the encounter between gay fathers and the social sciences and the impossibility of maintaining the division between self and other by way of theories of kinship or sexuality. After all, Tim's comments about going out and roaming remind us that we cannot assume that the men pictured in the window are not fathers, or that the social world of family is hermetically sealed from and exclusive of the social life the photographer frames for viewing.

My image, in the eye of the other, pushing a stroller down the summer streets of Provincetown reveals both the limits on and possibilities for understanding relationships and intimacy through such categories as "gay," "straight," "father," and "anthropologist." My image reflected in the eye of the other displaces the autobiographical "I" as well as the distinction between self and ethnographic other. From the perspective of the men pictured in the window, I was virtually transposed and transported into the imagined life of a gay father—complete with a stroller, two children, a supportive network of friends, and even an interested anthropologist studying my life and relations. The passive interpolative force of this gaze teaches us that the subject emerges as vulnerable to kinship because discursive circulations positing kinship as originating in birth carry the capacity to moor and unmoor the body to identities and obligations that are not necessarily one's own or of one's own making. It is the repetitive machine-like quality of biological kinship and its capacity to bring certain relations into and out of being that make kin relations somewhat uncanny.

The meaning of paternity in the present, as well as of the "I" of the fieldworker, dissolves when we hear Jon and Tim reflecting nostalgically on their participation in the alternative form of relatedness represented in the window. In its place we find excess, and the three questions—"Are you gay?" "Do you have children?" and "Does it matter?"—become impossible to answer. In other words, all objectivity disappears because the construction of sex and kinship as crucial sites of contestation that break identity and knowledge into charged binaries is revealed to be a trick of the eye (Sedgwick 1993). By gazing through the storefront window, we learn how sexuality and kinship have nothing (and yet everything) to do with knowledge and belonging.

Michael Taussig (1993) argues that we are not in a position to derive the meaning of such an encounter by increasingly layering on more and more contextual details to later strip bare through analysis. Such would be the case if one were to engage in the professional deconstruction of the researcher's desires to know and be known (Marcus & Fischer 1986). Instead, one is left no choice but to react and acknowledge that something crucial about what makes one a self is "implicated and imperiled in the object of study, and in its power to change reality" (Taussig 1993:217).

For Taussig, this moment of excess prefigures the possibility of ethnography and, once revealed, signals the end of a certain history of social science. Finding myself caught in mimetic excess, or framed by kinship, signals to me our coming to sense how the very categories we, as social scientists, use to attach bodies to words, and words to worlds, are imperiled by the senses and by sensual forms of education, whether in the register of kinship or of sexuality. To shift the assemblage, we need to enter into the mimetic magic of being in two places at once and recognize that words and photographs transform the self not only into an anthropologist but also into a (gay) father, the son or daughter of a (gay) man, and back again. They also transform the self from child to parent and back again.

The three questions—"Are you gay?" "Do you have children?" and "Does it matter?"—now seem to beg an additional question (if not more than one). And, while the question seems to follow logically from the others, none of my informants or my university's research oversight committee ever asked me if my father was gay, even though this information would seem to impinge equally on what could and could not be learned through conversation. I suggest it is the impossibility of providing a satisfactory answer concerning how and if this truth matters when things like belonging in kinship, paternity, and sexuality are visceral entanglements that take the form of "chimeras of possible longings" (Taussig 1993) that works against posing the question. In the face of such fragility, it becomes impossible to determine who is or is not a father and who is and who is not gay, as it becomes impossible to claim knowledge of natality and just who the children of gay fathers might be. All that can be done, I guess, is wait and see.

2

Anthropologists have long been invested in understanding the terms people use to name and categorize kin. For instance, Lewis Henry Morgan, often recognized as the founder of American anthropology, built an entire comparative approach to the study of culture around the words different peoples use for kin relations. Morgan's method developed from his interest in the origins of the various indigenous North American "tribes" and their differing social orders. It was while Morgan was trying to prove that all Native Americans were descended from a common Asiatic people—an effort he pursued through a global comparison of kinship systems—that he discovered six different classificatory "schemes" for grouping and organizing kin relations (Kuper 1988; Morgan 1870). While there may be an uncountable number of names available across the globe for kin, Morgan found that the ways humans have devised to group and classify kin are essentially variations on these six systems. According to Morgan, these systems (he named them Hawaiian, Sudanese, Eskimo, Iroquois, Crow, and Omaha) reflected differing degrees of knowledge concerning nature or the "true" biological order of relations. For instance, Sudanese kinship terminology had a specific name for nearly every conceivable biological relation, which demonstrated a close alignment between the classificatory system and natural facts. This close alignment made Sudanese kinship, according to Morgan, the most "descriptive" of all kinship systems as well as the most modern or recently devised. Hawaiian kinship, by contrast, was the least aligned with nature and was thus the most "classificatory," grouping and distinguishing relatives only according to gender and generation (Morgan 1870).

Morgan (1877) considered systems of classification with little or no correspondence to the facts of biology the most ancient because they display ignorance of the "true" relationship between heterosexual sex, biological conception, birth, and the creation of relatives. Descriptive systems, he thought, developed more recently since they display clear knowledge of the actors and actions involved in sexual reproduction and the creation of blood relations. In classificatory systems, for example, an ego might call multiple figures "mother" or "father," drawing no clear distinction between those actors who were involved in his or her conception and birth and those who were not (Morgan 1877). For Morgan, and a whole generation of anthropologists, the use of kin terms that make no distinction between biological and nonbiological relations was a holdover from earlier primitive social arrangements. Classificatory kin relations, even when found in the most "modern" social orders, were seen as relics of the "primitive promiscuity," or *hetaerism,* thought to define the earliest state of human society (Bachofen 1967 [1861]).

While Morgan's analytic trajectories and intellectual commitments might seem antiquated by current standards, and as having little or no relevance to an analysis of queer parenting, his initial insights concerning the importance of sex and sexuality, reproduction, and knowledge of biological relations—especially biological paternity—to social organization continue to operate in the public and political culture and to influence the discipline of anthropology (Fortes 1970; Povinelli 2002a; Schneider 1968; Strathern 1992a, 1992b, 2005). Contemporary anthropologists may reject many of the ideas orienting Morgan's thought, but his initial division between classificatory and descriptive forms of kinship, based on the correspondence between kin terms and sex, remains pertinent both in and beyond the discipline. The rules and logic of biological kinship, elevated to the status of the norm, continue to serve as a point of departure for rendering certain families, such as those formed by gay men with children or those formed through interracial adoption, "alternative" and, thus, legible on the basis of their exceptional status (see Butler 2004; Schneider 1997; Weeks, Heaphy, & Donovan 2001; Weston 1991). The implications of defining such forms of kinship and intimacy as exceptional are quite striking, given that, for a growing number of people in the Western world and beyond, the formation of family relations and the making of relatives does not entail procreative heterosexual sex, anatomical birth, or marriage (Franklin 2013; Rapp & Ginsburg 2001; Stacey 1998; Strathern 2005).

As these early anthropologists discovered, kin terms can and do name relationships that do not necessarily correlate with physiological or legal relations, and confusion often results when words like "mother" and "father" are assumed to describe biological, or even kin, relations (Maine 1861; McLennan 1885; Morgan 1870; Rivers 1900; Tylor 1889). David Schneider's (1984) critique of the study of kinship, in which he argues that kinship is an invention of Western anthropology that holds no correspondence to any indigenous category, was perhaps most responsible for pushing anthropologists to reckon closely with the biases found in modes of analysis that place decidedly Euro-American folk beliefs about biology and biological notions of relatedness at the center of efforts to understand different social structures, institutions, and forms of kinship. In the wake of Schneider's critique, many anthropologists have come to think of differing modes of delineating and emphasizing relational categories, whether in a Malay fishing village or among same-sex parents in the United States, as representing different "cultures of relatedness" (Carsten 2000a). Kinship is no longer seen as indexing, or expressing, the workings of a wider, perhaps superorganic, human culture but as a modality and technology that brings lives, their value, and their connections into being (Carsten 2000a, 2000b; Franklin and McKinnon 2001; Ginsburg & Rapp 1995).

My brief detour through the anthropological archive is meant to demonstrate two things: first, that anthropologists have always found kin relations and kin terms to be shrouded in uncertainty, and second, that they have known for a long time that few people track heterosexual reproductive careers when accounting for the origins of their kin relations. Since the very inception of the field, anthropologists have understood that one cannot presume to know the meaning of kin terms in advance and that the connection between kin terms and lived relations must be learned (Beattie 1968; Kuper 1988). Anthropologists have also known that kin terms, such as "mother" and "father," do not necessarily name singular relations (Firth 1969; Rivers 1968; Schneider & Homans 1955). What I hope to demonstrate in this chapter is how the need to discover, translate, and learn the meaning of kin terms is far from an obscure anthropological concern. Rather, it is an ordinary task tied to maintaining everyday life in contemporary Europe and the United States.

In the pages that follow, I explore the uncertainty that surrounds the use of kin terms in queer families. I am interested in understanding how one learns what words apply, and what words do, when one describes queer family relations. I think of my task as learning the terms of kinship—both as vocabulary and as the conditions of possibility enabling same-sex couples to bring children into their lives and to live as family. I want to understand the limits and possibilities offered by established kin terms for transmitting knowledge of familial relations when the everyday modalities of building and living in kinship are incommensurate with dominant cultural notions about the origins of family, paternity, and the making of relatives. To understand the families of gay men with children, it seems helpful to know how and when words like "father" come to be matched with relations and what using or not using such established kin terms might mean when describing or naming one's relations. As Jon and Tim's efforts to express the intricacies of their relationships on a birth announcement showed, the association between biological kinship and established kin vocabularies works to undo the meaning of the belonging and intimacy they brought into being. After all, the language and logic of biological kinship are often deployed by those who wish to exclude same-sex families, whether they include children or not, from citizenship and participation in civil society (Butler 2000, 2004).

For example, one often hears the claim that the families and kinship formed by gay men are merely creative fictions, that they are not worthy of state sanction or protection because procreation, and, thus, true biological relations and kinship, does not, and cannot, come about through homosexual relations As a result, queer families are often understood "as if" they were real, rather than granted an ontological status comparable to that granted biological kin relations in the public sphere. Distinctions of these sorts are crucial since becoming a parent and taking up the responsibilities of raising children continue to be equated with attaining full adulthood and responsible citizenship in the Western world and beyond (Borneman 1996; Franklin and Roberts 2006; Sedgwick 1993).

I examine these issues by chronicling scenes from the everyday life of two gay families, exploring how both parents and children gained knowledge about the meaning of kin terms and how these words came to be matched with relations. Through these scenes, I comment on what kin terms can and cannot do, which kin terms can and cannot be made to express the nuances of gay family life, and the horizons revealed by taking up relationships to which particular kin terms are attached. Like many anthropologists before me, I begin by assuming a position of uncertainty about the meaning of kin terms and kin relations and look toward the moments when a temporary resolution is found for the uneasiness that accompanies questions of kinship.

George and Stephanos

George and Stephanos lived in suburban New Jersey, forty-five minutes outside New York City. They had three adopted children, two girls and a boy. Two of their children were born in China and one in New Jersey. All were born within sixteen months of one another, and they were between the ages of five and seven when I became acquainted with them in the summer of 2002.

When I met them, George and Stephanos had known each other for more than twenty years, and their relationship had passed through multiple phases. The two had met as college students, in a bar in New York City, and from this beginning their relationship moved through a period of casual noncommittal sex to nonexclusive dating, exclusive monogamous intimacy, cohabitation, and, eventually, legally sanctioned domesticity and the common guardianship of three adopted children. The pair benefited from the 1994 legal ruling in New Jersey that allows same-sex couples to jointly adopt children—which they did—but it was not until 1999 that they legally formalized their family relationship by holding a commitment ceremony and performing a civil union in the state of Vermont.

George and Stephanos tended to articulate the movements in their relationship as coinciding with changes in their professional lives and financial standing. The braiding of the professional, the financial, and the personal into a family narrative indexes the ways notions of achievement, success, and failure—often, as defined by managerial and administrative discourses—infuse and inform ideas about building and maintaining kinship (Stacey 1998; Strathern 1992b). I understand the infusion of professional managerial discourses, and of ideas about property, with notions of kinship as indicating the way intimacy and family are partially built on the freedom and the principles of choice imagined to define free-market relations (Strathern 1992b). Here, the making and administration of family is thought of in terms analogous to the free will, rational choice, entrepreneurialism, and investment defining private enterprise (Franklin 2013; Franklin & Roberts 2006; Strathern 1992b). As a result, the class-based ideologies and references to capital at work in the creation of George and Stephanos's family narrative exist alongside the particularities of an "enterprise culture" (Strathern 1992b, 2005), and the legal and financial notions used to build and administer relations in the public domain of free-market capitalism provide logics and vocabularies for articulating the formation of intimacy and for crafting domestic life (Stacey 1998; Strathern 1992a, 2005). The infusion of managerial and administrative discourses into the domestic, and vice versa, illustrates that what are often assumed to be separate and distinct domains become blended in kinship, asking us to consider how biology and capital merge in ways that complicate previously established ideas about class and the operation of capital in determining the meaning and form of family relations (Carrington 1999; Franklin 2013; Rapp 1978). The families of gay men with children demonstrate how biology and capitalism merge in ways that extend beyond the manufacture of genetic therapies and reproductive techniques (Rajan 2006; Franklin 2013); this includes the melding of the managerial and administrative techniques found in free-market capitalism with the formation and organization of familial life.

For example, George and Stephanos described their family life together as emerging in the early 1980s from the milieu of professional political activism devoted to expanding queer forms of sociality. Throughout college, and directly following their time as students, both devoted time and energy to grassroots political organizing, directing their efforts to broadening the place of queer sexuality in the public sphere and to causes such as securing federal funding for HIV/AIDS prevention and housing for those suffering from AIDS. Graduate school and professional education followed their time as activists, and after acquiring MBAs and PhDs, the pair launched careers that provided them with freedom from certain financial constraints, giving them the moral authority and capacity to choose where and how they might live as a family.

Their movement from a "bohemian life," devoted to exploring and expanding queer forms of sociality, to cohabitation and monogamy dovetailed with their professional advancements and acquisition of the capital needed to jointly purchase a large apartment in Greenwich Village in New York City. Greenwich Village is, of course, recognized as one of the birthplaces of gay politics in the United States and for its thriving queer social life (Chauncey 1994). It is also well known for its desirable and expensive real estate.

While enjoying their life together in the Village, the two began planning a family with children. The pair described property ownership, material comfort, and the secure financial future promised by high-level professional positions in the arts and in advertising as establishing the necessary material grounds for undertaking what they saw as the serious task of raising and providing for children into adulthood. While the couple articulated their material achievements as crucial to their vision of family life, they remained acutely attuned to the ways their personal financial standing enabled them to exercise choice—in kinship, in domesticity, in career—when others could not.

Their initial efforts at family planning led to further, often unexpected decisions. Once they decided to have children, they also decided to sell their apartment in the city and buy a house in the suburbs. Before laying the foundations for their own family, neither man had realized the importance he placed on open spaces, wooded parks, large freestanding houses with yards, and easy access to (and exit from) the cosmopolitan life offered by a major metropolitan area for building and maintaining a happy family life. The move out of the city was consciously undertaken to re-create the physical environment each associated with his own childhood. Stephanos had grown up outside the United States and George in the Rocky Mountains, but both had been raised in solidly middle-class families in semirural areas on the outskirts of major cities. Once this shared imagination of the optimal family environment was revealed, Manhattan began to appear to them as dirty, hectic, overly chaotic, and insecure.

Their discovery of their shared vision was a surprise, since each had fled the suburban environment of his childhood in pursuit of the freedoms promised by the sexual forms of citizenship and community imagined to exist in Manhattan. While the suburbs of New Jersey might not seem an obvious place for two gay men to choose to raise children, the area where they now live is home to a large number of gay and lesbian families, and the town where they chose to settle is known as a center of lesbian and gay parenting. As a result, moving to New Jersey did not entail giving up or leaving the queer forms of community each man desired and had devoted a portion of his life to extending. Suburban New Jersey simply offered a different aspect of the forms of sociality they had both enjoyed and worked to expand as younger men.

Commitments

George and Stephanos began living together in 1988, and they adopted their children in 1996, but they did not legally formalize their union—in essence, making their family a state-sanctioned nuclear unit—until 1999, when same-sex civil unions became legal in Vermont. When I asked about their decision to form a civil union, they explained its appeal as lying partially in the fact that it was not a marriage. Marriage, as formulated in the law, was deeply problematic and difficult for the two to embrace. At the time, marriage was an exclusive heterosexual legal arrangement, and it remains so today in New Jersey. For George and Stephanos, the appeal of a civil union was that it awarded same-sex couples state sanction, protection, and recognition of their family relations but in ways that did not participate in the exclusionary politics and violence enacted against queer subjects by the state through the institution of marriage.

The legal distinction between marriage and civil union appeared to free the pair to obtain state sanction for their family relations without compromising their earlier efforts to expand the public and political domain to accommodate openly queer lives. At the same time that the couple consciously engaged in finding and building kin relations that did not participate directly in heterosexual institutions and norms, they ordinarily used the vocabularies of established heterosexual familial kinship to describe and name their relations and kinship. For instance, both George and Stephanos regularly described themselves as "married" and used terms and phrases like "my husband" when referring to one another. They also wore matching wedding rings to publicly display their participation in a cultural institution and their status as family men, even though the symbol could very easily have been read as indicating the presence of a woman in both their, and their children's, lives. The everyday use of established kin terms, such as "marriage" and "husband," to name and describe queer relations draws attention to the different ways meaning can become attached to words and to the descriptive capacities of kin terms in North America.[1] When George and Stephanos use such terms, even though the state's definitions do not apply, we gain a sense of the multiple meanings and relations that can be and are referenced by kin vocabularies (Schneider 1968; Firth 1969).

When George and Stephanos describe themselves as married, and claim one another as husband, they evoke the ordinary quality of their family relations, even though, in a strict sense, the intimacies defining their family life do not sit easily beside the established use of these words. The ways in which different meanings are evoked by kin terms might best be understood by turning to W. H. R. Rivers and his 1912 description of kinship among the people living on the Murray Islands in the Torres Straits (Rivers et al. 1912). According to Rivers, when the Murray Islanders speak *of* kinship they denote an entirely different set of relations than those classified when they speak *about* kinship. I understand this distinction to reside in the difference between speaking of one's relatives in experiential terms, meaning what one's relatives do and perhaps say in daily life, and speaking about one's relations in abstract terms, meaning providing information about who one is related to and how. What Rivers discovered is that the Murray Islanders evoke completely different registers of meaning when kin terms are used as a form of address and when kinship or kin terms are the object of a sentence.

A similar operation seems to be at work in queer families but with different implications. When George and Stephanos spoke with me *about* their family relations, the terms "husband" and "married" carried mean-

---

[1] David Schneider has described how kin terms in the United States are used as verbs, adjectives, and nouns. As a result, a boy can "complain that his father 'mothers' him" (Schneider 1968:99). For Schneider, the different ways kin terms are applied grammatically speaks to the fundamental distinction in American kinship between relationship as substance and relationship as code for conduct. In the United States, "kinship terms can mean either the substance element alone, the code for conduct or role element alone, or it can mean both at once" (Schneider 1968:99). As a result, gender and sex often slip free from kin terms, and the words "mother" or "father" can describe a kind of person and the role they perform as opposed to one's place in anatomical conception and birth. The same can be said of terms like "marriage," where phrases like "she is married to her job" make sense. Yet, Schneider does not discuss how words are made to carry meaning and what words do when spoken. It is the way kin terms are made meaningful and the performative aspects of kin terms and their experience that I am interested in here.

ings counterposed to those that emerged when they inhabited these terms and used them as names for their own relations. When speaking with me *about* kinship—that is, when kinship and kin terms were the objects of discussion—the use of words such as "marriage" and "husband" carried a history that included the politics of exclusion and the shifting nuances that establish gay families as different from state-sanctioned norms. When used to denote their decidedly queer kin ties, these same words evoked intimacy and the ordinary everyday life of the family relations being named. Yet something more was taking place. Clearly, George and Stephanos were not following a wider social convention, in which meaning is known to shift registers when kin terms are used in the genitive as opposed to the dative case, as one might assume of the Murray Islanders. Rather, the shifts in register seemed to accompany the men's own efforts to express the quality of family relations and the form of an intimacy they themselves did not necessarily know how to name or to describe—especially to a social scientist. In such circumstances, established notions of the family and of kinship serve as known and existing sets of relations that one can point toward when elaborating the qualities of the family at hand.

For instance, in my first telephone conversation with George, when we were trying to arrange a time to meet, he said, "Yes, come by after six. That way you can meet my husband, Stephanos, and the kids." His next words qualified this statement: "Well, we're not really married, you know, but I call him that [husband] anyway. Just come by at six and I'll explain. We have lots to talk about." As my subsequent conversations with the couple demonstrated, the meaning of a word like "husband," "married," and even "father" is a moving target.

The shifting meaning of "husband" and like terms is demonstrated by George's sense that he has to qualify his use of the word and to explain how and why he uses it as he does. The qualification, and subsequent reflection on the meaning and use of kin terms, draws attention to the pragmatic aspects of making kinship and to the place of language in the making of kin relations. It also draws attention to the suspicion that kin terms carry too much meaning, and that their meaning must be made explicit when used. By using an established kin term to name his relation with Stephanos and by later explaining the use of this term, George both builds and thickens the ties he has named.

Following the insights of J. L. Austin (1975), we can understand how George and Stephanos are *doing* kinship when they use words such as "husband" and "married" as names for their relationship. The use of these kin words is clearly a constative one in the sense that the words refer to a set of relations that existed prior to their utterance. Yet, when George engages in an explanation of his use of terms, he draws attention to the way words like "husband" and "married" are also indexical and to how the indexicality of kin terms can be used creatively and pragmatically to make relations legible and to point to social identity.

Following Michael Silverstein (1976), we might think of George and Stephanos's use of kin terms as drawing attention to the shifting referents that serve to establish the meaning of kin terms. So, while the word "husband" might ordinarily be used to name the man a woman is married to, the form of intimacy it indexes when George and Stephanos utter it is only referentially linked to the legal definitions and operations configuring marriage as a heterosexual institution. Not only do George and Stephanos identify as homosexual but their relationship is also codified by the law as resting on notions of intimacy that are different from, but still reference, those associated with heterosexual marriage. In Vermont, after all, a civil union awards and ensures the same protections and benefits that accompany a marriage—as it is most broadly defined by law and policy—but the union remains explicitly distinct from the norms defining marriage as exclusive to heterosexual couples.

I think of this condition, in which ordinary kin terms are used to name and describe relations that fall outside the expected norm, as emblematic of the relationship of queer kinship to those associated with the norm. Queer kin relations clearly overlap with, and sit alongside, established forms of family while simultaneously holding elements that can and often do emerge to disrupt congruence. We might think of George's need to qualify and explain what he means when he refers to Stephanos as his husband as indicating how queer family relations touch but also introduce a fissure in established definitions of kin terms.

The importance of remaining attuned to the different meanings brought about by shifts in the use of kin terms is not new to anthropologists. Yet anthropologists often proceed as if the meaning of words like "father," "husband," or "married" is stable, readily known, and amenable to translation (Borneman 1996; Schneider 1968). Alternatively, borrowing from Elizabeth Povinelli (2001), we might think of George and Stephanos, along with the majority of queer parents, as "relaxing into" the vocabulary and symbols of familial kinship to elaborate legal and relational categories that simultaneously align with and stand counterposed to known institutions.

It is perhaps the easy commitment to the idea that "husband," "married," "family," and the like are stable, or at least relatively so, and express clear and known sets of relations that fosters the sense that George and Stephanos's arrangement is ironic or indicative of a paradox that makes their relations unintelligible. Oddly enough, members of the conservative Right as well as scholarly champions of queer sociality make the very same claim about the ironic quality of queer kinship, although they aim that claim toward different ends (Butler 1990; Viefhues-Bailey 2010). George and Stephanos's use of kin terms, of course, reflects broader social concerns, but it is also something else. The easy use of the terms "marriage" and "husband" to name their relationship also reflects the movements entailed in taking up, and installing oneself in, a vocabulary and an interpretive frame (Povinelli 2001; Silverstein 1976). Using kin terms as the couple do exposes the permeability and malleability of existing forms of familial kinship and points to the risks that established kin vocabularies and institutions pose to efforts at elaborating nonnormative relations. Using words such as "married" and "husband" as names for nonheterosexual kinship might promise shelter from institutional forces that threaten to render queer forms of kinship and sociability illegible, but it also operates as the vehicle for rendering queer relations incomprehensible. When the terminology is understood in this way, the political convictions informing George and Stephanos's arrangements might retain traction alongside their efforts to elaborate their family relations in ways that provide relief from the personal risks of finding one's self and one's relations threatened by unintelligibility.

The two men were well aware of the capacity of their words to confuse and become unintelligible in everyday encounters, and they knew the catastrophic as well as comedic potential carried in their efforts to match words with their relations. For instance, Stephanos recounted an episode that had unfolded the previous summer, when he had applied for a family membership at the local swimming pool, run by the city's parks department. Difficulties arose when the person processing the membership assumed Stephanos had made a mistake when filling out the application form. The form, it turned out, was obstinately heterosexual and relied on the gendered norm that family was exclusively constituted by one man, the woman to whom he was wedded, and their children. As a result, Stephanos had no choice but to name George as his spouse, which meant configuring George's sex and gender as female.

The woman processing the application had never encountered a woman named George and had to be convinced that Stephanos had not made a mistake when filling out the form. A second problem arose when the park worker discovered that the software used to register members and to print membership cards could not accommodate same-sex families. A family, according to the software, was either one man married to one woman or a single parent and that couple's or individual's children. Accommodating families comprising two men or two women with children proved impossible. When the computer application was asked to do so, it reported an error, and blocked the registration.

Stephanos recounted with a degree of delight how the park worker laughed when she discovered that the only way to proceed was to create a transfamily: either Stephanos or George had to pose as a woman for the pool membership to be processed, which seemed to bend institutionalized notions of family and gender even further out of shape. In the end, Stephanos registered himself as George's wife and was identified on their plastic membership cards as female, which meant he was unable to access the men's changing room, as his card would not unlock the door. To Stephanos, the inability to access the locker room seemed a small inconvenience to endure to receive the reduced rates provided to families wishing to use the swimming pool.

Stephanos did not relate the story as an encounter with violence or as a defeat dealt by a chauvinist heterosexual society. Rather, he recounted it with humor and as marking the changing character of the couple's struggles against sex and gender norms in the United States. Whereas, Stephanos and George joked, they had once endured getting thrown in jail for their activities on the frontlines of the life-and-death struggle for federal funding for HIV/AIDS patients, they now found themselves struggling against the sexist software used by the local parks' department and bending to accommodate gender norms so they and their children could enjoy the local swimming pool.

The story ended with Stephanos remarking that the park worker must have been converted into a "devoted activist," because no problems surfaced when the couple renewed the family's pool membership the following year. And neither he nor George found himself locked out of the men's changing room.

The couple's descriptions and accounts of their daily family relations, and the ordinary prospect of their relations being misrecognized, speak to the complexity involved in naming the relationships found in queer families. His pool membership card aside, Stephanos does not regularly refer to himself in public as George's wife, even if both men take a certain degree of pleasure in the way doing so muddles established gendered and sexual hierarchies. Despite their gender-bending use of established kinship terms and notions of marriage, the fact that Stephanos and George are not married, and do not wish to be, introduces an additional complexity into their efforts to match words with their family relations. The pair are joined in a civil union, which legally does not make one either a husband or a wife, or married, but "party to inclusion within such terms."

At the time of our discussions, same-sex marriage was not yet legal anywhere in the United States, and I do not know how George and Stephanos feel about marriage now that it is, but their embrace of a political critique of marriage and their use of the vocabulary of that institution to name their relationship index how kin terms such as "husband," "married," and even "father" can and do float free from what are often assumed to be institutionally grounded moorings.

George and Stephanos were not the only couple I worked with who upheld a critique of marriage, as an overtly political institution, while describing themselves as married and as husbands. The quite ordinary negotiation of the discrepancy between institutionally codified and administered forms of relating and the ordinary use of kinship terms to render queer family relations intelligible grows from the semantic elasticity and expressive capacity of kin terms as they shift registers and move between naming, describing, and classifying. The shifts between registers are what allow the multiple political connotations of using established kin terms to name queer relations to be retained along with the shelter they promise from the standing threat of misrepresentation and illegibility and unintelligibility that accompanies the formation of queer families.

When George and Stephanos use established kin terms as names for their family relations, they not only confuse the expected referents and usage of these terms but they also open to speculation what else these words might mean. The often assumed "natural history" (Silverstein and Urban 1996) of kinship, in which kin terms are supposed to index a single and exclusively heterosexual field of relations, is shown to be contingent and as holding multiple alternative possibilities (Povinelli 2001). The uncertainty that accompanies these contingencies and linguistic operations takes root, and demands negotiation, in George and Stephanos's efforts to build family relations and come to an understanding of themselves as fathers. This uncertainty is among the risks that accompany living in kinship.

The Other Women

While George and Stephanos embraced and performed the image of a legally sanctioned nuclear family, their participation in family making went beyond their own household. Stephanos had helped a lesbian couple, "Anna" and "Unna," conceive a child through artificial insemination. Anna and Unna's child, David, was born roughly a year after Stephanos and George became fathers, but, because of a complicated series of events, the two families were no longer on speaking terms. When we were in regular contact, Stephanos and George knew very few details about Anna, Unna, and David's daily life, even though they lived only a few blocks from the other family. What they did know came from mutual friends who kept them informed.

It was apparent that the experience of helping Anna and Unna form a family was deeply woven into George and Stephanos's understanding of paternity and kinship. The rift between the couples, and the undefined quality of the relation between the two families, spilled into the men's own efforts to both define themselves as fathers and establish what it means to be a relative. As a result, the use of kin terms like "dad," while perfectly ordinary, also provided for moments of reflection on the meaning of family and of being a relative.

George and Stephanos met Anna and Unna shortly after moving to New Jersey. When the couples were first introduced, the women were also planning a family with children and were debating the pros and cons of using sperm from a bank, as opposed to sperm from a "familiar" donor, to make Anna pregnant. At the time, George and Stephanos were ready to adopt, having already completed the necessary legal work, mandatory home study, and seminar for prospective parents run by the adoption agency they had selected in New York City.

The capacity of Anna and Unna to give birth to a child and the place of biology within North American notions of relatedness configure the place of choice in the making of kinship differently for the two couples. The grounds for knowing how and if one is a relative, then, as well as the correspondence between kin terms and kin relations, have a gendered aspect. For instance, biology and established ideas about kinship configure Anna's relation to any child she carries as self-evident. Anna's child may not be recognized as belonging to a legitimate family and Anna may not be regarded as a proper mother because she is lesbian, but the status of her relationship to the child is not questioned (Richman 2010; Schneider 1968; Strathern 1992b). Sexuality might put the social expression of maternity in question, but the biological relation remains beyond doubt. Anna remains the child's mother. Maternity is material; it is in and of the body.

The same does not hold true for gay men. If anatomical conception and birth secure the biological aspects of maternity, anatomical conception and sexuality introduce doubt into paternity (Cavell 1996; Dean 2009). I am not suggesting that the maternal relation is immune to doubt or that birth secures words to relations. Rather, I am suggesting that sexuality and gender articulate with ideas about the origins and existence of kin relations in ways that establish the paternal relation as in need of verification (Cavell 1996;

Elshtain 1982). Paternity, unlike maternity, is shadowed by doubt because of the place of biology, of conception and birth, in the making of kinship. Stanley Cavell (1996) has described this decidedly gendered form of skepticism as registering in the doubt that one's conceptions are one's own and that one's creations are the result of one's own doings. The need to negotiate such forms of doubt was reflected in George and Stephanos's experience of biological kinship and of family making.

Expecting, Part I

Anna and Unna were drawn to using a "familiar" donor to become pregnant because it allowed them to sidestep the expensive bureaucratic and medicalized procedures used by sperm banks and fertility clinics when administering reproductive assistance. By stepping outside the medical environment, they extended their capacity to choose and increased their ability to tailor the form of their future kin relations and speculate with a greater degree of precision about the possible physical attributes, personality traits, and even the intelligence of their future child. By not using the services of a clinic, they were also able to uphold their romantic ideal of conceiving a child in the intimate setting of their own home, which they did by using the rudimentary technology of a baby-food jar, a small syringe, and a bit of pornography for Stephanos.

In a manner that recapitulates many scholarly claims about the place of biological knowledge in kinship, Anna and Unna drew from their understanding of genetics when selecting how, and with whom, they would make a child. They proceeded on the assumption that they could craft not only the form of their future kin relations but also the physical qualities and attributes of their future kin by selecting the person who would make Anna pregnant. Their ability to speculate on the physical attributes of their future child rests on the place of biological substance in kinship, which explains that a child conceived between Anna and Stephanos would be physically composed of the pair's biological material and that kinship comes about through biological conception (Carsten 2000b, 2004; Schneider 1972; Strathern 1992b).

Obviously, when Anna and Unna were planning their family, they knew the decision to become pregnant and carry a child to term entailed establishing biological relations. They were also aware that their family arrangement would index the absence of a man and, thus, a missing paternal figure. The place of biology, conception, pregnancy, and birth in dominant notions about the making of kin means their family would always be marked by the presence of an absent kin member. This is also true of families created through adoption, surrogacy, and other biotechnologies (Eng 2010; Franklin 2001; Franklin & Roberts 2006; Ragoné 1994). Finding they were more comfortable with the idea of being acquainted with, and thus knowing something about, the "missing" father figure, Anna and Unna decided to ask Stephanos to donate the semen to make Anna pregnant.

Their decision was not based on the desire to build kinship with Stephanos. They had no desire to make a hybrid family comprising themselves, as two lesbian women, and the biological father of their child. Stephanos, a trusted friend whose intelligence and good looks the couple found compelling, was simply asked to assist in making a child but not kinship. The job of making kinship, or the social relations constituting a family, was to be the exclusive task of Anna and Unna. By donating his semen, Stephanos enabled Anna and Unna to have a child, and thus a family, but this did not entail making a paternal relation. In other words, Stephanos and his semen would be engaged in making a person but not a relative. And, after the process was complete, even though Stephanos would not be "just any person" in relation to Anna, Unna, and their child, he would not be related to the child in any traditional sense. Separating the making of persons from the making of relations challenges earlier anthropological formulations that rest on the assumption that persons, relations, and words align and that structures can be derived from these orderly alignments. Where anthropologists might be trained, and expected, to find structure, what they face instead are questions about etiquette and the place of affect in obligation.

Expecting, Part II

In contrast to Anna and Unna, George and Stephanos had limited expectations about what they could and could not control when making a family with children. Anatomically unable to give birth to a child, the two had to operate within the institutional and legal environment defined by the state's administration of families and their formation. How and when, even if, they would become fathers would be determined in accordance with legal procedure and the institutional processes that regulate adoption, their chosen means of bringing a child into their lives. As a result, their capacity to choose was greatly constrained and restricted by the state's administration of the family (Donzelot 1979).

At the outset, they had been counseled to believe the entire adoption process, while open ended, would most likely be complete within 12 to 18 months from its start. In the end, they waited far longer than anticipated. George and Stephanos had initially worked exclusively with an adoption agency that specialized in placing Chinese-born children in U.S. homes, but the adoption officials in China failed to adhere to established schedules. After two and a half years of regularly broken and postponed agreements, the couple contacted a second adoption agency that operated exclusively in the United States.

If the first agency had been unable to deliver results, the second agency proved exceptionally efficient, and the couple was preparing for the arrival of a newborn boy within a few months of contacting that agency. Three weeks after the child arrived in their home, an official from China contacted them to ask if they were willing to adopt two children—a boy and a girl born to the same mother. The boy had just been born, and the girl—thirteen months old at the time—had been in an institution since birth. George and Stephanos agreed almost immediately and went from having no children to having three in a matter of weeks.

A few months later, Anna and Unna asked the pair if they would consider helping Anna become pregnant. George was deeply uncomfortable with the idea, but Stephanos was willing to entertain the possibility. George later explained that he had experienced a great deal of hostility and antagonism from the members of his own biological family when he came out as teenager and, later, while establishing himself as a gay man, and, as a result, he was averse to the idea of making or maintaining biological family relations. His aversion to biological kinship was partially responsible for his and Stephanos's decision to adopt rather than work with a surrogate when bringing children into their lives. When describing his disposition toward biological kinship, he said,

> One of the beauties of being gay is that no one expected me to have children, or to even want kids, but me. So, when it came time to make a family, it was always going to be by my own design and no one else's. It was never about—or going to be about—biology for me. That was out of the question. My whole life, I dreamed about making something else—some other kind of family than the one I had. For me, I always imagined adopting. I didn't like my biological family, and they certainly don't like me, so why would I want to make one like that?

Stephanos, in contrast, said he was flattered by the invitation and felt drawn to the idea of helping Anna and Unna make a family. He described coming to be part of the women's plans as an easy process:

> I didn't really think too much about it. It wasn't like we sat down and had a long detailed discussion about every single detail. It was all really casual.

They had us over for dinner, floated the idea by us, and I just drifted along with it. At that time we were really close, and I don't remember either of us being particularly surprised by the question. I think we both knew or sensed it was coming for a while. I guess George had pretty much made up his mind already and said no right away. I kind of mulled it over for a while and then went along with the idea. We discussed lawyers a couple of times, but I didn't even really ask George if it was all right or even if he cared. I just assumed he wouldn't since we had our own thing going on. I just followed along with their plan without really saying yes or no, which turned out to be a bit of a problem, but everything's mostly worked out fine, well, for the most part anyway. At least, at first.

George was initially shocked and confused by Stephanos's decision. He couldn't digest the idea that his partner would, in essence, begin a second family with Anna and Unna right after adopting three children with him.

I said no right away, and when Stephanos didn't [say no], I didn't know what we were getting into. I didn't know what was going on. Our whole life had just been turned upside down by these three babies, and the first thing Stephanos wanted to do is go off and make another family? I couldn't wrap my mind around it. It seemed like he was turning everything upside down after we were just getting settled. Honestly, I was baffled, but everything worked out, up to a point. Sure, I was hurt, but I wasn't devastated. It wasn't something that was going to tear us apart. It seems petty, but it just didn't seem like a good idea to me at the time. I didn't know where his decision was taking him. Where did he think he was going? Was he going? At the time, I couldn't tell. Yes, things are a little messy right now, but we're dealing with it. We're okay with where things are. It's better the way things are right now.

George eventually came around to supporting Stephanos's decision, reasoning that the choice to help Anna and Unna become pregnant was his alone to make. As he put it,

It's not something I would ever do, but it's his body and his decision. I figured, I love him, and I support him, and I respect him, but it's his body and his life. It's something he has to live with. So, why not? I'm not one to stand in his way. It was ultimately his decision, not mine.

In the preceding excerpts, the uncertainties that accompany making family relations bring to light the place of language in kinship. Part of making and living in kinship entails negotiating unanticipated questions concerning who is a relative and what constitutes a kin relation. Scholars of kinship will recognize that Schneider (1972) built his analysis of American kinship around these two questions. What Schneider failed to recognize is how these questions are far from exclusive anthropological concern. As George's and Stephanos's narratives indicate, negotiating the affect that accompanies what Cavell (1987) calls the "unknowability" of a kin relation, and determining who is related and how, is an integral part of making family relations and living as kin. In the couple's elaborations about the feelings that accompany building family relations, the unexpected aspects of being a relative gain voice, illuminating the work of language in making kinship legible.

The couple's efforts to negotiate the meaning and implications of Stephanos's decision to help Anna and Unna form a family reflect what might be termed a "metadiscourse" (Povinelli 2001; Silverstein & Urban 1996) about kinship and its meaning. I am calling George and Stephanos's narratives "metadiscursive" because the men actively comment on making kinship itself and on what constitutes family relations in the process of bringing these relations into being. The movements of their narratives index the subject's relationship to kinship itself, as a discursive field.

By paying attention to "meta" moments—for instance, when George questions where Stephanos's decision to help Anna become pregnant might lead or when he assesses his concern about Stephanos's decision as petty—we learn how kinship and kin terms exist in an indexical relationship to other forms of social organization and obligation. We also learn how what might best be described as "etiquette" comes into play when the pragmatics of using language to express the meaning of kinship proves risky or threatening. The expression of such etiquette is found in constraint, which Meyer Fortes (1957) might argue implies consent to a moral form of obligation.

The questions raised by George's and Stephanos's comments about making family relations do not focus on the use and meaning of individual kin terms. What the above narratives bring to attention is a duality originally described by Claude Lévi-Strauss (1963): the way kinship operates as both a system of terminology and a system of attitudes through which various kinds of relationships and prescribed behaviors are indexed and expressed. If Rivers and others emphasized the importance of recognizing the different registers revealed when kinship is spoken *of*, as opposed to spoken *about*, George and Stephanos's concern over the meaning of making relations indicates how speaking *in* and *with* the vocabulary of kinship has certain consequences or brings certain things about.

In a manner that echoes many of Povinelli's (2002b, 2006) claims about intimacy, the couple's narratives demonstrate how discourses of kinship work to make particular relations legible and livable and others not. Linked with these forms of recognition are notions of sovereignty that establish certain aspects of forming kin relations as taking place by design and as unfolding through choice, while other aspects are positioned beyond the reach of reasoned action and planning (Povinelli 2002b, 2006). For instance, George and Stephanos, as sovereign subjects, are able to freely choose adoption as a means of bringing children into their life, and thereby live in kinship with them, in lieu of their inability, as a couple, to anatomically conceive and give birth to a child. The same cannot be said when considering George's relationship to his biological family. Sovereignty does not extend to his being able to actively choose his way off the genealogical grids that define him as a biological relative, regardless of his preference. Just as Anna will always be biologically related to any child she gives birth to, George will always be anatomically related to his mother and father. Euro-American cultural configurations do not allow for autogenesis or immaculate conception and birth for anyone but a god (Leach 1966b).

Sovereignty does, however, work in coordination with discourses of kinship so that the couple is able to build kin relations that are not defined by biological notions of being related or by marriage. Yet, the fact remains that they are actively engaged in making familial kinship, as opposed to something else, which positions them and their children as participants in sets of relations that overlap and intersect with those that emerge from tracing ancestry through biological descent and marriage. As a result, kinship and kin terms emerge as a pragmatic grammar and vocabulary available for expressing and indexing specific sets of social relations based on an established set of relations between terms (Lévi-Strauss 1963).

That George and Stephanos have consciously chosen to make familial kinship demonstrates the constraints placed on the sovereign subject by genealogical forms of recognition and the vocabulary and grammar of familial kinship (Povinelli 2002b, 2006). Since George and Stephanos have chosen to adopt, they must craft their relations in conformity with established notions of the family. If they are to be and to remain fathers, they must configure themselves and their relations in the image of legally defined familial kinship and paternity (Borneman 1997; Carp 2000; Donzelot 1979). If they were to build relations that did not index established notions of paternity, family, and kinship, their relations would be at risk of becoming illegible, and inexpressible, within and through the vocabulary and grammar of kinship. Perhaps obviously, if this were to occur, their family would be in danger of dissolution by the various surveillance mechanisms of the state (Donzelot 1979; Foucault 2009). It is the enfolded quality of the sovereign subject within discourses of kinship that configures the meaning of kin terms as flexible and contingent on use, but not infinitely so. As Lévi-Strauss (1958, 1963) argues, there might be an endless variety of possible configurations of relationships, but there are only a small number of possible kin arrangements.

Kin terms must be made meaningful, or made to index specific relations, but their plasticity in this regard is not infinite (Strathern 1996). Since kin terms and the relations between them exist independent of lived relations, there is always discord and distance between words and the relations they are used to describe. It is the indexical capacity of kin terms, and the ability to project kin terms into unanticipated contexts, that enables the vocabulary of kinship to be brought into close alignment with lived relations, but the relation between terms themselves remains autonomous and an obstacle to be overcome when one expresses the nuanced qualities and history of a lived relation (Lévi-Strauss 1963). It is the "autological" (Povinelli 2006) aspect of making kin relations and making these relationships intelligible that establishes Stephanos's decision to help Anna and Unna become pregnant as a contested act. Here, the meaning of kinship and kin terms is at risk because the relations being created are precariously balanced on the brink of becoming unintelligible.

George's sense of trepidation and his uncertainty about the relationships that Stephanos is making speaks to the delicate work of using kin terms to express the intricate sets of obligations and commitments that define familial relations. George's feelings also speak to the way kin terms and the relations between them become objects of discussion when making kinship and the meaning of doing so is at stake. The metapragmatic function of language is at work in George and Stephanos's narratives, because there are no immediately available terms or references to describe or name the affective terrain or values on which to rest the relations being made. As a result, appropriate words and meanings had to be searched for and found, and this took place through a discussion of sovereignty and the different ways sovereign subjects are and might become enfolded in affective fields.

It is important to note that the men did not discuss the meaning of kin terms. The uncertainties raised by Stephanos's decision were not put to rest by exploring the lexicon of established kin terms and finding an appropriate word to describe and name the relations being made. Rather, the couple found temporary resolution by exploring the limits and extent of sovereignty in kinship and the limit and extent of feeling as a basis for making claims to another's life. George was able to make peace with, or at least come to terms with, Stephanos's decision to help Anna become pregnant by reflecting on the qualities of his love for the man, the extent and limit of its reach, and the place of the body and its ownership in relationships. His search in these domains indicates the difficulty of knowing the terms of kinship, even one's own.

We might think of his reflections on love, sovereignty, and the ownership of the body as positioning George in relation to Stephanos such that the improvisational language of affection and desire, as opposed to the more structured and juridical grammar and vocabulary of kinship (Cavell 2006), establishes the context for understanding the relations being built. When kin terms are used to index affection, the fixed and structured quality of the grammatical relation between terms becomes plastic and unbound from such things as biology and the body.

When George shifted the context for understanding the implications of Stephanos's decision from the grammar of kinship to the improvisational language of desire and affect, addressing the uncertainties raised by that shift became a matter of etiquette rather than one of determining the meaning and value of a relation based on its place within a preexisting structure. Displaying such etiquette is both a matter of language and behavior, since it is brought about through the use of words and rests on the linguistic expression of a formality or on actively using language to index specific formal structures of moral obligation and positioning the speaker and the addressee within their frames of reference (Fortes 1957). Paraphrasing Clifford Geertz, we might understand such etiquette as sheltering both George and the inner life of his relationship with Stephanos by "surrounding both with a wall of behavioral formality which protects the stability of each" (1976:255). It is the force of such etiquette, one that respects, while refusing, the capacity of kin terms and kin grammars to obstruct the life of relationships by obscuring their expression, that holds sway in George and Stephanos's understanding of their place in Anna and Unna's life.

Etiquette and Obligation

Once Stephanos agreed to help Anna become pregnant, a legal agreement was drafted to prevent the possibility that the existence of a biological relationship might become the basis for making legal claims to care. In the document, Stephanos was referred to as the child's "progenitor" and Anna as the "progenitress," terms that evoke notions of descent, ancestry, and the genealogical organization of relationships but not the attitudes and affective bonds carried in the vocabulary of established kin terms like "mother" or "father."

The words "progenitor" and "progenitress" are descriptive of relations, and they exist within the lexicon of established kin vocabularies but as purely descriptive terms for an objective relation, and their use thus evokes different affects and implies different forms of etiquette. In other words, they do not function as terms of address or as the names for relations but, rather, serve a "meta" function by referencing and describing an existent functional biological role in the creation of relations. By using the words "progenitor" and "progenitress," as opposed to "father" and "mother," the force of legal pronouncements forecloses the possibility that the existence of a biological relationship of descent might be transformed into an affectionate familial relation that carries social obligations. Legal force ensures that the two registers of kinship, that of terminology and that of attitudes (Lévi-Strauss 1963), remain distinct and separate. We might think of the oppositions and values made explicit in the legal arrangement as analogous to those that distinguish a civil union from a marriage in George and Stephanos's discussion of the matter. In each case, the legal enforcement of distinctions that might seem trivial, even negligible, are crucial to the relationships being formed. What the force of law is unable to ensure is etiquette and the proper approach to future desires and the affect that accompanies making and being relatives.

Puzzles

After the legal papers were signed and filed, Anna began charting her ovulation and Stephanos donated semen on the days when she was most likely to conceive. It took two cycles of ovulation and donation for her to become pregnant, and David was born almost one year to the day after George and Stephanos had completed their adoption.

After David was born, the couples began spending more and more time together and sharing the duties of caring for two households and four children. According to George and Stephanos, for the first year, it seemed as though they "were well on their way to inadvertently creating that big gay rainbow family that we all said we didn't want." Then, things began to change. The men increasingly felt that Anna and Unna were criticizing them for their parenting skills and that the women did not entirely trust them to care for David. George said, "It was as if we were also children and continually needed to be educated about the ins and outs of being good parents—as if they [Anna and Unna] were the only ones who knew what they were doing [when it came to child care and being a parent]."

George and Stephanos felt deeply challenged and increasingly provoked by Anna and Unna, and this tension led to a series of confrontations and eventually heated arguments that unraveled the bonds between the two families. According to George, Anna and Unna seemed to believe they held a certain degree of expertise when it came to parenting, by virtue of Anna having given birth to David. The women's embrace of the idea that the ability to properly nurture and care for a child, and thus to be a parent, flows directly from anatomy—what the men saw as a "phony" moral authority based on fundamentally conservative principles—made George and Stephanos feel as though their own family relations were being diminished or disparaged. According to Stephanos, the suspicion being directed toward their family—based on the idea that maternal forms of authority arise naturally from birth and thus trump paternal forms of care—proved so antagonistic, hostile, and, ultimately, destructive, that the men consciously removed Anna, Unna, and thus David from their social life.

I do not know the other side of the story, but George and Stephanos's feeling speaks to the implications of breaching etiquette and disrupting the formalities that sheltered their relationship from evaluation by the strict grammars of biological kinship. The disruption indicates how the force of law may be effectively used to maintain and administer oppositions inherent to the grammatical structure of kinship itself but proves ineffective in governing the shifting formalities on which relations rest.

Stephanos was elusive and evaded direct questions when I asked him about his place in creating a lesbian family with whom he no longer had contact. I did not press the issue, but when I asked him to elaborate on the meaning of his decision to help Anna become pregnant, he spoke elliptically, offering the following thoughts:

> Well, it's so easy to fall into the negative, to think in terms of regrets or something like that, but that's not it at all. I don't even like how that sounds, or what it even means . . . to regret what I did. What does it mean to regret bringing a life or a family into being? Sure, I wish I had some kind of "magic eight ball" that would have let me see what was coming. You bet. But I don't know what that eight ball would really have done for us. Questioning everything—every little detail and possibility—just wasn't the spirit of things. It was about helping two people make a family and a child. They asked me for help, and I wanted to help. You never know where a relationship is going to go or how it will turn out. I was flattered and happy to help.

George added that the insemination was "something he [Stephanos] just did—trusting in whatever would happen." He went on to say that Stephanos "tries not to dwell on what's happened [between the two families] so he can maintain that same 'open spirit' that made it possible [for Anna to become pregnant]." It was my sense that George and Stephanos worried that dwelling on the split and their confused feelings about what remained a significant set of relationships in their life threatened to overwhelm other possible meanings those relationships might come to acquire. It seemed as if the etiquette that defined as open ended the couples' mutual experiments in forming families and making kin could be foreclosed if Stephanos allowed himself to regret his decision. Dwelling on the split, I think, threatened to define the relations between the two families in the very concrete terms of a lost or broken kinship or by the terms of a dominant discourse of "real" kin relations that could relegate their own family relations to a subordinate status.

To think of one's kinship as lost or as broken, one must first assume that one knows what effective, working, or properly functioning kinship is. In other words, one needs to know the proper correspondence between words and relations and to ignore the way the meaning of kin terms is actively made with and through language. The risk Stephanos seems to signal when he warns against the all-too-easy negative portrayal of his helping Anna become pregnant is assuming that the initial endeavor was undertaken with the intent of creating a known and named set of relations and attitudes, which would then be lived out in accordance with a predictable and structured set of expectations and obligations. As Stephanos makes clear, the kinship and family he helped create were never intended to include him, George, or their children. Rather, the project was about helping Anna and Unna become pregnant, about forming a family by bringing a child into someone else's life. It was never about becoming a father or establishing paternity, and thus living in kinship, but about giving back after having received the gift of a child.

The danger of assuming the initial endeavor was automatically about making kinship, and thus paternity, is mortal, and making this assumption risks defining the relationships brought into being by the two couples through established notions of what a family and kinship are and are not. To assume Stephanos and Unna were making kinship is to configure the subsequent strained relationship between the two families as a deviation or aberration constituted by lack, on either Anna and Unna's or Stephanos and George's part. This is precisely what Stephanos and George hope to avoid.

When I pushed Stephanos further, he offered the following thoughts on his place in Anna and Unna's family. I understand his words as providing an explanation for his reluctance, even refusal, to provide the greater detail I hoped to find. He said,

I try not to think about it too much. It only leads to trouble. The plan was never for me to have another family, well, it was about making another family, but I was never going to be a father in that family—or even be a part of it. I wasn't making the family; they were. I just wanted to help. I was trying to give back. He [David] was always going to be their child, and they were always going to be the parents, not me. Sure, I'm part of his life—their life—but I'm also not. Where will I be [in the future]? I don't know. Who can say? In that house, technically, I'm a father, but I'm not. In this house, I'm not a father, but I am. It also goes the other way around. [In that house, I'm not a father, but I am. And, in this house I am a father, but I'm not.] See what I mean? Puzzles.

Stephanos then excused himself from the conversation, offering to refresh our drinks as he left the room. After he left, George steered the conversation away from their relationship with Anna, Unna, and David, and we quickly took up different topics.

In Stephanos's account, how one is present or absent in another's life and whether one is related to another as kin are open questions that arise partially from the indexical quality of language and are addressed through the pragmatic use of language. By listening to Stephanos, we learn how addressing such questions entails exploring both established ideas about the structure of familial kinship, or the relationship between terms within the larger grammatical arrangements of kinship, and embracing an etiquette that protects and shelters the individual formalities that define the inner life of relationships. The puzzles Stephanos confronts—and seemingly avoids solving—arise, perhaps, from the known capacity of kin terms to evoke biological notions of descent and affiliation—thereby overtaking and enveloping other possible forms of organizing family relations—and from the deep sense that the meaning of kin terms and their use is far from transparent or obvious, even for their active users. The sheltered formalities on which kin relations rest, those formalities that might establish the context for using and expressing the meaning of kin terms, are not readily assessable. And, as George and Stephanos's experience shows, the failure to acknowledge them is not only rude and offensive but also grounds for one's removal from the life of a relation. Embracing others as kin means accepting the profound difficulty of understanding the protected and sheltered affections and formalities on which kin relations rest.

Careful Criticism

Directing attention toward the shelter provided by kinship, and the risks associated with kin relations, might enable anthropologists to glimpse the way affect unsettles established discourses about the relationship between kinship, gender, and sexuality. If, as has been argued, queer kinship disrupts, or unsettles, established notions of social organization by rearranging such elementary principles as descent and affinity (Borneman 1996, 1997; Weston 1991, 1993), then the use of kin terms in queer families should push scholars to revisit the place of sexuality and gender in kinship.

Scholars working on topics related to kinship or gender are often urged to work toward a unified analysis of these two domains because of the convergent and mutually constitutive social phenomena within each category (Peletz 1995; Collier & Yanagisako 1987). By conducting a unified analysis, the thought goes, the broad structural configuration of human and social reproduction, familial kinship, and marriage as natural, and thus universal, can be placed within the operations of historically specific matrices of power (Donzelot 1979; Foucault 1978; Yanagisako & Delaney 1995). It is through the unified analysis of kinship and gender that anthropologists have come to critically evaluate the different ways anthropology "naturalizes" such phenomena as the violence associated with the patriarchal family and the exclusions that come from privileging marriage and familial kinship as the primary modality of societal reproduction (Borneman 1996; Herzfeld 2001; Rapp & Ginsburg 2001; Sullivan 2004; Yanagisako & Delaney 1995).

According to John Borneman (1996), predicating human reproduction and societal reproduction on kinship and marriage has led to the emergence of a universalist notion of the human being as heterosexual. By propagating such universalist principles, Borneman (1996, 1997) says, anthropology has gained an administrative capacity over life and the philosophical management of society. The cost of staking notions of the human being, and of life, to marriage and reproductive kinship is the relegation of queer forms of sociality to the space of social death and dying, or abjection, which gains a particularly disturbing political salience in the age of HIV/AIDS (Borneman 1996).

Borneman suggests that if anthropologists championed care over sexual reproduction and marriage, they could move the field away from jurally informed notions that link sex between a man and a woman and marriage to life and that which does not comply with these institutions to abjection and death. Such a move would open a broader range of intimacies and forms of sociality to anthropological analysis by separating the reproduction of individual subjects from the reproduction of society as a whole (Borneman 1996, 1997). As a result, procreation might be seen as a process that takes place independently from the sexual mandates and gendered divisions of labor associated with marriage and kinship. In this way, Borneman (1997) claims, the creativity and innovation of queer subjects who are working toward gaining societal recognition and acknowledgment for their relationships might gain critical purchase in and on the social sciences.

Below, I revisit anthropology's orientation toward a unified analysis of gender and kinship, and Borneman's claims about kinship, life, and death, from a perspective that takes into account the etiquette and affection revealed by the use of kin terms. Does such etiquette make it difficult to locate, let alone describe, the dispersed sets of obligations and expressions of affection that configure the use of kin terms and the meaning of being related as kin? Do the dispersed forms of obligation and affect associated with kinship relocate the place and agency associated with care and the creative crafting of kin ties? If so, does the place of heterosexuality and, by extension, the death-dealing violence identified by Borneman need to be reconsidered?

To demonstrate the implications of considering etiquette when studying kinship, I draw from two encounters in which the way kin terms were used was felt to be out of place or out of alignment with expectations by their users. Because they seemed out of place, their utterance brought reflection more generally on the meaning and appropriate use of kin terms as well as on the meaning of relations. By following the movement of these reflections, I show that the obligations, affections, and forms of care compelling the use of kin terms are far from transparent and that the place of sexuality and gender in the intimacies associated with kinship are far from certain. When the multitude of affections and obligations sheltered by kin terms is recognized, the strict alignment between such things as gender norms, heterosexuality, and notions of descent and the genealogical organization of life and death become less defined and more open than is often assumed.

I first return to George and Stephanos's narrative about family formation, focusing specifically on the men's negotiation of gender and sexuality in their kin relations. Then I consider an experience recounted by another man, Stephen. He and his partner Rayan lived in New York City. The pair brought a child, a little girl named Chris, into their life through a surrogate, and Stephen was subsequently forced to negotiate the place of sexuality in his relationship with Chris.

Empuzzlements

George described the use of kin terms by his children as "quite weird." I take his assessment as indicating his reflection on as well as his relative uncertainty about, perhaps even vexation with, the appropriate use of kin terms in his family.

George said that, as his children have gotten older, they have begun to use the terms "mom" and "mother" in unexpected ways. The children, it seems, have begun calling both him and Stephanos "mom" at certain times and in certain locations, apparently using the word as a form of direct address as well as a classificatory kin term. George recounted,

> Now that the kids are older, and they have more friends in and out of the house, we hear the words "mom" and "mother" a lot. It's quite weird, but what the hell? When a whole group of kids is in the house, after soccer practice or something, I'll be making sandwiches and cookies, and the kids will just start calling me "mom." The same is true for Stephanos. He is definitely more butch than me, so we were laughing about the irony of this big Greek man being called "mom." We were joking that we had succeeded in raising a whole bunch of hip gender-bending children, but there's more to it. We would be driving the car pool, or all the kids would be here at the house for snacks after school, and suddenly one of us would be mom. They would just say, "Mom, can you give so and so a ride home?" Or, "Ask your mother if we can have some more cookies." I don't know who started it, maybe it was our kids, maybe not, but I didn't even blink an eye when I first heard it. I just played right along. Now "mom" and "mother" pop up every once in while when no one else is here. It's kind of sweet. Adrian, our little boy, has started calling us "mommy" in the middle of the night when he's crying and wants comfort. That's the kind of thing that takes the funny out of it. These kids obviously know we aren't women, or moms in any traditional sense of the word, but we get called "mom," especially when we're taking care of a pack of kids, driving the car pool home and making everybody snacks. I think the kids in our house probably just grabbed a familiar word, pasted it on, and made it fit, but it's taken on a life of its own. I never thought I'd become a mom in drag when I became a father, but here I am. It's never occurred to me to ask what's going on or what they mean, if anything. We just go with it. I say, "Okay, sure. More cookies coming up." Or, "It's fine, I'll take you home." It's like they have a sense of what mothers do, and they see us doing it, so we become moms. We just go with it.

The use of the term "mom" to refer to two erotically involved men is consistent with Raymond Firth's claims about Euro-American kinship, based on his work with working-class families in London (see Firth 1956; Firth, Hubert, & Forge 1970). For Firth, this kinship is far from a descriptive system, since terms like "father," "son," "mother," "daughter," "brother," and "sister" all operate as terms of address not only for members of one's immediate nuclear family but also for members of religious orders and other nonkin bodies. When used as forms of address, these terms operate as names for relations that are of integral importance to ego and to the social order, expressing relative status and value in ways that do not imply genealogical or biological relations. David Schneider (1968) has also described how kinship terms in the United States are often applied to persons who are not kinsmen or relatives. Such usage, for Schneider marks a code for conduct.

The theoretical importance of recognizing the way kin terms operate as forms of address concerns the widely held assumption that kin terms, when spoken in different settings and contexts, refer to the same or similarly structured relations (Firth, Hubert, & Forge 1970; Needham 1971; Schneider 1968, 1972). Why, after all, should anthropologists assume that two individuals, called by the same kin term—say, "father" or "mother"—share a role that is transferable, not only from one relation to another but also from one person to another? In other words, why should anthropologists assume two people called "father" are socially congruent and, therefore, in a sense interchangeable (Firth, Hubert, & Forge 1970)? Through assumptions about the transferable quality of kin terms, scholars such as Schneider (1997) and conservative journalist Andrew Sullivan (1996) are able to claim gay and lesbian families are virtually the same as heterosexual families because of their common participation in societal norms and structures.

Firth does not suggest anthropologists pay detailed attention to the infinite ways relationships might be personally negotiated and intellectually explored. Kin terms, after all, are not radically singular in their use, and neither is their meaning self-consciously crafted. Rather, Firth suggests, anthropologists recognize the tendency of kin terms to change in their usage and that social scientists attend to the ways kin terms and their possible uses are learned and projected into and onto new relational settings. From this perspective, studying kin terms and their usage comes to be about expressed opinions of what people "think [kinship] is, or used to be, or would like it to be" (Firth, Hubert, & Forge 1970:335) as opposed to being about representations of what kinship *is*.

George and Stephanos demonstrate how those who are addressed, or those who are named, as kin do not necessarily know why they are addressed as they are. As a result, when they are addressed by an unexpected term like "mom," they are uncertain how and why the term applies to them, since its use arises from creative alliances that are independent of their own sense of self and relations. Rather than searching out the meaning of being addressed as "mom," the two men "just go along with it," placing their understanding of the emerging relationship and its formalities above norms, verbal consistency, and correction.

If one were to follow more contemporary thinking about kinship, and view queer families as displaying a particular "culture of relatedness" (Carsten 2000a), in the "culture" displayed above, the logic defining the relation between terms such as "mother" and "father" and the value of using one term in the place of another is not readily available or transparent to those who are addressed or those who use these terms to elaborate their relations. Instead, one's own creative efforts to make and express kinship are met by others' efforts to do the same, and one often finds one's own formulations trumped in the process. In the place of verbal consistency and disciplinary efforts to establish the correct use of words, one finds the shelter of an etiquette in which expressions of kinship are free from the constraints of such things as gender and sex norms or codes of conduct. The affection and care guiding the use of "mother" is taken seriously, in this case, because it holds a child's desires, provides shelter and comfort, and evokes the terrifying splendor of the visceral entanglements brought about by consenting to the moral obligations of caring and being cared for as kin (Lingis 2000, 2011).[2]

It is when George is speaking *about* kinship, that is, speaking in a metadiscursive register, that the term "mother" becomes distanced from the nuances or intimacy and affections constituting lived relations. It is this relationally distant register that a child's use of "mother" to address a gay man appears ironic, subversive, or as enacting the performative force to undo gender norms. In pondering the implications of two gay men being addressed as "mom," George and Stephanos may draw on the ironic mode for their expressions and, in so doing, comment on gender norms, but any displacement of these norms is secondary to the splendor of protecting and maintaining the order of their family relations and sheltering their children's sense of well-being. As a result, the political implications of their finding themselves to be "mothers in drag" operate in a separate and distinct metadiscursive framing of kinship from the affective language that enlivens and informs the term's intimate use and meaning. It is the splendor of words spoken in the affective register, and in this case the gift of etiquette returned in exchange, that undoes the connection between the terms "mother" and "father," gender norms, and biological reproduction. When the connections between kin terms and biological relations come loose, so do

[2] Of course, the (mis)pronunciation and (mis)application of kin terms can also be met with competing forms and expressions of etiquette in which violence is enacted in the name of maintaining the established codes of conduct associated with sex and gender norms. This is a common experience for many gay men and children who have been forcefully evicted from their families.

grammatical projections in which relations between words are assumed to index relations between people. In the place of these projections, we find the splendor of a gift, or a kinship based not on the exchange of words or material protections but on bodily comportments and affections, like care, that might best gain expression through the conscious removal of one's words from speech (Cavell 1987; Lingis 2000).

It becomes apparent that "mom" can be used, as it is in George and Stephanos's family milieu, as a classificatory term that names persons who perform specific tasks associated with caring for children, such as driving a car pool, making cookies, and preparing meals. These affections draw attention to the place of nonhuman actants in making kinship and to how the creativity and agency associated with becoming kin emerges from alliances formed between such things as the cars, schools, work schedules, cookies, and kitchens that establish the conditions of possibility of care (Bennett 2009; Connolly 2010). It is the place of the nonhuman in caring and being cared for that shifts the site of creativity entailed in making kinship away from the individual and agential subject to a dispersed set of actors and actants whose connections and relations are neither readily nor necessarily apparent.

The implications of expressing kinship through the removal of one's words were made apparent in a story Stephen told me.

Generation(s) of Difference

I first met Stephen at an adoption seminar I helped organize while working as a volunteer for the Lesbian and Gay Community Services Center in New York City in spring 2000. Stephen was attending the seminar to support a friend who had been invited to participate in a public panel discussion of being openly gay, or "out," and a dad. Stephen is a Jewish man who works as a fundraiser for a very large international charity. Rayan, his partner, is Palestinian. He immigrated to the United States from Israel with his family when he was a teenager. He works as a painting contractor in and around New York City. Their daughter Chris came into their lives through the services provided by a surrogacy program for gay men run by a lawyer in Boston. She had been carried to term by a young woman attending graduate school, made pregnant through artificial insemination with sperm Stephen donated.

During the lunch held for workshop participants, Stephen recounted the following story. At the time of our conversation, I had yet to meet Rayan or Chris, who was three years old at the time.

Well, I had an uncomfortable thing happen a couple of weeks ago. Let me tell you the story and see what you think. It happened in a parking garage in midtown [Manhattan]. This older man who was parking the car started the whole thing off. I was waiting by the car with Chris in the stroller when she looked up and asked me, "Where's Daddy? I want my daddy." You see, Chris has a daddy and a Stephen—that's me. It just happened that way. For some reason, she's always called me by my first name. It's been this way since she first began to learn words and names. She chose the terms, not us. I was hoping for "Dad" since Rayan was already Daddy, or even "Papa," or "Pops," something like that. But, she calls me "Stephen" or "Steph," so that's the way it is. Anyway, the guy who was parking the car started joking around with her, saying, "Where's your daddy? Who's your daddy? Am I your daddy? Is that your daddy over there?" You know, like a lot of people do when playing with kids. But, Chris got kind of upset and said, "No, I want my daddy." And the guy just looked at me, and I kind of froze. In that look, I knew he was asking, "Who the hell are you?" It shot through my head that this could be trouble, and I got scared. I had no idea what to do; my own homophobia just took over. I knew at the time, as I usually do, that I should have said, "No, Chris has two daddies, and I'm one of them." He never really did ask me who I was, but I said, "I'm Stephen, we're going to meet her daddy. He's at work." As I'm saying this, Chris is just looking at me. Not only does she get really uncomfortable and agitated when people she doesn't know take an interest in her, but she was visibly confused. She was probably thinking: "Why did this guy care? And, why isn't he [Stephen] telling the truth?" The situation was really only weird for me, not for him or her. She was just annoyed. Anyway, she was really confused and kept looking at me, looking for some response to defuse the situation. I still fell terrible because I let her down. I balked because of my own doubts and homophobia. The funny thing is, she yelled out, "I have two daddies," as we were walking away. But there was something about this situation where I had to assess and think about whether or not I was going to come out, and I didn't. I just wasn't sure if I should come out as both a homosexual and a father, and I didn't do either. But the really crazy thing is that she wasn't wrong. She was looking for her daddy and that wasn't me. I'm a Stephen to her. I'm something else— another. To this other guy in the garage, I might have been dangerous — a strange man with a child. She was obviously comfortable with me, but I couldn't be placed [with this child] immediately, and I didn't rise to the occasion and explain things because I was scared and completely uncertain about what to do.

My initial reaction to this story was that many adoptive parents, especially those who adopt internationally, must experience similar moments of mistaken identity and confusion. In my mind, such "mistakes" had an origin in the visual appearance of physical features and in the lack of visually similar characteristics that might be used to link parents to their children (Howell & Marre 2006). When Stephen explained that he and Rayan had worked with a surrogate and that Chris was his biological child, I realized my assumptions about mistaken identities were an artifact of the realist epistemology born of the overlapping grammars of biology, sexuality, and kinship.

When Stephen reveals that he is not Chris's "daddy" but is someone and something else, people assume that the two are not part of the same nuclear family, and are thus unrelated, even though Stephen appears to be performing the tasks of a father. They assume that he does not belong in the sphere of affection and intimacy that accompanies a parent's relationship to a child, because Chris seems to signal linguistically that her kin are elsewhere. The rules of biogenetic kinship say that little girls can only have one daddy, so when she says, "Where's Daddy? I want my daddy," Stephen is transformed into an unknown figure whose presence is potentially menacing. This very logic is recapitulated when Stephen describes himself as "something else" or "another" to the daddy Chris calls out for in the parking garage. In this scenario, etiquette might include enacting violence in the name of protecting a child and its kinship.

When Stephen removes his words for kinship from the conversation, a gesture we might understand as enacted for the purpose of sheltering Chris and her affections from the violence of homophobia, he is caught in circuits of uncertainty that lend themselves to anxiety and other forms of violence. To define himself as Chris's parent after she says "I want my daddy" is to reveal an intimate relationship between himself and her daddy, which means coming out to a strange man in a strange situation. Doing so makes him nervous because he fears his words might be met with physical violence. Yet, to remain mute about the quality of the relationships at hand is to both remove himself from Chris's sphere of kinship and to risk becoming a stranger to Chris and, thus, to be opened up to societal suspicions. Stephan configures his actions as akin to having made a mistake about the correlation between speaking certain words and provoking violence.

Chris picks up on Stephen's uncertainty and trepidations about how best to proceed and alleviates the tension by blurting out her understanding of the scenario: "I have two daddies." The effect of her utterance is to render the biogenetic logic predominantly used to define family members, the logic that configures the relationship between a child and a father as singular, inappropriate for interpreting the relationships at stake. Once the biogenetic basis for understanding the term "father" is undone, the affective register is opened to consideration, and the confusion defining the encounter as a crisis temporarily subsides.

When Chris shouted, "I have two daddies," as she and Stephen were walking away, it no longer mattered if there was or was not a reproductive sexuality founding her family relations. Her words did not cause Stephen's homosexuality to disappear, nor did they defuse the dangers of homophobia defining the encounter, but her voice undid the binary logic that makes having two daddies, or a Stephen and a daddy, incommensurate with kinship. Chris was able to perform these operations by drawing attention to the splendid order of her affections. In this moment, Stephen suffers a small death that takes along with it the idea of a pure kinship, whether gay or straight.

In Stephen's account, we learn that the close language of affection, and the etiquette it seeks in return, does not lend itself to knowing the appropriate use of kin terms with certainty. Rather, the delicate balance of terms and affections sheltered by etiquette are shown to be at risk from the violence of kinship and sexuality. Such standing threats make the conscious management of meaning a necessary part of living in kinship for gay men with children. The problem is that such violence configures language itself as an impediment to determining the appropriate words to best protect and shelter the intimacies and affections defining kinship. In the place of certainty, we are left with laughter that draws on the sense of the fragile balance that might be achieved through the delicate work of aligning words with actions and affection with behavior, or the etiquette enacted by Stephen as he struggles to determine the context in which he becomes, unquestionably, Chris's father.

3

When I began researching the family life of gay men with children, my colleagues advised me to pay close attention to ethnic, racial, and class differences and to seek out consciously the effect of these factors on the lives of those with whom I worked. Their concern, I believe, arose from the widely held impression that gay parents are predominantly white, live in urban settings, and maintain middle-class lifestyles—that is, that they are essentially similar, and that their lives recapitulate many established social norms. If I were to proceed without questioning how this appearance of similarity is produced, my study would gloss over the complexity and heterogeneity found in the families built by gay men with children (Weston 1991).

As it turned out, the majority of the families I came to work with had children who were readily recognizable as racially or ethnically distinct from their parents. In fact, many of the parents who served as my informants understood and described their intimate family relationships as built across the divides associated with nationality, religion, race, ethnicity, and class. The building and maintenance of such relations were seen as a success and were very often cited as evidence of the strength and enduring character of the bonds constituting the family.

The gay adoptive parents I knew saw the maintenance of familial bonds across racial, class, ethnic, and religious divides as enriching family life as well as the lives of those with whom a family associated. Here, diversity within and across family relations provided a model of acceptance of and respect for difference that the greater community might follow toward the betterment of society as a whole. It was as if the capacity to love and care for another, in light of and because of their known differences, provided a means for healing a social body that was suffering unnecessarily from the violence of its own divisions.

When I asked the men with whom I worked to explain the prevalence of such cultural, racial, and ethnic diversity in queer families, they often suggested that it was partly a reflection of where I was conducting fieldwork. The East Coast, and particularly the Northeast, is known for its dense heterogeneous population. The region has a long and well-known history of im-migration from all over the globe, and this has resulted in a certain degree of acceptance toward, and willingness to make, "mixed" family relations. In this explanation, the violence of society's hierarchical divisions—the very divisions living in a "mixed" family is imagined to assuage—is occluded by fortuity, history, and the imagined future offered by an emerging pluralist society.

I was also told that the contingencies of the adoption market into which gay men often enter when bringing children into their lives are responsible for the creation of so many racially and ethnically diverse families. It is often assumed that U.S. adoption agencies and their policies are extremely normative and thus prone to excluding gay men who wish to bring children into their lives on the basis of the widely held idea that gay men are not fit to be parents. The exclusions that result from such policing, it was said, drove many gay men to pursue international adoptions when seeking a means to bring a child into their lives. In this explanation, diversity is a symptom of violence itself and a sign of institutional practices.

A different picture of the policing capacities of adoption agencies emerged when international adoption was considered. International adop-tion agencies are commonly thought to be less regulated and less prone to enforcing the sexual norms that are imagined to exclude gay men in the United States from adopting children domestically. This imagination takes form in the widely held belief that international adoption is the only sure way for gay men to bring children into their lives, since reduced gov-ernmental oversight and lack of administrative capacities make it difficult for foreign agencies to effectively survey the sexuality of U.S. citizens. The lack of effective or total administrative oversight of the adoption process in international settings is assumed to make it easier for members of a sexual minority to negotiate, or perhaps even manipulate, the placement of a child in their care. It is as if holding the status of U.S. citizen and having access to capital trumps concerns about sexuality and its place in the family for those in the developing world who are in need of placing children in a caring home.

The legal environment in which international adoption takes place, I should say here, is quite complicated. The Hague Convention, which sev-enty countries have signed, seeks to regulate the movement of children across national lines for the purpose of preventing human trafficking and protecting the best interests of children who are made available for adop-tion. The convention is designed and drafted to establish safeguards to ensure that international adoptions take place in accordance with mutually agreed-upon standards defining the best interests of the child with respect for his or her fundamental human rights as recognized in international law. Signatories to the Hague Convention agree to conduct a thorough evaluation of the environment into which a child might be placed to ensure the best interests of the child will most likely be served and to assure that competent administrative experts follow recognized and agreed upon legal procedures when transporting children across international lines for the purpose of adoption. While some countries that have "supplied" many Americans with adoptable children are relative newcomers to the Hague Convention, such as Guatemala (2008), Peru (2007), and South Korea (2013), the U.S. government signed onto the agreement in 1994 and renewed its enforcement of its commitment in 2008. As a party to the agreement, the U.S. government must assure that children brought into the United States for adoption have been deemed eligible for adoption in the child's country of origin, that consideration has been given to finding an adoptive home in the child's country of origin, and that all efforts are made to assure that the best interests of the child have been met throughout the entire adoption process and transfer of guardianship. As a result of the U.S. government's membership in the Hague Convention, all adoptions taking place in this country are held to the same legal and administrative standards whether the child's origin is international or domestic. What this means for our purposes is that international adoption does not provide a shortcut for those who wish to bring a child into their life through adoption. When people attempt to adopt a child from countries that do not participate in the convention, the U.S. government's participation assures the appropriate administrative and legal procedures are followed before allowing a child to be placed in a home here.

The veracity of claims that gay men must limit their expectations and accept the likelihood of rejection when attempting to adopt domestically or that they must operate outside the purview of the domestic institutions charged with regulating adoption when searching for a means to bring a child into their lives is vague at best, if not outright untrue (Green 2000; Martin 1993; Savage 2000).[1] The same holds for the idea that adoptions taking place in developing countries are somehow less administered or

---

[1] The experience of William and David (see Introduction) demonstrates how various moments in the adoptive process serve as scenes of instruction through which prospective parents gain knowledge of the institutional landscapes, legal parameters, and administrative procedures defining adoption. The familiarity with institutional protocols and institutional figures that comes from partaking in these forms of instruction results in expertise that enables participants to navigate these arenas and to put the

regulated by the state and its actors, and thus less policed, than those taking place in the United States. It is also untrue that state institutions in this country operate exclusively to enforce norms that prevent gay men from forming families with children (Richman 2010). While one might feel uncomfortable with the logic, gay men are often sought out by the state to adopt or provide foster care for children who are in the state's custody and are either HIV-positive or identify as gay (Galluccio & Galluccio 2001).[2] State actors recognize that gay men, precisely because of their sexuality, may well be the most "fit" and the most appropriate parents for children whose needs cannot be met by the state's own institutions.

What none of these views seemed to adequately address, to my ear at least, was the hope that accompanied discussions of diversity within the family and the sense of healing offered by forging family ties across the lines of difference that are commonly construed as violently dividing the social body but deployed by the state to ascertain the norms utilized in governance (Foucault 2009). Might such an attachment to what I saw as indicators of the institutional administration and regulation of U.S. family life illuminate the melding of subjectivity and institutional discourses in the creation of adoptive families by gay men?

The central location of violence and suffering in gay men's imagination of family makes the relationship between the categories of the normal and the pathological central to a consideration of the intersection of the state's regulatory apparatus with same-sex families. If the categories of the normal and the pathological provide a means for the state to gain a living regulatory presence in adoptive families, as well as a vehicle for putting the desire of gay men who wish to form families with children into the service of the state, as Jacques Donzelot (1979) might argue, we can think of the suffering endured in the name of founding a family as indexing the operation of the state's regulatory regimes on the subject (Donzelot 1979).

It is in this light that I came to understand my colleagues' questions and concerns about diversity as pushing me toward providing an account of what Michael Herzfeld (2001) describes as the role of the family in in-

---

various agencies and administrative offices to effective use when it comes to obtaining their desired familial forms.

[2] Placing children in a nonnormative setting for the purpose of addressing a known "problem" is a well-established practice. Interracial couples, recent immigrants, older persons, or single parents are often turned to by the state to provide sanctioned familial care for children whose needs extend beyond the capacities associated with normative figurations of the family.

scribing the rules of society on the body. The project is particularly salient because bodies are categorized differently in the eyes of the state (and in the eyes of anthropology), following the well-known fissures of race, ethnicity, and sexuality. Tracing the mediation of such forms of diversity in the family allows us to see how those who occupy different categories are positioned differently in relation to public institutions, such as adoption agencies, courts of law, and clinical practices. Members of racial, ethnic, or sexual minorities stand in different relationships to the regulatory arms of the state from members of the white, heterosexual, middle classes, and the experience of family reflects this difference.[3] Folding the state's regulatory apparatus into family relationships decisively configures the experience and meaning of family.

In this chapter, I complicate the homogeneous image of gay families by looking past assertions of success—defined as having achieved a nuclear family that resembles the (multi)cultural ideal—that accompany the majority of representations of such families. I do so to speak to a broad range of issues that arise from the melding of institutional discourses into the family lives of gay men with children. My analysis is drawn from an extended conversation I had with a man I call "Steve," who is white, middle-aged, single, and the father of "Peter," who is Native American. Steve adopted Peter when Peter was twelve years old, and his description of becoming a father included scenes of suffering that continued to reverberate through their relationship. Steve's narration complicates the commonly held assumption that the societal enforcement of cultural boundaries, such as those pertaining to race, sexuality, ethnicity, and class, constrain and impede the pursuit of happiness.

Steve's story shows how the happiness promised by building family relationships is less a product of the triumph of agency over repressive social forms of power that differentiate and divide and more a condition of possibility promised by the successful folding of institutions and institutional actors into lived relationships. As I demonstrate, the complex folding of public institutions into family relations takes place through a commitment, on the part of those institutions, to deriving the relationship between the normal and the pathological by way of established objective

---

[3] Sylvia Yanagisako and Carol Delaney's (1995) acute critique of David Schneider's (1968) attempt to render U.S. kinship as all of a piece is important to recall here. By ignoring the different ways in which family comes to be aligned with the state, and the different ways family relations operate at oblique angles to state discourses, Schneider (1997) assumed that the U.S. experience of family is fairly homogeneous.

criteria. I argue that such an operation configures suffering as crucial to accepting the existence of a family relationship.

The willingness to suffer in the name of the family unsettles narratives that equate achieving happiness—whether within family relationships or otherwise—with activism directed toward relieving the constraints of cultural discourses on the subject's ability to form relationships (Foucault 1978). When attention is turned toward the suffering that accompanies building and maintaining family relations, one becomes aware of how the state's efforts to regulate society "plays upon the family" (Donzelot 1979). Might the juridical sanctioning of specific cultural ideals of the family and kinship intersect with clinical discourses in such a way that the subjective experience of family relationships becomes impossible to separate from institutional forms of power?

For gay men, successfully adopting is not simply a matter of demonstrating a commitment to actively achieving and maintaining established and accepted images of family relations. To bring a child into one's life through adoption (as well as through pregnancy), one must also be willing to have one's sense of self, or one's subjectivity, defined through the operations of public institutions and the law. The embeddedness of the family within the operations of the state, I maintain, is what makes it impossible to locate the impediments to achieving happiness, something often imagined as a product of the strict political enforcement of cultural boundaries, such as the one between heterosexual and homosexual identities.

I look at the anxiety generated by the gaze of the state on gay adoptive fathers by analyzing Steve's experience of family. For Steve, the perfect family did not materialize. As will be seen, Peter did not sit comfortably within the image of the family held by Steve or the frames of reference used by the state to define a familial relationship. This resulted in a series of conflicts and challenges to accepted notions of family, paternity, and state based forms of authority. By focusing on a familial relationship that was brought into being through adoption, approached dissolution, and then reemerged transfigured and transformed, I hope to show how the long history of the state's involvement with the family mandates that images of success and happiness be placed within a matrix of institutional practices (Butler 2002; Donzelot 1979; Foucault 2003). It is due to this involvement, I claim, that the happiness associated with family relations is linked to social regulation and the administration of norms. After all, coming to embody dominant images of family life, as defined and regulated by public institutions and state agencies, is configured as the condition of possibility for achieving happiness.

Steve's relationship to Peter and the various "officials" who became involved in his family does not necessarily represent the "dark side" of gay adoption, since the outcome of his story is ultimately one of success, if not happiness. Yet, the challenge Steve's narrative poses to our understanding of the state's regulatory mechanisms speaks to societal investment in particular forms of familial authority and the trouble that results when such forms of authority are challenged. It is toward understanding the presence of institutions within the family that I now turn.

The Struggles of Daily Life

"Steve has a story to tell." Rodney and David brought Steve's situation to my attention after I mentioned that everyone with whom I was working described their family relationships as nothing less than the perfect embodiment of the family life they had dreamed of. Rodney and David were no exception, and they jokingly confirmed my impression, describing how they really were happily living out their lifelong dream, even though they struggled with the physical and psychological legacy of the neglect one of their children had suffered in an orphanage in South Asia and even though David was HIV-positive and his survival depended on strict adherence to a pharmaceutical regimen of care.

"Sure, we struggle," David explained. "But ours are the ordinary struggles of family and parenthood. We're really very happy. We have our problems and our issues, but we've never really struggled like Steve, and hopefully we never will." According to Rodney, the importance of Steve's story, particularly for an anthropologist, resided in the challenge his experience poses to "the idea that gay men are all perfect overachievers whose family lives are fairytale stories of success." David went on to tell me that, "if Steve will talk to you, you'll see that the reality of gay parenting isn't all perfect and happy."

From Rodney and David's words, we learn that suffering is a perfectly normal, anticipated, and accepted part of family life and that struggling to find a harmonious compromise between conflicting individual desires and collective needs is the ordinary work of maintaining family relations. Yet the couple spoke of certain forms of suffering, such as Steve's, in an entirely different register. For Rodney and David, Steve's experience evoked notions of trauma, and thus of extraordinary pain that holds the capacity to fragment the enduring character of family bonds. I understand David's hope that he and Rodney would never suffer like Steve as resting on the cultural configuration of pain as having the potential to undo family relationships by rendering them incomprehensible (Good et al. 1994; Kleinman 1988; Young 1995).

With the help of Rodney and David, I contacted Steve. He agreed to meet with me, and a couple of weeks after our initial telephone conversation, I sat down with him in Rodney and David's backyard. Over dinner, Steve recounted his story.

He was in his early fifties and had lived his entire life in and near the same small college town in the northeastern United States. His son, Peter, twenty-one years old at the time, was away at college attending summer classes when Steve and I met. I never met Peter, but I learned he had been adopted through state social services when he was twelve. Before his adoption, Peter had been removed from the care of his biological family because of a history of physical and sexual abuse in the home. Peter's biological family lives in a large city a couple of hundred miles from the town where Steve resides.

I have not summarized or reduced Steve's narrative but have left it largely intact, presenting his words as he spoke them. My intent is to show the affect carried in Steve's words and the "pitch" of their delivery and, so, to preserve the relationship between the words, their aesthetic configuration, and the truths they evoke and to make that relationship accessible to the reader. I have also left Steve's words as he spoke them because the narrative itself, in its form as well as content, seemed to perform as a quilted surface on which Steve allowed himself to find rest and comfort after a prolonged period of agitation. In other words, to understand Steve's story and to follow its implications, one needs to encounter his words as he delivered them.

Steve refused to speak with me any further after our initial conversation. My one and only encounter with him ended when he said, "Whew! I've had enough. I'm done! If you come back in three or four years, I might tell you more, but right now I'm done!" I understand Steve's refusal to revisit our conversation, or to say more about his life and relationship with Peter to express the fatigue that arises from revisiting complicated and intense experiences through their narration.

> STEVE: Yeah, I adopted Peter when he was twelve years old, and we went through some shit. But the truly remarkable thing is that after five or six years of all the crap you can imagine, we're now okay. He calls me "dad," he visits regularly, he's in college, and we are a family again. I still find it really hard to believe this is how it's turned out, that this has actually happened . . . given what we went through, but here we are, and I'm just so relieved you can't believe it. I have so much respect for that kid, but man, I also carry around a lot of guilt and crazy contradictions, but, hey, that's what you get when you go through the shit storm we hit. But we came out on the other end, and we're all right. Like I said, we're a family again, he thinks of me as his father . . . he calls me "dad."

A.G.: Yeah, you know Rodney and David told me a little about what you went through. I hope you don't mind, but I already know a bit about what happened.[4] I guess I'm really interested because everyone I've spoken with so far seems to have such perfect families. Nobody seems to have struggled. Maybe that comes later when everybody's kids get older and become teenagers?

STEVE: Damn right it will, with kids it all comes back sooner or later. So you probably want to know the who, what, where, when, and how, don't you? Rodney and David also told me a little about you and your research too. So I've got a pretty sound idea of what's going on here and what you're up to. So let's get into it. Okay, I'm an art teacher. I have an MFA and a master's degree in childhood education and development and another in psychology. I built up all those letters behind my name so I could be a parent. Before that I was a builder, a trade that doesn't give you the stability to be a proper parent.

A.G.: Oh yeah? When I'm not doing this, I'm a carpenter. I know all about that.

STEVE: Fuck, it takes all types, huh? You can tell me about going from carpenter to anthropologist later, that's one I've never heard of. But, you know, it's either steak or ramen and nothing in between when you're in the trades, and that doesn't make for being a good parent. It's boom or bust, and sure the money, when your making it, is great, and, man, do I miss it, but having that paycheck arrive like clockwork, tick-tock on the minute every month, every year, makes up for a lot of sleepless nights. I sure as hell don't miss walking back and forth pacing a trench in the living room floor worrying about paying the bills when I didn't know when that next check is going to arrive. You know what I'm talking about.

A.G.: Yeah, I do. I can only imagine trying to raise a kid in that whole boom/bust thing. It's hard enough keeping myself alive working in the trades.

STEVE: That's why I went to art school and got the teaching degree. I knew I wanted to be a parent after I had a few jobs working for social services when I was in high school and when I first got out of college, back in

---

[4] Rodney and David had told me on a previous occasion that Steve had struggled to maintain custody of his son after Peter began having troubles with the law while in high school. Peter had been arrested on multiple occasions on charges ranging from underage drinking and public intoxication to trespassing and the destruction of property. He had also been expelled from school for selling drugs.

the day. I worked in a boys' home, basically a halfway house for juvenile delinquents, right over there, across the valley. Started mopping the floors and moved up from there. It was there that I began to learn about kids and learned the possibilities of being a parent. Now, included in all that was learning what a parent could do and what a parent could not do for a kid. And when I say *could*, I mean that in every sense of the word. I saw everything that goes on and what its effects are [on kids]. I saw it all— neglect, abuse, hunger, drugs, sex—I saw it all. And you know what? I also saw the successes. I saw what the right ratio of a little bit of love and little bit of care can do for a kid. I saw how the right circumstances can turn a real son-of-a-bitch kid around, and how that kid can come out the other end all right. Sure, that big beast, the system or whatever you want to call it, sometimes just eats kids up. But sometimes it also works. And that's what I'm talking about. How it sometimes works.

So, seeing all this, I learned what families can and what families cannot do. I saw how a little love and a little bit of values can really change a kid around. I also saw how some kids simply get so fucked up, so tweaked— by the system, by whatever—that nothing is going to help them. That's why I got Peter. I'd been waiting and watching for years. I lay all the groundwork so when my friends in social services called, I was ready to go. So when that call came, and I went in and met him [Peter], I realized that here was a kid with a basic set of values and instincts . . . that he could be turned around. Given the right circumstances, I knew he could be turned around, and that I could do that for him. When I met him, I knew we had a fit.

A.G.: So why adopt an older kid? Did you toy with other options, like surrogacy or anything else?

STEVE: Yeah, I thought about it all, and I got to see a lot of the fallout from those things when I was working in social services. I knew I didn't want to foster. I'd seen the mess that makes for the whole lot, for everyone involved. The parents suffer, the kids suffer—it's just too much back-and-forthing with no sense of permanence for all involved, and that doesn't even include all the weird sex and abuse stuff we all know about with foster kids. And I just didn't have the cash to adopt that perfect little newborn. That shit's expensive. I also knew I didn't want the added mess of a third family member, so I said, "Screw the surrogacy thing. I want to do this alone." So I went in for adoption—went all the way with it. At the time, I knew I didn't want a baby. Fuck that, I thought, I want a person. I want a kid. I didn't think I wanted to go through the diapers, and midnight feedings, and the toilet training. I later learned that all this has its unique charms, but that's a different story.[5]

Anyway, I went off looking to adopt an already grown kid as a single gay man. I never lied about it, and it was never a big deal. Nobody really cared. Everybody knew anyway, so I never denied anything, and nothing was ever denied to me . . . at least that I can figure out.

A.G.: I hear that a lot. Nobody ever says sexuality plays a major role in adopting. Do you think the state cared?

STEVE: Oh yeah. They cared, but that came later, after the shit really hit the fan. At first, they were just happy to not have another teenager on their hands, growing up in an institution heading down that life of crime we all know about, but we'll get to the other part later. So I wind up meeting Peter, and they originally just wanted me to be a foster parent, but I said, "Fuck that, it's all or nothing." So when Peter did actually decide to come home with me it was to stay. It was permanent. So, I knew Peter was going to be okay when I met him. He wasn't one of these kids who had no hope. You could see it in his eyes, he knew the difference between right and wrong and he wanted a home. A stable home. He was one of the ones who was going to make it, and you could just tell.

A.G.: And you knew all this from working in the halfway house?

STEVE: Pretty much. That and a few years of schooling in childhood development and psychology. You could see he wasn't a lost cause, and all the social workers and case workers backed me up there. They all said he bonds well with people and that he wants to be loved. Sure, he had a long history of abuse and was literally Dumpster diving for food when he was a kid, which I discovered later after all hell broke loose and the court opened his records, but he was essentially okay because he had a few basic values.

That he's all right now is just amazing. [In his other family,] Peter had it made for the first two weeks after the welfare checks came, and then for the rest of the month, he and his brothers and sisters were on their own, literally. Shit, these kids were living on their own in the streets fighting with the cats and rats and dogs for scraps of food. It was rough,

---

[5] Steve later became intimately involved with a man who had recently adopted a newborn baby. Steve had taken on the duties of changing diapers, bottle feeding the child, and attending to the child's needs while the father was at work. Steve had since broken off his relationship with this man, and he was suffering as a result of the young child's removal from his life.

and this kid knew it. Not only was there neglect but there was physical abuse and sexual abuse in this family, and this is what proved to be the real monster. This kid had to fight and, because of it, he had absolutely no sense of boundaries and no sense of controlling his impulses—sexual or otherwise. But, as it turned out, this kid also had a fierce protective loyalty and aggression that also caught up with him and had to be harnessed.

A.G.: Harnessed. What do you mean?

STEVE: Well, as it turned out, and I don't know if Peter knows I know this, but he used to sleep across the bedroom door to protect his brothers and sisters from whoever was coming in to get them. I mean . . . think about it. That's all about loyalty, aggression, and self-sacrifice, and when dealing with all this crap in his past, that aggression was a side that was going to factor into how he was going to deal with whatever came his way. And, believe me, it all came out eventually, and it came out with a vengeance. He acted out as fiercely as can be imagined, but all that sense of loyalty, and what's right and what's wrong, also came through.

A.G.: Wait, what do you mean?

STEVE: Well, look. Everything was fine and good until just about his sixteenth birthday because everything that happened, happened at home. And then all hell broke loose. We had assault and battery, theft, burglary, and destruction of property all in one week. That's when I knew we were in for trouble. I shit you not. We had problems before, but we went to a whole different level. Suddenly, he was acting out against other people and other people's property. It was all public, and it showed we were now playing in a different league. Obviously we needed help, and I wasn't about to fuck around. But you know, we came out the other side of this all right. I'm not sure how or why—well, yes I am. We were very lucky to have some very excellent and understanding people step in. You know, it's one thing for a kid to be fascinated by smoking pot and its paraphernalia and to be taking a few drugs, but when you realize your kid is capable of hurting other people you really wake up.

At this point, our conversation shifted to the advantages of living in a small town as opposed to a big city for dealing with the problems Peter was having. The officials placed in charge of administering Peter's rehabilitation were familiar with Steve's work in the community and his professional standing in the schools. These same officials also knew the individual strengths and capabilities of the various state officials and other professionals with whom Steve and Peter would have to work as they labored toward reparation through therapeutic and legal interventions. Such familiarity, Steve speculated, allowed for a degree of flexibility within the normally rigid bureaucratic structure of the courts in deciding how Peter's problems would be handled. Steve attributes the successful outcome that was eventually achieved, or the (re)making of his family to such flexibility.

The specific events or incidents that define Peter's behavior as problematic are not relevant to my analysis. In fact, Steve does not provide a detailed account of what Peter did to get into trouble with the law, beyond the legal category of the offenses. What interests me is the way Steve weaves a narrative around enduring a series of events that led to the brink of dissolution of the familial bond he had established with Peter and the subsequent reemergence of their relationship. I understand Steve's sense that he does not need to provide forensic detail as indicating how, in many ways, his and Pater's experience is quite ordinary.

I focus here on the work of institutions such as the family and the courts in Steve's emplotment of the near-destruction and eventual reemergence of kinship. Steve's story demonstrates how in specific circumstances the institutions that cause injury and pain through their administration of family relations hold out the promise of healing the very hurts they inflict. It is the double operation of institutions, which inflict pain in the name of providing restorative care, that constitutes the subject as split or as divided from subjectivity. This paradox, I claim, undermines Steve's sense of certainty concerning the status and the agency of his paternal relationship to Peter.

In the previous chapters I argued that uncertainty haunts kin relations due to the difficulty of securing the meaning of words and of determining the appropriate words for naming, describing, or expressing the meaning of relations. I now suggest that the operations of the state and the simultaneous excessive capacity and failure of its apparatus to subjugate make it difficult, if not impossible, to establish if one's experience of kinship is in fact one's own. Such uncertainty makes the meaning of living under the signs "gay" and "father" impossible to gauge by objective criteria.

In Steve's story, the paradox by which the very institutions that cause suffering hold out the redemptive promise of healing the pain they inflict provides the condition of possibility for identifying the costs of coming to embody the regulatory apparatus of the state. Following Talal Asad (1993, 2003), I suggest that the multiple layering of condemnation and confirmation that arises through Steve's reflection on his experience as a father can be heard as giving voice to an asceticism within kinship that configures knowledge of familial forms of belonging and the truth of family relationships as emerging through suffering. At the same time, Steve's words challenge Asad's (1993, 2003) idea that modern forms of sociality are predominantly shaped by the historical movement away from pain as a form of knowing.

Steve's narrative demonstrates that suffering in the name of the family is not antithetical to the development of the moral forms of living associated with kinship. Rather, it is integral to these very forms of belonging. Steve's words also show how suffering in the name of the family need not be associated with error, perversion, or sickness, as many public institutions would lead us to believe—including those with which Steve became involved. Rather, the pain and suffering of the kind inflicted on and endured by Steve seems to provide both an agency and a medium that enables family relations to emerge and to become meaningful.

Three distinct movements figure in the evolution of Steve's knowledge and embodiment of fatherhood and the operation of the state's institutions vis-à-vis his experience of coming to embody the paternal role. These movements follow Steve's changing knowledge of himself as he prepares to take up the legal status of father and then must address Peter's difficulties as a paternal figure.

In the first movement, Steve describes the transformations he underwent to become a father. Here, Steve teaches us that public institutions define the proper characteristics of a father, and he describes how he consciously set out to form himself into the state's image of a paternal figure so he might one day legally take up such a position. He undertook self-transformations so that he could prove he possessed the objective qualities that define a good parent in the eyes of the state.

In the second movement, Steve explains the consequence of having his capacity to be a parent cast into doubt by Peter's unlawful actions: He was forced to reestablish that he did, indeed, possess the qualities of a good father. The cost of establishing this proof was his authority to define what it means to be a father in terms that are not inflected by institutional discourses.

Steve's reflections on his treatment by institutional figures, after his status as Peter's father had been restored, forms the third movement. In this final movement, his experience of being in a relationship with Peter, that is, his subjective knowledge of kinship, is evacuated as externally imposed criteria determining the meaning of family relations dominate his voice. Steve's reflection on his experience of institutional figures shows how the law's reliance on supposedly objective diagnostic categories to determine if his relationship to Peter is or is not familial splits him, as a subject in such a way that suffering and uncertainty become necessary to knowing if he is, in fact, Peter's father.

First Movement: Becoming a Parent

From his descriptions of himself before adopting Peter, we learn that institutional ideals and practices provided Steve with an image for defining the proper characteristics of a good parent. It was the operation of state-sponsored institutions and the image of the father they promote that provided Steve with a basis for determining that his life as a builder was incongruent with accepted and established ideas of good parenting. Steve describes consciously embarking on a project of self-formation that included leaving the building trades, going back to school, becoming an art teacher, and gaining the credentials of an expert in childhood development to align himself with the institutional image of a proper parent. Steve consciously underwent a process of transformation so that he might one day legally take up the position of father in his own family. If Steve had maintained a division between institutional notions of a good father and his own understanding of what a good father looks like, then his own subjectivity would have remained suffused by dominant cultural images, including the notion that homosexuality and participation in a boom/bust employment sector are incompatible with parenting.

Steve came to learn the qualities that define a proper parent by participating in the operations of a state-sponsored institution. While working in a halfway house for boys, he came to know both what the state considered the proper function of a family to be and what a family could and could not do for a child.

For Steve, attaining the financial and temporal predictability associated with the state's image of a good parent meant having access to more wealth than the salary of a civil servant allows. But he readily exchanged his earning potential in the building trades for the more predictable economic relationships promised by taking a job as a schoolteacher. To display that he was qualified to be a father, Steve transformed his image and mapped his identity in accordance with the contours of paternity in state-supported institutional settings. In a quite literal fashion, Steve took up the qualities attached to the state's image of a good father and brought them to life in himself, so that he could then present these very qualities back to the state as his own.

When Steve takes up the state's image of paternity, state forms of power come to overlay his sense of self in such a way that experience becomes inseparable from the operations of the state. As a result, when Steve speaks, he speaks not only as a father, and thus as what Legendre (1997) calls "the living voice" of state-sanctioned familial authority, but also as an institutionally credentialed expert, one who holds a degree in childhood development and the education of children. It is the utterances of such experts that are constitutive of the state's image of the family and of the proper position of the father within its folds (Goodrich & Carlson 1998). The convergence of such forms of power within Steve, as a subject, means that both his imagination of himself and his experience of fatherhood have to be understood as embedded within the state's efforts to regulate the social order.

Steve's story provides evidence of the embedded quality of the family within the operations of the state, testifying to the necessary collusion between public institutions and paternal figures when it comes to creating adoptive families. From Steve's words, we learn how the family floats as an agency within the state's apparatuses of power and how, in the eyes of the state, belonging in a family comes to equate with participating in the forms of life sponsored by the state (Biehl 2004; Borneman 1996; Donzelot 1979). Steve alludes to the floating agency of the family when he recalls the education he received while working as a social worker. Here, participation in the state-sanctioned forms of living equates with life, and the withdrawal or refusal of kinship and family forms of care equals abjection, the foreclosure of life's chances, or social death (Carp 2000).

In Steve's narrative, the state's utilization of the family to assure the production of sociable subjects is depicted in the negative image and abandonment of the child whose obligations and relationships exist outside kinship and the family. Such a child does not know the difference between right and wrong and is "so fucked up" and "so tweaked" that he or she is beyond help. It is well known that the biological family often produces these very qualities in its participants. All that remains for such a child is a life of institutions and crime, or a drawn-out social death. It is when Steve comes to embody state forms of paternal care that he pronounces those who exist outside the frame of familial care as beyond the reach of help and, in essence, as dead, dying, or death-dealing. Steve's figuration of (the adoptive) family as a form of life arises in conjunction with his articulation of how institutional forms of power operate on the subject, transforming him into the embodiment of paternity and, more generally, transforming those who exist outside the authority of kinship into sociable citizens.

The proof of the collusion between institutional forms of authority and the family is found in the state's apparent lack of concern about Steve's homosexuality, or, at least, his obvious status as a single man, when granting him the legal status of father to Peter. In Steve's experience, it is by possessing the qualities inhering in the state's image of a paternal figure and objectively showing a commitment to raising responsible and respected children that one successfully achieves the status of a parent in the eyes of the state. The state's concern when granting Steve paternal authority over Peter seemed to reside in finding the best possible means of assuring the future of the social order, in light of the known failures of its own institutions (Donzelot 1979). In this instance, the state's role in regulating and policing sexuality is secondary to providing a home for a child whose preexisting family relationships are known to be detrimental to reproducing the social order and the future promised by the state. The same can be said of the state's role in policing the adoptive family, which is associated with coming about through the traumatic disruption of biological kinship.

By listening to Steve, we learn how raising a "normal" child equates with being a successful father, whether gay or straight, and how the law and public institutions create conditions in which adoptive fathers either make themselves into the image of a good father or they are not fathers at all. Institutional commitments to biogenetic notions of being related allow biological fathers to have unsuccessful children or to be less than perfect fathers and still remain in possession of their parental status. The fact of a biological relationship cannot be dissolved in the eye of the law, only the social component of the relationship. In the case of adoption, achieving and maintaining the status of parent is not based on sexuality and the reproduction of biological bodies but on institutions and institutional actors deriving the relationship between the normal and the pathological. It is the person who is objectively shown to possess the qualities necessary to raise a normal child or to make a troubled child "come out the other end all right" that is allowed to become a parent and to remain one.

The possibility that Steve's sexuality would lead to the production of abnormal children or cause him to fail as a parent was of little or no concern to the state until Peter's unlawful behavior brought Steve's sexual orientation into consideration. Before Peter's troubles, Steve found his desire for a child to operate in accordance with the state's investment in the family and the state's need to address its own institutional inadequacies. Therefore, he willingly placed himself in the service of institutional efforts to ensure the future forms of society promised by the state.

Peter's failure to abide by the law equates with Steve having failed as a father to properly bring the life of his child into alignment with the rules of the social order. As a result, Steve finds himself held accountable in unanticipated ways for his son's life. To unpack the implications of this account-ability, it is helpful to return to Steve's description of having the regulatory vehicles of the state overtly become part of his family relationships.

STEVE: You know, this one time Peter had been gone for two or three days. He had a court date coming up that he knew he couldn't miss, so I'll be goddamned if he didn't go out and get himself arrested just before all this had to happen. He didn't just accidentally get caught—he was smart enough not to get busted—but he knew that I would be there if and when he got arrested. The symptomology of it all was that he had to test me. He knew he still wasn't ready for me, but he knew he had to see me. He had to check in. So I get this call in the middle of the night from the police two days before the court date telling me they had him locked up and I should come down and pick him up. Christ, you know, I hadn't seen the kid in three or four days . . . he had just walked out of the house in the middle of the night and not come back. So I go down there and he looks at me, and I looked at him, and I saw a glimmer of something in his eye, but I knew he wasn't ready. He was just buzzing too hard . . . too much emotion, too much everything. He and his little buddy in that cell were just vibrating too hard and I knew I couldn't handle him. He would be gone again before I could get him in the car, let alone to the court date, so I just walked away. I just said, "Fuck it. I'm not in control here, and I'm leaving you here." It hurt like all hell, but I knew he wasn't ready for me. I could see it in his eyes. But at the same time, I knew there was a beginning. I saw that in his eyes too. He looked at me and he knew I had his number, and I saw it in his eyes. And it took another three years, and another patch of shit I couldn't believe, but we made it through.

A.G.: What happened with the court date? How did that play out?

STEVE: Well, after we went to court, a whole bunch of people got involved. Everything from counselors to probation officers to social workers; they were all over us. I mean they were on us like flies on shit. Now, while they didn't allow him to return to my home, essentially institutionalizing him in a halfway house like the one I used to work in, they also saved him and they saved me. You know, you have to appreciate a certain irony here. When I took a twelve-year-old boy into my home and life with the intent of forming a family, right at the age when kids begin individuating and making moves away from their parents and family—and this is an irony I never forget—he left and came back. He left and came back to me, to the family. He came back to me and to the family; and he came back to the values of the family in the end. And, you know, it was something that had to happen. That's the only way I can make sense of it. I'm not talking some New Age bullshit here—like everything happens for a reason. But what happened had to happen.

A.G.: What do you mean, it had to happen?

STEVE: He had to act this shit out to define himself as a family member. It was something that had to happen on his terms or not at all. All that shit he dragged me through were the terms of being in a family for him. He had to test everything, and, man, did he know how. He was too damn smart for most people. He could just manipulate around them. I'll never forget the first time we sat down with that social worker. The first thing out of that kid's mouth was, "My dad's a faggot and he didn't tell me until after I was adopted. I hate him for lying to me and now I have to live with him." You know, he played the homo card, lied through his teeth, and turned the social worker against me right off the bat. Right then, I just thought, "Oh shit, here we go. Hang on. I just have to have faith that this person hangs around long enough to realize that this is all a crock of shit, and that he [Peter] was never lied to, and that he [Peter] doesn't have a homophobic bone in his body." I had to have faith that this social worker wasn't a dumbass and was smart enough to realize that she was being played by one pissed-off kid. Anyway, this would all eventually prove true, but the social worker immediately took his side and came after me, asking me to verify that what Peter was saying wasn't true.

A.G.: So what did you do?

STEVE: Basically, I had to prove that I never lied to the kid and that it was him [Peter] who wasn't in control, and not me. We eventually took care of this, worked through it, but it took a long while for the social worker to trust me and believe what I was saying. And, you know, when this was all happening, when that shit was pouring out of his mouth, I was sitting there across the table from him and—son of a bitch—you know, I saw that same damn glimmer in his eye again. That glimmer in his eye from jail that said he knew I had my thumb on him. He knew he wasn't going to get anything over on me. Again, it was that look that gave me faith that he was going to come around. That we were going to be all right. It was a connection, and, as long as that was there, it was worth the struggle. Sure, we were going to give each other hell, and we both knew it, but we were also in it together, and he had to know that of me. And you know what, after a few more sessions that seemed to be going nowhere, this crap-faced probation officer called me into his office and sat me down and said, "You do know that at some point you have to decide whether or not you're going to father this boy." And I just thought, "You little shit!" What you're saying is that since I'm gay and single, you don't believe that I'm a responsible parent. I was so pissed off, but at the same time so uncertain of my reading of the situation, that I just turned around and walked out of the room. But, again, I just had to have faith that this guy wasn't a complete idiot and that he would come around. And eventually he did. After talking to Peter's teachers and a few other people around town who I work with and know in the community, he realized that, hey, it really was beyond my control. And no matter what I did, Peter was on his own journey and he needed to step back and let it take its own course. But to say I needed essentially to "step up and parent, you faggot" was just too much. I just bit my tongue and walked out.

A.G.: What do you mean you didn't know how to read it? A lot of people say they don't know how their sexuality factors into things like adoption and home studies, and things like that, but this seems different. People usually say it matters somehow and somewhere, but they can't quite put their hand on it and usually end up saying something like "everybody has a hard time adopting." Even straight couples suffer and have horror stories.

STEVE: I know exactly what they're talking about. You know it's funny living here in [our] liberal little [town], where everyone is so damn politically correct that they would never say anything like, "Faggot, you can't be a parent and it's your fault this kid is so screwed up. You should have known better." Instead, you get a polite suggestion that sounds value free, neutral. But I'm damn sure if I were sitting there with wifey and we had both raised our hands and shrugged our shoulders and said, "We've done all that we can. This kid is out of control," that he [the probation officer] wouldn't have said, "Step up, mister and missus, you've got to be a better parent." And, this is that double irony I always find myself in. While I want to say that my being gay doesn't affect how all this has gone down, how Peter and I have been treated—and it hasn't overtly—I never know if my experience is either the same or different from a straight couple's. I could have been treated just like everybody else, but, at the same time, I just don't know. In my mind, in my heart, I know that I'm being treated differently. I continually think and respond as though I'm accused or held to a different standard. In my head, I hear this man's words as saying I shouldn't be doing what I'm doing because I'm gay. I hear him telling me this even when his words might not say that at all. And the symptomology of all this goes back God knows how far. I've been out and open about all that crap for so long I usually don't even think about it anymore. But there it is: Bam! Right in the middle of my consciousness and in the middle of my dealing with all these agencies and institutions. And the damnedest thing is that it's my voice that's doing this. It's me not necessarily hearing the words that are being spoken. This makes it really hard to figure out exactly where my gayness factors into all this. Am I doing the work of the institution for them, and in a way against them, by kicking the crap out of myself? Or is the institution actually telling me this, and I'm receiving the message loud and clear? I can never tell. I honest to God don't know, and that's something I think about all the time. While I'm as liberal as the next guy, I would never say I trust these institutions, or have faith in what they do, but I have tremendous respect for the individuals who stepped in and helped me and Peter. So where is the boundary? People worked for me and for Peter, and we came out all right. We're a family again. But these same people are part of the beast, man, they all work for that big beast, so what is what here? I have no idea.

The Second Movement: The Subject vs. Subjectivity

In what I have identified as the second movement in Steve's narrative, his ability to be a father is contested by Peter having broken the law. The state's initial response is to search for the origins of Peter's troubles in his relationship with Steve. The state's search for the origins of Peter's troubles in Steve's sexuality is certainly ironic. Peter had been removed from his biological family by the state as a result of the physical and sexual abuse he suffered in their care. Placing Peter in Steve's care provided a means of addressing a sexual pathology known to take place within biological kinship. The state's response to Peter's accusations against Steve arises from the collusion between public institutions and the family, which together produce the conditions in which a child's actions and behaviors bear witness to the capacities and capabilities of his or her parents and the quality of his or her family relations. Once Peter breaks the law, Steve is called on to prove that Peter's troubles do not trace back to flaws in his person and care.

Grounds exist in the eyes of the state for dissolving the parent/child relationship if Steve is found to be contributing to Peter's unlawful behavior. The grounds for dissolving the relationship are the legal framing of adoption as contractual and the state's imagination—informed by the psychological sciences—that a child's primary affective states and moral disposition arise from, and even mirror, operations within familial relations (Carp 2000). While the contract is not an individually negotiated transaction between a prospective parent and a child, of the sort accompanying the exchange of goods for services, the law constructs adoption as the legal binding of a parent to a child on the basis of the parent's promise to align his or her authority with the state's so as to raise sociable subjects (Eng 2010).

The capacity of a prospective adoptive parent to fulfill the obligations imagined as necessary to raising a "normal" child is ascertained by experts in childhood development before the state approves an adoption. If a state expert does not pronounce an adult capable of raising a normal child, an adoptive relationship will not be legally formed. If an adoptive parent is found no longer to possess the qualities necessary to raising a normal child, grounds exist for dissolving an established family relation. Of course, the same stricture applies to nonadoptive families. If a "biological" child cannot be cared for within the structures of the family, the parental relationship may be dissolved and the child made a ward of the state. In each instance, it is the state's need and promise to protect the child's well-being that guides legal action.

Steve's sexuality surfaces as a problematic element that may lend itself to the dissolution of his family relations when Peter gets into trouble with the law. Peter knows Steve is vulnerable to accusations about the place of his sexuality within the family, and he exploits his father's vulnerability by declaring to state officials that Steve lied to him about his homosexuality at the time of his adoption.[6] Steve's reaction to Peter's allegations shows how vulnerability to claims about sexual impropriety configures the experience of fatherhood for gay men. Steve's response to Peter's claims was not one of shock or surprise but of resignation to and acceptance of a known possibility. Steve's immediate thought, "Oh shit! Here we go," indexes a preexisting cultural narrative in which the revelation of a parent's hidden homosexuality is known to provide a basis for questioning, if not undoing, existing kin relations. It is clear that Steve anticipated this very scenario and that he holds a sense of how such words might be received outside the context of his relationship with Peter. It does not seem a stretch to say that formulating a response to allegations of this sort is crucial to Steve's capacity to be and to remain a father and that his understanding of what it means to be a father is inflected by his knowledge of being vulnerable to such accusations.

---

[6] It is the known ability of the child to activate the forces of the state against their parent or guardian, and the mutual vulnerabilities that arise as a result, that point toward the freedoms and constraints that serve as the basis for an ethics within kinship. These topics are addressed in the following chapter, where I discuss the lives of children in gay families.

The state responded to Peter's accusation by investigating Steve's character and inquiring into his honesty regarding his sexuality and into whether he had, indeed, disclosed the truth of his homosexuality to Peter prior to the adoption, or if he had fabricated fictions. Determining the temporality of Steve's disclosures and ascertaining the meaning of Peter's claims rest on objective criteria. Steve either did or did not tell Peter he was gay before the adoption, and Peter either was or was not lying when he claimed that Steve had not done so. If the state determined that Steve had lied to Peter or that Peter had lied to the social worker, an identifiable cause would emerge for Peter's unlawful behavior, based on objectively discernible events and truths.

If the state were to have proven that Steve had, indeed, failed to tell Peter the truth of his homosexuality prior to the adoption—and that Steve knew, at that time, that he was gay—then its findings would have constituted objective evidence, by its own criteria, that Steve does not possess the qualities of a good father. Garnering such evidence requires assessing the relative likeness of Peter and Steve's relationship to the categories found in the law and provides a means of locating Peter's pathological behavior in Steve's sexuality. Establishing the degree of congruence between Steve and Peter's relationship and the categories of the law and clinical discourse equates with a type of healing, since it places the relationship within the law's lexicon of concepts concerning social relationships, their proper operation, and available corrective courses in the event of malfunction or misalignment. Placing intersubjective relationships within this lexicon enables painful events, such as disclosing one's homosexuality to one's child, or being called a faggot and a liar by one's kid, to be understood as specific acts of deviation from the law's order, thus setting the stage for the law and its agents to bring about restoration and restitution.

From the state's perspective, proof that Steve is not the cause of Peter's difficulties resides in factors that are external to Steve's and Peter's own understandings and experiences of their relationship. If it is discovered that Steve is not the cause of Peter's troubles, then the pathology can be linked to events that took place in Peter's biological family, which allows Steve to be transformed back into a therapeutic agent of the state. The social worker sets out to determine if Steve, in fact, did embody the law's image of the father, which she does by seeking out other people's testimony about his character and parenting qualities. The search denies Steve the ability to voice the knowledge he holds of being in a relationship with Peter, since it is Steve's very capacity to speak truthfully about his relationships that is in question. The search for objective truths disregards Steve's knowledge of that "little glimmer" in Peter's eye and the relevance of that little glimmer to Steve and Peter's future as a family.

Since state institutions employ objective criteria when determining the existence and meaning of a relationship, a child's description of an adoptive father as a "faggot" who "lies" does not and most likely never will qualify as a statement that defines the qualities of a good father. A child uttering such words, whether true or false, does not display the proper socializing effects of good fathering. All Steve can do in the wake of Peter's accusation is "wait and see" if the social worker "sticks around long enough" and is "smart enough" to realize that things as they are and things as they appear are not the same.

The Third Movement: The Return of the Subject

The third movement in Steve's narrative shows how institutional knowledge operates to establish suffering as a modality through which Steve comes to learn the meaning of being a father to Peter. Steve gives voice to the reconfigurations in his knowledge of paternity when he narrates his response to the probation officer's command that he decide if he is going "to parent" Peter. Steve is angered by the accusation that his lack of parental attention is the cause of Peter's difficulties and that Peter's well-being is tied to his choices. One can assume that Steve sees choosing to "parent" Peter as embracing the state's image of kinship at the expense of his concern for Peter's well-being. Steve displays his feeling about being forced to make such a choice by "biting his tongue and walking out," rejecting the probation officer's interpretation of events and refusing to respond to the man's figuration of the agency and temporality of paternal authority in his relationship with Peter.

Peter's formulation of choice within kinship stands in marked contrast to anthropological portraits of queer kinship that understand choice as providing a means of undoing the constraints associated with the heterosexual norm (Carrington 1999; Sullivan 1996; Weston 1996). In such portraits, the flexibility associated with agentially creating and maintaining family through reasoned action is supposed to allow subjects to live in relationships unencumbered by the operations of power associated with the state's sanction of marriage and biological notions of kinship. Through Steve's words, we learn that the edict to choose kinship, or choose to kin—meaning to father Peter—is directly aligned with the imperatives of the state and the imagined agency of paternal authority in the eyes of the law. Far from providing liberation from the constraints imposed on the subject by normative discourses of relatedness, the obligation to choose to be kin operates as the very vehicle of state regulation. What anthropological portraits of chosen kinship do not account for is Steve's inability to locate the origins of his kin relations or the source of his suffering in kinship. Steve's righteous indignation speaks to the compulsion of a father to care for his child and Steve's enactment of this anger by "biting his tongue and walking out" to a pragmatics of affect.

When Steve reflects on his encounter with the probation officer—and the probation officer's command that he must choose to parent Peter—he describes elusiveness in the relationship between words and the suffering they cause. Steve is not certain if the words that hurt him—words that formulate his relationship to Peter as a matter of choice—emanated from the personal views of the probation officer or from his own (mis)interpretation of them. Ultimately, he locates the injury in his own (mis)interpretation of the probation officer's message and in his own uncertainty about whether, as a gay man, he should be a parent.

Steve's uncertainty demonstrates the law's active removal of subjectivity from the process of determining the meaning of family relationships, just as it illustrates the state's reliance on objective criteria for placing subjects within the categories of the law. Just as Steve could not locate the source of his injury outside his sense of misunderstanding and misapprehension, the probation officer and social worker could not recognize that Steve "had his thumb on Peter." Neither could they recognize Steve's sense that Peter knew he was not going to "get anything over" on him—meaning paternal authority was actively being enacted. These two "facts" went unaccounted for by the probation officer, since they reside in Steve's experiential knowledge of being a father to Peter, in Steve's understanding of that "little glimmer" in Peter's eye and the future relationship it signaled.

The cost exacted by the law's investment in the cultural image of paternity as containing known properties and qualities is Steve's ability to narrate his own knowledge of what it means to be a father. As a result of the connection between state-sponsored institutions, the law, and clinical discourses, Steve does not hold the authority to define the meaning of being a father to Peter or the capacity to voice his experience of being related to Peter as kin. All he can do is surrender to institutional efforts to establish a correlation between his life and relations and the law's image of paternity. In other words, for Steve to continue being a parent after the family's disruption by violence, he must submit to the authority of the state and its judgments about whether his relationship to Peter is normal or pathological.

We learn of Steve's ultimate capitulation to and embrace of the state's efforts to identify the causes of Peter's behavior in his sense of indebtedness to the social workers who helped him and Peter through their difficulties. As Steve said, he may not trust state-administered institutions, but he has "tremendous respect for the individuals who stepped in and helped out." Despite Steve's mistrust of institutions and his ultimate trust and faith in specific individuals, his experience as a father speaks of forms of suffering that the state's narrative of healing cannot approach. The excessive suffering that falls outside dominant narratives of family is given voice when Steve speaks of the radical uncertainty surrounding his treatment by institutions.

When Steve's experience of suffering is registered as something other than the product of individual psychology or a contingency of intersubjective relationships, we hear a critique of the idea that the family exists as an objectively known and actively made set of relationships. To trace the implications of this critique, we can consider Steve's claim that "we're all right now. He [Peter] calls me 'dad.'" Steve suggests an alternative narrative about the place of suffering in the family and of healing when he says he and Peter are "now okay." Here, the meaning of relatedness is located in the experience of caring for another person over time, as opposed to possessing a set of qualities or living in alignment with an objective set of criteria (Borneman 1997). By listening to this alternative narrative, we may understand why the healing promised by the state does not provide Steve comfort or rest.

A Respite for the Family

With the words, "We're now okay. We're a family again. He calls me 'dad,'" Steve draws attention to the temporality involved in maintaining family relationships and to healing itself. From the "now" in which Steve speaks, the violent disruption that brought the family to the brink of dissolution has been temporarily repaired, affording Steve a moment of rest. He finds rest not because of the healing promised by embracing the state's institutions, but because of Peter's return to the family. Steve describes Peter's return as ironic because the institutional models of childhood development he studied and has come to embody claim the appropriate trajectory for Peter, at this stage in his life, is to leave the family. Peter's departure is to be expected, given the pain he and Steve have inflicted on each other.

Yet, the rest Steve has found is contingent on the words Peter speaks. After all, it is Peter's speech that signals, as well as brings about, the family's reunification. Steve can only experience healing and feel that the family (and that he, as a father) is "okay" as long as Peter consents to kinship and opts in by calling him "dad." Steve's words imply that his sense of well-being, as a father, is based on his vulnerability to Peter's accusations that he is not a proper parent and on the need to continually demonstrate that he is one.

The point is not that one could lead a pain-free life by rejecting membership in the family or that membership in a family automatically brings suffering. Rather, Steve's words illuminate how belonging in kinship is based on what others do with language and consenting to being subject to another's words. Steve's knowledge of belonging in the family, as a father, then, is based on his vulnerability to Peter's words. Such vulnerability is particularly vexing, since Steve knows he must inflict pain on the very person whose words legitimate him as a father and thereby establish grounds for revoking their consent to kinship.

The emotional conflict Steve suffered when leaving Peter in the jail cell speaks to this predicament. While Steve believed, at the time, that Peter's actions were indicative of a family relationship that was yet to emerge, his decision to walk away and leave Peter "vibrating" with his "little buddy" in the jail cell, awaiting his appearance before a judge, inflicted pain for the sake of nurturing a relationship that was yet to arrive. Inflicting such pain can easily be construed as neglect, just as it can be construed as expressing care.

Because injury itself founds Peter and Steve's family, one cannot say pain disrupts a preexisting and stable set of relations (Asad 2003; Butler 2006; Das 2000). Instead, for Steve and Peter to continue as a family, each must knowingly suffer pain and inflict it on the other, and each must endure the injuries the other inflicts. That Steve can only experience family in the ironic mode illuminates the impossibility of directly expressing the meaning and source of belonging in family relations, just as it reveals the impossibility of knowing for a fact, other than through suffering, that one is related to another as family.

We need to keep track of the sites in Steve's narrative that the family has not yet emerged because they reveal the work of time in enabling experience to return as a basis for defining relations (Das 1990). Returning to my conversation with Steve, we learn how pain operates as agency in familial forms of care. The following excerpt reveals how the agency of suffering allows Steve's subjectivity, or experiential knowledge of living in kinship with Peter, to return as a basis for knowing the meaning of being a father.

A.G.: Wow, that's a tough story. It's really hard to know what to do with it. All that second-guessing about who's who and what's what. I guess everybody wants to believe that institutions work, whatever that means, but to know they're also working against you—especially when given what you guys went through—is just tough.

STEVE: That's what I mean by I carry around a lot of shit from all this. I've got so many conflicting emotions, sometimes my head just spins. But somehow we're all right now, and that also makes my head spin. You know these damn experts, whether doctors, shrinks, or lawyers, they don't know their asses from their elbows most of the time. Christ, at one point in the middle of this whole mess, Peter was put on this medication because he was just acting out all over the place. Shit, I was to find out later—after all hell had really rained down—that one of the side effects of this medication was the breakdown of inhibitions. Christ, here's this kid who has absolutely no sense of boundaries to begin with because of all this violence and sexual abuse, and they put him on a medication that prompted a loss of boundaries. God, when I found this out, I felt so awful. Here I was pushing this medication on him, thinking it was the best thing since sliced Wonder Bread, and this is what I get. Everything I knew and read seemed to point towards this being the one [the right doctor to care for Peter], and then I find out that he's getting into deeper shit because of the medication he put him on. Man, did this result in a contradictory set of feelings. I felt guilty and pissed, caught in a double bind. Suddenly, I was contributing to his falling further, but that fucking doctor couldn't find his ass—even with both hands. They [the clinicians working with Peter and Steve] didn't know any differently than I did, but he [the doctor] really failed to act responsibly. Those fucking people were equally uninformed as me, and that's not right. It's unacceptable. I actually conspired to put the kid in a position to act out further. It just kills me to think about it. Me, the one who was supposed to be protecting him, the one he's supposed to trust—his dad is the one who set him up to fail further. Man, I never thought I'd hear that word again—*dad*—whatever that means. After all this shit, I'll never really know.

A.G.: Yeah, it's tough to know what to say. A lot of people have told me they have a hard time figuring out what happened as they go through an adoption, or what's happening in their family lives, but this is different.

STEVE: All you can really do is listen, because let's face it, unless you've gone through something like this, you don't know shit. And even after you have, it's not like you come out the other end squeaky-clean, grinning. You get dirty, and you just have to somehow live with it. One thing that I find very funny is that I hear about people who have done these cultural trips back to the countries where their adopted kids came from. You know, taking the Cambodian kid back to Cambodia to look at where they were born. And I just laugh because we used to take cultural trips back to [the city of Peter's birth]. We used to go back every year, for like three years in a row—to see Peter's family and particularly to see his brothers and sisters. But after a few of those trips, I said, "no more." It was way too confusing for him to see his brothers and sisters, who were still living in a culture that was completely antithetical to the values of our home, of the place where he was now living. For him to go back to a culture or society where everything was all right as long as you got away with it, as long as you didn't get caught everything was cool, was just too much. You know, from anything goes until you get busted to a place where I was on him like white on rice and not letting him just walk out of the house at 11:00 at night all by himself. Can you imagine that? A twelve-year-old kid that would just leave the house in the middle of the night, just go out without saying a word and just go wander around wherever. Not having that right seemed like the biggest violation in the world to him because that was how he was used to living. He fundamentally didn't get why it might be a problem in a family setting. He had to learn this, and going back to [his hometown] didn't help his cause. He would come back and struggle and struggle and suffer and suffer until he got acclimated again. So, finally, I said we aren't going to do this anymore. I told him that when he turned eighteen I would help him find his parents again and help him get in touch with his brothers and sisters again, no matter where they were. And we did. After he was eighteen, we found everyone and we all got together. And, bless his heart, when the time came, he said he didn't want to see his parents yet because he simply wasn't ready. So just about a year ago, we went over there and had a wonderful reunion. He got to see what was going on, and he had learned to translate that set of family values into what we have here, so he was okay. We made it through that spell just like all the other shit, and he still calls me "dad." He had learned and knew the value of particular family cultures.

I view Steve's struggle to be recognized as a father, by himself and by others, as echoing concerns about legitimacy within kinship. Doing so allows me to address the stakes of achieving congruence with the categories of the law, what Judith Butler (2002) has called "landing the desire of the state." We can begin thinking about what it means to embody the regulatory apparatus of the state, as opposed to dealing with the operations of the regulatory apparatus in the abstract, by examining how Steve's subjectivity always seems to spill over and exceed the legal and institutional imagination of the categories he occupies.

Attempting to understand the operations of the state within the intimacy of Peter and Steve's familial bonds moves the ethnography of the state away from its more traditional moorings in geopolitical regions and social territories associated with regulatory regimes aimed at control and with structured modes of rule (Das & Poole 2004). To position an ethnography of the state within the intersubjective bonds of the family is to acknowledge that subjectivity cannot be separated from the operations of the law and that the distinction between state forms of rule and familial forms of obligation, or the inside/outside distinction on which anthropology has traditionally relied when defining the family's relationship to the state, is a blurred distinction at best (Das & Poole 2004; Goodrich & Carlson 1998; Sarat & Kearns 1995).

I begin by addressing how their kinship becomes known to Steve and Peter and how the institutional narrative of the family becomes incongruent with Steve's experience of being a relative and becoming a father to Peter. By asking how kinship becomes known to Steve, and how it becomes unknowable, we can see how one's recognition as a family member, what I am calling "legitimacy," entails more than garnering state approval of one's desire and reaping the awards of state sanction for one's intimate bonds (Butler 2002). I believe Steve and Peter's uncertainty about the meaning of their relationship offers an intimate portrait of the law's operation in everyday life and indicates the need to think about how the state and its categories, at times, become marginal to the subject in everyday life (Das & Poole 2004). If legitimacy were only a matter of legal recognition, the proof of Steve's likeness to the state's image of a father would provide him with the rest promised by its narratives of healing, and Steve could be certain of the meaning of the term "dad" when uttered in the context of his relationship with Peter. Steve's experience obviously differs from this scenario, since the state went to great lengths to prove to itself that Steve was indeed a legitimate "father" to Peter, as it does with all adoptive parents, and yet Steve did not recognize himself in the state's definition. Steve's case does not easily conform to the logic of the exception, because it is the mechanisms deployed by the state to prove that he is in fact Peter's legitimate father that deny Steve the promised pleasure of landing the state's desire.

Instead, the state's mechanisms of proof and its institutional pronouncements split Steve's knowledge of the content and form of his own relationships—relationships he has consciously constructed in alignment with state-sanctioned forms of family and paternity. Although it remains essential to Steve that his relationship to Peter be legible to institutional actors, the image of relatedness sanctioned by the state lies adjacent to his own knowledge of what defines him as a father. After all, it is Peter's signature, and not the imprimatur of the state, that proves essential to Steve being and remaining a father. It is the legitimacy found in the register of subjectivity, as opposed to the legal pronouncements of the state, that enables Steve to recognize his relationship to Peter as familial.

The necessary turning away from the law and its pronouncements, if Steve is to be acknowledged as a legitimate father to Peter, resides in the fact that subjectivity always exceeds the law's imagination of family relationships. The excess produces conflicting notions of self that continually elude, and perhaps violently oppose, the enunciations of the state (Butler 2002). Such a spilling over, on the part of the subject, means the state's promise of forging legitimate family relations—in which the subject is publicly recognized and recognizable as a father despite difference—is impossible to attain through legal pronouncements alone. Steve's sense of never knowing the meaning of the term "father," even when acting in alliance with the state and its institutions, demonstrates this point. One result of the conflicts that arise from Steve's efforts to be a father to Peter is the violent removal of Steve's notion of himself as a father and the resultant injury to Peter. The violence associated with the conflict between state actors and Steve, as a father, renders the appearance of the term "dad" in Steve and Peter's relationship uncanny, since it is a word that forever seems out of place and out of time when applied to Steve.

The uncanniness of being called "dad" arises from the incongruity between Steve's own image of himself as a father and the image of fatherhood promised by the machinations of the state. For Steve, losing the state's image of fatherhood as a referent for defining his relation to Peter means that he becomes illegible as a father in his own eyes. As a result, Steve must turn elsewhere to find the meaning of his actions in the life of his child.

The loss of meaning is the result of the paradoxical position in which Steve finds himself when acting in alliance with institutional figures. In doing so, Steve repeatedly fails to protect his child's well-being and, thus, to perform his paternal function. It is while aligned with the state's image of a good father and "pushing" Peter to take the medication prescribed by the court-appointed psychiatrist that Steve most overtly contributes to Peter's harm. He fails to protect Peter from the violence state actors can and do enact both passively and actively. The result is the loss not only of Steve's ability to define the meaning of the term "dad" but also of his ability to distinguish between the illegitimate violence of the state's neglect and what is imagined as the necessary and legitimate founding violence of paternal authority. The cost to Steve is the ability to know if his actions as a father are enactments of paternal authority or if he is unwittingly colluding in the excessive violence of the state.

Steve's uncertainty is a product of the law and of the need for him, as an adoptive parent, to prove his alignment with both the state's actors and the state's image of a good parent if he is to achieve and retain the legally recognized status of parent. The alignment between the state and adoptive parents makes it necessary for Steve to surrender his ability to know if the violence of enacting paternal authority is oriented toward creating a sociable subject or if it is legitimating the excessive violence of uncaring state institutions. The guilt associated with the state's failure to protect Peter's well-being is directly transferable to Steve, in both an affective and a juridical register through the forfeiture of such knowledge.

Steve gives voice to the predicament of occupying this position when he informs me that, unless you've experienced what he has, "you don't know shit," alluding to the idea that only after finding one's body and subjectivity within such a conflict can one know the meaning of the state within relationships. Steve goes on to show how being an integral player in the unfolding of the plot does not provide the clarity necessary to establish a correlation between the causes and the effects of the violence that gives birth to inclusion in specific categories and their history. Instead, Steve's "head just spins" when he attempts to attach meaning to the events in which he has been enmeshed and that define him and Peter as part of the same family but different.

The Birth of Legitimacy

The final movement in Steve's narrative develops around Steve's coming to know that he is Peter's legitimate father. Steve's sense of legitimacy comes from learning that he has acted to ensure his child's well-being throughout the "shit storm" he and Peter have weathered. Steve becomes legitimate when he can say Peter "calls me 'dad.'" The pronouncement allows Steve to rest because it signals that they "came out the other side all right." His knowledge that Peter is "now okay" signals the transfiguration of the pain and violence Steve has knowingly inflicted on Peter into the founding violence of parental authority and kinship, as opposed to an illegitimate and gratuitous form of violence enacted, perhaps, for perverse pleasure. Temporarily naming the violence he has enacted as a necessary byproduct of care enables Steve to heal, since the pronouncement frames his actions as something other than pathological. Instead, Steve is able to picture his actions as necessary to the formation of a family and to the transformation of a child into a sociable subject.

The legitimacy Steve finds, as a father, should not be thought of as durable, since it rests on Peter's consent. The perilous quality of paternity is supposedly assuaged for heterosexual biological fathers, since the "fact" of birth, of reproductive sexual intercourse, establishes biology as an objective basis for knowing without a doubt that one is or is not a father. For Steve, knowledge of himself as a "dad" is dependent on the continual incremental assignation of meaning to the suffering he has inflicted on Peter (and that Peter has inflicted on him) by Peter's acts of speech. As long as Peter is speaking—and continues to speak—as Steve's son, or as long as Peter calls Steve "dad," Steve is Peter's legitimate father. In other words, Steve is legitimately (re)born as a father to Peter as long as Peter calls him "dad" or lends his consent to the term.

The point at which Steve recognizes that he has been reborn as a father occurs when he hears Peter reiterating the rules and values in the name of which Steve has caused Peter to suffer. Steve describes discovering that his ethic—perhaps paternal authority—has come to life in Peter when he negotiates the meaning of the "cultural" trips he and Peter took to visit Peter's biological family. The trips caused Peter pain because Peter was unable to "translate" back and forth between two different sets of "family values." Peter struggled after these visits because acceptable behavior for a child in his biological family and in the family setting established by Steve were completely antithetical. As Steve describes, for Peter to go back and immerse himself in the culture of his biological family, where "everything was all right as long as you got away with it," was overwhelming. Afterward, Peter would struggle and suffer until he was again acclimated to the rules of Steve's paternal authority.

Steve finds the cause of Peter's pain in the violation the boy felt when Steve refused to allow him to do the things his biological brothers and sisters were doing, such as walking out of the house "without saying a word" at 11:00 at night. As Steve saw it, not allowing Peter such freedoms seemed to the boy like the "biggest violation in the world." Peter did not understand that such actions were "problematic in a family setting" precisely because they signal a disregard for paternal authority and the mandate that this authority be exercised to protect a child's well-being.

According to Steve, Peter had to learn the difference between the value of the rules upholding the family in which he was living and those of the family from which he had been removed; and, until he did, visiting his biological family "didn't help his cause." In other words, it was a reminder of the difference to be overcome by forging legitimate kinship ties. By Steve's logic, at the age of eighteen, Peter would be in a position to make his own

choices about familial forms of obligation and belonging. As a legally eman-
cipated adult, he would be in a position to evaluate and decide for himself the value and structure of family relationships. But, until then, Steve
held a position of authority over him and was in charge of protecting his
well-being.

Proof that Peter has embraced Steve as a paternal authority emerges
when Peter begins to "translate" between the values of his biological family
and those established by Steve in the name of the law. For Steve, it seems
Peter's ability to understand different sorts of family organization and recognize different sets of family values resides in Peter's deferment to the
normative rule of kinship sanctioned by the state, to the image of the father
on which Steve has based his authority. Peter's deference to the abstract
authority of the state, and this authority's manifestation in rules, enables
him to compare the competing values of each family, in terms of a universal
equivalent, and to weigh them in accordance with the life offered in each
case. Peter demonstrated his ability to translate back and forth when he
returned as a young adult to visit his brothers and sisters and saw "what was
going on." Steve characterized the visit as a "wonderful reunion" because
Peter was able to get in touch with his brothers and sisters while retaining
his sense of the "value" of his relationship with Steve.

For Steve, the truth of Peter coming to embrace him as a paternal figure
came when Peter rejected Steve's offer to visit his biological parents when
he turned eighteen. When Peter said he "wasn't ready" to see his parents, it
indicated to Steve that Peter had come to embrace the rules underpinning
Steve's authority as the basis for determining the value and meaning of
family relationships. When Peter told Steve that he was not ready to visit
his biological parents, he transformed the violence in his biological family
into an illegitimate and destructive force, or pathology, and the pain and
suffering in his relationship with Steve into parental care, or therapy. Steve
seems to find peace knowing that the violence and pain he has inflicted on
Peter is a legitimate kind that founds Peter as a sociable subject, just as it
founds him as a father.

4

An expanding body of literature links renewed interest in kinship studies to a series of crises affecting the epistemological scaffolding that supports knowledge of kin relations. Judith Stacey (1998), for example, argues that the epistemological crisis affecting family relationships is an outgrowth of the reorganization of capital and care in neoliberal states, the increasing use and availability of biotechnology to assist conception, and changes in the legal organization of adoption, marriage, and the family. According to Stacey and others, these shifts have introduced flexibility into a domain once thought immutable, certain, and immediately knowable—namely, the origins of one's kin.

In preceding chapters, I have tried to show how gay men with children navigate this ambiguity, and how the ways and means devised for address-ing such uncertainty determine whether and how relations are recognized as familial. Such recognition proves crucial to gay men with children, since the possibility for attaining full citizenship and adulthood rests in its ex-pression.

In this chapter, I listen to children's voices and to their figurations of inheriting a world that is ambivalent about the sets of relations constituting their families. I draw from three institutional settings—a daylong sympo-sium for prospective lesbian and gay parents held at the Lesbian and Gay Community Services Center in New York City, the yearly "town meeting" organized by COLAGE (Children of Lesbians and Gays Everywhere) during Gay Family Week in Provincetown, Massachusetts, and two separate sup-port groups organized to address the specific needs of queer parents—in which members of the LGBT (lesbian, gay, bisexual, and transsexual) com-munity publicly discussed the various techniques available for bringing children into one's life and the dilemmas parents face when the lives and relations they create are pictured as inappropriate or not in the best interest of children.

When families are created through reasoned action and agential choice, the parental gift to children of life and the world, given in exchange for the affect and care of kinship, becomes problematic (Das 2006; Foucault 2003). When the life gifted to children by their parents is not socially sanctioned and the world is not accepting of the relations that brought those children into being, the legitimacy children are expected to confer on a parental relation becomes problematic. Might the public performance—and criticism—of family and its creation provide a means of preparing the world for children whose relationships do not arise from heterosexual reproduction? Is there a place in anthropological discourse for children's understandings of kinship? What might a child's interest in kinship be?

The need to understand a child's investment in kinship arises in conjunction with the need to distinguish between the suffering inflicted on a child inadvertently—perhaps in the name of familial love, as was discussed in the previous chapter—and that perpetrated by a society that sanctions the eradication of homosexuality. I am interested in the institutional efforts geared toward mediating the tensions inherent in embracing a logic of kinship in which deriving the meaning of social relationships is understood to be essential to their creation. Might an allegory for anthropological inquiry be found in the efforts expended by lesbian and gay parents to understand the meaning of family?

Talking about Family

The committee in charge of ensuring ethical human subjects research at Johns Hopkins University—an external body called the Homewood Institutional Review Board (HIRB)—explicitly forbade me from speaking with anyone under the age of eighteen while I was conducting my research.[1]

---

[1] When I applied for IRB approval in summer 2001, Johns Hopkins University had stopped conducting its own review of what constituted ethical human-subjects research in response to the U.S. government's suspension of all federally funded human-subjects research at the university. The government's actions were in response to several well-publicized incidents over a period of three years in which human subjects were harmed, some fatally, while participating in research being conducted by Johns Hopkins faculty. The most striking of these incidents was the death of a participant in an asthma study administered by the Johns Hopkins Medical School. In response to the suspension, Johns Hopkins contracted with the external, independent Western Institutional Review Board to review and ethically evaluate new or ongoing research involving human subjects. WIRB's orientation was directed toward restoring the flow of federal funding for medical research, as opposed to evaluating the anthropological research, and it did not consider established protocols that enable ethical ethnographic fieldwork to be conducted with minors when evaluating my application. As a result, HIRB prevented from having any contact with minors that was not supervised by a parent or guardian.

This restriction is obviously problematic when one is working in the homes of gay parents, where children are active contributors to the creation of family and its meaning. I initially thought that I would be able to incorporate the workings of children's lives into my research in a way that did not breach the lines defining the ethical treatment of human subjects by attending public events at which the lives and interests of children were openly discussed. I also thought these public settings might provide sites for exploring the moral and ethical grounds for the view that children's lives and relationships are best left untouched, kept from the prying eyes of the anthropologist—except under the exceptional circumstances of endemic disease, extreme political violence, or domestic abuse. Under such extreme conditions, it is often ethically imperative that children's lives be transformed into objects of knowledge for the purpose of therapeutic intervention.

The children of LGBT parents occupy an ambiguous position on the ethical terrain maintained by HIRB for this very reason. Often, ethical discourses are put into the service of societal anxieties about the place of sex in family relationships, and the sense that only those who are appropriately married or properly identified as heterosexual should form families orients research on nonheterosexual families toward the establishment of measured outcomes (see, for instance, Patterson 2005). Such anxieties arise in part from the imagination of same-sex eroticism as pathological and of those who identify as anything other than heterosexual as erotic predators whose attentions can easily turn toward children (Donzelot 1979; Foucault 2003; Sedgwick 1993). When a parent's sexuality provides a means for defining him or her as pathological, and thus worthy of diagnosis and eradication, what might the impact be on that parent's child?

Since I was not conducting a comparative study based on objective measures, HIRB held me accountable to an ethical practice derived from the adult's imagination of the child's imagination of the adult—to borrow a phrase from Michael Taussig (2003)—that configures intimacy between adults and children in the family as necessarily private. In such adult imaginaries, inquiry into the family lives of children is a violation that risks harming a child's successful transformation into a normal adult by altering the ways a child knows its world and relations. It seems imperative to ask about the tension between leading a publicly queer family life and maintaining the societal imagination that children's lives unfold in a private world, sep-

---

This restriction prevented me from conducting participant observation among children, which I had planned to do by volunteering my time as an au pair to several gay families.

arate and apart from public view, when silence, for sexual minorities, has come to so powerfully equate with death. It also seems imperative to ask why it is automatically assumed that children grow up and become adults. Scholars such as Michael Moon (2012), Myra Bluebond-Langner (1980), and Pamela Reynolds (2000) have each described how children actively create ethical figurations of the self and live in moral worlds that do not orient towards those associated with the labors, symbolic economies, and affective structures figured as adulthood.

Michel Foucault (2003) and Michael Taussig (2003), in separate ways, have established that institutional maintenance of secrecy around children's lives is integral to the societal masking of the disciplinary techniques that subjugate desire to the aims of the state and citizenship, or adulthood. What silences, binaries, and ethical positions are allowed to go unchallenged by maintaining the idea that children's lives are best lived under an institutionally guarded and administered veil of secrecy? What is so fragile about, and possibly so dangerous to, the lives and relationships of children that institutions must ensure they unfold in privacy and secrecy? What questions arise when children publicly discuss and perform their agency in the creation of family?

Talking Families

Center Kids, the center's children's program, organized a symposium for prospective lesbian and gay parents at New York's Gay and Lesbian Community Services Center. The event was designed to provide prospective parents with information about how to bring children into their lives and what they might expect once they had. The symposium was not the first of its kind. Center Kids had organized similar events in the past, but nothing of the sort had been held in at least four years; it has since become a yearly event. Previous events had been structured as informal round-table discussions held in the living rooms and kitchens of the various interested parties. This symposium was much larger in scale and broader in scope. The meeting brought together prospective parents with representatives of queer-friendly professional organizations, both public and private, that provide adoption and family services to people living along the East Coast. More than two hundred prospective parents and roughly thirty organizations, including religious charities, governmental agencies, nonprofit groups, and private law firms convened for the day.

The symposium was the brainchild of Terri Bogus, the director of Center Kids. "Garrett," a member of the center's board of directors, had made the event possible, securing grants to help fund it from American Express

Financial Services and the Gay Financial Network. Garrett had become personally invested in addressing the issues facing prospective LGBT parents after witnessing what he described as "the ongoing struggle" of a friend trying to bring a child into his life through adoption. Garrett organized the symposium to provide what he saw as both a needed service to prospective LGBT parents and an opportunity for the center to raise money. The event carried a suggested admission price of $40 for individuals and $60 for families—meaning couples attending together.

The admission fee, corporate sponsorship, and emphasis placed on the dissemination and circulation of "information" during the symposium were emblematic of the expanding professionalization of kinship and its creation in contemporary Europe and America (Rapp & Ginsburg 2001), in which the formation of family and its maintenance increasingly entail entering fee-for-service relationships with trained experts in the fields of reproductive biology, medicine, the law, psychiatry, and social work. The paid assistance of experts is often needed to help with the gathering and translation of the information that enables individuals to make the decision about how to form families with children. The assistance of experts is also necessary to negotiate the institutional, legal, and clinical matrix through which children become family members (Franklin & Roberts 2006; Ginsburg & Rapp 1995; Rapp 1999; Strathern 1992a, 1992b).

The symposium was geared toward providing pragmatic answers to questions that have oriented anthropology since nearly its inception, such as "Where do relatives come from?" "What makes a family?" and "What does it mean to be related?" The answers provided drew from the known capacities of professionally applied biosocial technologies, the law, and institutional procedures to make children available, place them in homes, and, thereby, create legitimate family relationships. In the symposium, family relations were seen as both readily obtainable for LGBT subjects and capable of being tailored, or handcrafted, to meet the individual needs and specific circumstances of prospective parents through the application of known biological and cultural techniques.

The possibility of providing pragmatic and technical answers to questions concerning the origins and meaning of kinship is an outgrowth of some forty years of activism and scholarship challenging the idea that the creation of life and relatives is the exclusive work of heterosexuality (Carsten 2004; Ginsburg & Rapp 1995; Ragoné 1994; Stacey 1998; Weston 1991; Yanagisako & Delaney 1995). The relative success of this critical project can be measured in the symposium itself, in which the relationships formed between LGBT subjects and children—no matter the means—were unquestionably seen as legitimate ties of kinship. Such a position was available because symposium organizers and participants clearly understood the category "relative" to be culturally constructed.

"Emily", a well-known author and activist convened the symposium. Emily's opening remarks that day provide a sense of the cultural milieu in which queer family relations are imagined to arise. She had been invited to speak partly because of her celebrity status in the world of lesbian and gay parenting. She is famous for having written a very popular text on the subject of lesbian and gay parenting, and for her work as a political advocate and therapist for alternative families in New York City. As the words Emily spoke that day demonstrated, she is far more than an expert on queer families; she is, in many ways, the living embodiment of the image of queer parenting put forward in public and self-consciously queer political representations of LGBT families.

Having children is the most important decision of your life. The more time you've spent around kids, the more you probably know this. In fact, the closer you've been to kids, the more scared you probably are about having kids, and this is perfectly fine. It simply shows how you need to talk, talk, talk, talk, and talk it over before you do this. Really talk about how children will change your life to either your partner, yourself, or to anyone else who will listen. You need to know, or at least have a good idea, both about how a child will change your life and how it will not change your life. I tell people trial and error is the way to do it. Invite a child into your life and see how it feels for a few days. Then, talk to people you know who don't have kids and see how they feel. Ask them what they think about it. This way you can really get a feel for what you're in for and how you're going to deal with the ups and downs of parenting. Because once you're in, you're in. The decision is for life, and it's completely life altering. Once you have kids, you're in for the most honest, mystical, emotional journey of your life. I don't know of anybody who regrets it or who wouldn't do it again.

The queer model is ideal because it's spoken, it's a negotiated process. There is no pressure in the queer community to have kids, so it's an ideal model for making families. Kids just aren't expected, and nobody just winds up pregnant, so you can decide what it's going to look like, and how you're going to live it. So look into your heart and decide how much you long for a child because, ultimately, it's not about planning but about lust. The planning is really only secondary; it's really about realizing that longing you probably have in your soul, and going out there and taking care of it, and making it real. Just get ready because you have to ask yourself some more questions, and ask yourself honestly how badly you're longing for this. [My longing] was so intense that when my dog had puppies, I would look at her and get jealous. At that point, I had to look at myself and start asking exactly what I was going to do about these intense emotions I was having. I started asking exactly what I would and wouldn't do to have kids. Would I leave a partner, because he or she doesn't want to have kids? Yes. Would I quit my job and move to another city? Yes. It's this kind of passion that's going to see you through the heartbreaks and happiness of parenting. The intensity is not a detriment; it's a resource for the job. Passion allows you to start and passion takes you through the burdens and crisis points in the job because parenting is a labor of emotion. Queerness might suppress a longingness for children—we suppress because it's always said to be an impossibility—but in the end, it's an existential question. Where do we want to be at the end of our lives? Kids are about lifetimes, generations, and true guilt-free care and comfort.

Families of Choice

The language and logic of choice in Emily's remarks have been taken up and put toward productive critical engagements in the social scientific literature on nonheterosexual families. Anthropologists, sociologists, and political scientists have embraced the picture of nonheterosexual families Emily presents and developed portraits of kinship in which queer families figure as living examples of bold new "critical" types of kin relations that hold the promise to undo the forms of social suffering inhering in participation in the heterosexual nuclear family (see Borneman 1996, 1997; Carrington 1999; Lehr 1999; Lewin 1993; Stacey 1998; Sullivan 2004; Weeks, Heaphy, & Donovan 2001; Weston 1991). For instance, Sullivan (2004) argues that the work of deciding—meaning the willed, self-reflexive action that she understands as accompanying the decision to form a family—establishes a quintessentially different psychodynamic arrangement of power within nonheterosexual families than that found in heterosexual families. By rearranging these dynamics, Sullivan believes, queer family relations possess a means to undo the suffering associated with the societal endorsement of heterosexuality and its accompanying patriarchal forms of power that legitimate specific forms of exclusion and injury (see also Berlant & Warner 1998; Butler 2002; Lehr 1999; Sedgwick 1993).

The formulation of queer kinship as "an ideal model" for achieving less restrictive, and thus happier, family relations rests on the assumption that LGBT families and their members are inherently flexible and are amenable to change through democratic process, sovereign acts of choice, and dialogic negotiation. Such a picture of queer family relations is derived from the idea that homosexual unions are sterile or that "kids just aren't expected, and nobody just winds up pregnant" in same-sex unions. Since children are not expected but are readily available, gay individuals are presented with the opportunity to decide exactly what form family relations will take. Here, the presence of children, as unexpected but welcomed members of queer families, is understood to provide the opportunity to rethink the operations of kinship on subject formation. The restrictive and punishing elements of the heteronormative family, in which the subject—whether queer or straight—is understood to emerge through patriarchal power and its ac-companying violence (Pateman 1988; Reiter 1975; Rosaldo & Lamphere 1974; Rubin 1975), is thought to be undone by the flexibility promised by democratic action, sovereign acts of choice, and the free-market exchange of information found in queer families.

Emily's words bolster this image by encouraging the formation of rad-ically flexible forms of family that are referentially linked to the genealog-ical grids associated with biogenetic kinship but are independent of the dynamics of power and exchange found in kin relations associated with heterosexuality. Yet Emily's words also illuminate the limits inherent in such thinking when she claims that having children remains an "existential question" about "where one wants to be at the end of life," even when family relations are constructed in accordance with an experimental ethic that proceeds along the lines of trial and error. By following Emily's words, we learn how freely and willingly partaking in the gift economy that lies at the heart of kinship—in which adults give both life and the world to children in exchange for the unified temporality of "generations" and "true guilt-free care and comfort"—is central to securing the future forms of happiness associated with belonging in families of choice.

To embrace uncritically the language of choice, the spirit of invention, and the gift economy of kinship is to neglect the anxiety, sense of mystery, danger, dependency, vulnerability, mortality, and forms of oppression Emily describes as also accompanying the formation of family. Emily says we must choose when forming family because of mysterious longings, lusts, passions, and jealousies that carry the potential to destroy—the self, society, and children—when we act without critical reflection. When anthropolo-gists do not take the danger and darkness associated with forming a family into account, they run the risk of portraying nonheterosexual families as embracing a distinctly modern quest to attain pain-free family relations through reasoned action and dialogue, ignoring the agency of pain and the legacy of struggle that accompany the founding of family relationships, as I discussed in the previous chapter. Emily's description of the dark side of family formation calls on the social sciences to acknowledge how being willing to knowingly suffer in the name of the family accompanies the acts that bring children into one's life. The willingness to suffer for family should make us pause and reconsider ethical positions that picture the presence of pain in family relations as an aberration in need of correction.

The contrasting images of parenthood in Emily's remarks cloud the claim that relatives can be agentially chosen and created and that adults readily give the gift of life and the world to children. Emily's description of family as something that overtakes one, as opposed to something one enters through reasoned deliberation, dispels such thinking. How do the lives and voices of children intersect, traverse, and transform the very adult idea that forming a family with children is something that defies reason but can be managed through deliberate, reasoned action and creative dialogue and negotiation? Where do the interests of children reside in such a vision of family and kinship? What is the relationship between the demand to speak and that which must be concealed in queer families with children? Does Emily's directive that one talk about family to be family participate in the anxieties surrounding sexuality that Foucault (2003) argues transform the bodies and lives of children into objects in need of constant surveillance?

It's a Labor of Emotion

It was a hot August day. I had taken a seat on the edge of a very crowded meeting room in St. Mary's Church, beneath a fan. I had joined some 150 people who were taking part in the yearly town meeting held by COLAGE. The event was billed as providing a space for the children of LGBT parents to "speak out, tell stories, give advice, and tell the truth to parents and other youth who want to know about the experience of growing up with LGBT parents." The meeting was conceived as an open forum, where the general public could come and learn about the dynamics of families of choice "from those who know the details of their inner workings best; the children."

The "town meeting" figures centrally in the self-described "creation myth" of COLAGE. The idea of forming a group for children in lesbian and gay families and of holding a town meeting during which those children educated adults about the meaning of their kinship supposedly arose spontaneously when a small group of children "spoke out" during a conference organized by the Family Pride Coalition in Washington, D.C., in 1990. The conference in Washington had been arranged to develop a collective awareness of the issues affecting gay families across the country and to develop supportive social and professional networks for LGBT parents.

As part of the meeting, a series of workshops had been arranged for children. The events proved disappointing to all, since those who attended felt that the issues truly affecting their lives were not addressed. In response, the children organized themselves into a collective and voiced their concerns to the adults who had organized the conference. The children suggested that they formulate their own program at future events, as a way of attending to and addressing their own needs and concerns. The adult representatives of the Family Pride Coalition thought the idea was excellent, and the children set their own agenda at the following year's meeting.

It is from the initial efforts of children to "speak out" and define themselves as members of a unique community, one based on but independent from their parents' sexuality, that COLAGE was born. Today, COLAGE continues to be run exclusively by children with LGBT parents, and it remains separate from such adult-run organizations as the Family Pride Coalition and PFLAG (Parents, Families, and Friends of Lesbians and Gays). Since its founding in 1990, COLAGE has grown into an advocacy group with over 4,000 members and chapters in nearly every major city in the United States and in other countries.

Consistent with the initial act of speaking out that brought COLAGE into existence, the town meeting is defined by the sense that children have needs and concerns that are different from those of adults and that relations between parents and children contain an element of estrangement. The task of the town meeting is to bridge the "stranger sociability" (Warner 2002) of the family through public dialogue, in the hope of creating happier family and community relations.

Public speaking is integral to this process, reflecting the belief that the predicament of a child's belonging in an LGBT family can be reconciled by children publicly revealing the place of their parents' sexuality in their everyday lives. The process extends parental care beyond the domestic sphere to include considering the ways LGBT family relations are received by the general public and the world at large. Through this process, adults can address, in practical ways, the injuries children suffer as a result of societal ambivalence about the family relations their parents have brought into being.

The creation of public forums for discussing and discovering the efficacy of kin relations is understood as unique to queer families. Here, the building and maintaining of close family ties is linked to the dialogic exploration and expression of the meaning of kinship and sexuality and of their combined effects on the lives of children.

"Speaking out" in the town meeting, and publicly describing the place of one's parent's sexuality in everyday relationships, does not directly equate with the ego working on itself to alleviate painful or troublesome symptoms, as the therapeutic discourses of the psychological sciences might be glossed. In the town meeting, giving an account of oneself and of the meaning of one's family relations is partly a political project conceived to generate pragmatic solutions to the suffering society inflicts on children as a cost of their belonging.

Brian, a parent who attended the meeting regularly, brought my attention to the distinction I am trying to make when he rhetorically posed the question, "Where else but in families of choice can children get a chance to publicly grade their parent's performance?" Brian went on to say that a sense of mystique surrounds the town meeting because it is perceived as holding the power to bring about concrete changes in the ways children and parents in LGBT families relate to each other. Brian made this clear when he described how his own relationship with his teenage son had been transformed by what he heard while attending his first town meeting.

BRIAN: I couldn't believe what I was hearing. Here was a bunch of unbelievably well-spoken kids telling me about how my own kids probably feel about my relationships with other men. It was so honest. It kind of hurt, but it was also amazing. I definitely sat down and thought long and hard about the men I was dating and what my dating life was doing to my children. After that, I definitely changed what was happening and who I was bringing home on Friday night.

A.G.: What do you mean? What did you do?

BRIAN: Well, it turns out, even though my one kid technically isn't supposed to be with me on Friday nights—he's supposed to be at his mom's [at the other end of the block]—he really didn't like seeing strange cars in the driveway. I guess it really upset him. I only realized it after hearing what the kids were saying at that town meeting and then having a conversation with him about what I heard. He's sixteen, and I had no idea my dating life was still a big deal to him, but it was. He always played it off so cool, saying everything is just fine and nothing bothers him. That's just how teenage boys are. They'll never just tell you anything about themselves, but I guess seeing strange cars in the driveway really upset him. Now I make sure there are no strange cars in the driveway on Saturday morning. I'm no saint, but I am here for my kid always. So, no more strange cars in the driveway. He needs to know that I'm available to him all the time, even when he's at his mother's, and that's what I guess I really learned from those kids.

As Brian's words indicate, the conversations at the town meeting are understood to bring about change in the objective practices surrounding the family's relationships, as opposed to the subjective meaning of being a relative. In other words, the goal is not to change "how teenage boys are" or to transform a father into a "saint." Achieving such transformations would involve the reshaping of persons. Instead, the goal is to change how kinship is done, or performed, by devising techniques for identifying the mechanisms within a relationship that are malfunctioning and causing pain or difficulty. Brian is not trying to change who he is or who his son is. He is devoted to isolating problematic elements in his existing relationships, based on what he knows about his son and what his son knows about him, and so to alleviating the suffering brought about by specific isolated and perhaps unconscious tendencies. Central to this process is dialogue and speaking one's interests, needs, joys, pleasures, and pains.

The split between the interests and needs of adults and those of children is physically manifested in the spatial arrangement of the town meeting. During the meeting, children assemble and position themselves apart, occupying a different physical space than their parents do. When I attended, the children spoke from an elevated platform at the head of a large meeting room in a church to an audience of parents neatly arranged before them in rows. It is the operation of dialogue and participation in the circulation of discourse from stage to audience that bridges the divide between the needs and interests of parents and those of children.

The formation of COLAGE and the organization of the town meeting itself mirror Michael Warner's (2002) description of the formation of *publics* and *counterpublics*. Following Warner, we might understand the town meeting (and the creation of COLAGE) as formalizing the existence of a *counterpublic* of children within the more general *public* of LGBT families. The coming into being of such a collectivity of children establishes the split between the separate *publics* made up of adults and of children as a social fact. When children speak as members of a community defined by their parents' sexuality, the dialogic form of belonging associated with families of choice is delineated and defined, giving rise to the sense of an objective and identifiable set of organized relations that can be known and commonly shared. Through such modes of public address, nonheterosexual forms of relationship become known as familial. Children gain the quality of truth tellers whose spoken words seem to solidify the existence and legitimacy of family ties while simultaneously making statements about the normal and the pathological in LGBT family relations.

In the town meeting, the voices of children are able to solidify the meaning of queer kinship because of the assumed psychological innocence of children within Western developmental models (Das 2000; Das & Reynolds 2003). Within this imaginary, children are understood as unique and new individuals, innocent of their parents' social history but connected to their parents' lives, as witnesses, through their need for parental care (Strathern 1992a). Envisioned as witnesses who might speak the truth about family relations, children have the opportunity to hold their parents accountable to a more general public's sense of what is and is not appropriate behavior. The power of the child to bring down the forces of the state and other forms of authority through bearing witness to their parent's behavior or sexuality should not go unnoticed in this forum. The known vulnerability of parents to their children's words demonstrates a material form of violence that children and parents in gay households navigate. The constraint shown by children who have been given a forum and the freedom to speak demonstrates an ethics of care that is actively directed toward caring for vulnerable parents (Reynolds 2000, 2012). As the previous chapter demonstrates, this constraint is not always exercised, illuminating a competing truth about relatedness

Public testimony transforms the possibility that a child might hold a parent liable for actions performed in the name of kinship—a kinship defined as arising by "choice"—into an actuality. The town meeting is built on the philosophy that a child's kin relations are best served by publicly grading parental actions and seeking public modes of redress and accountability for parental shortcomings.

The possibility of a parent's being disciplined by a child for the choices that a parent has made rests on the potential for children to say too much and overexpose the confusing and conflicting acts entailed in maintaining intimate family relations (Taussig 2003). Might the potential of children to speak dangerously about their parents provide a means for children to participate in constructing the meaning of being related? It is often thought that such constrained speech amounts to a child's consent to kinship. Of course, the possibility for such participation rests on the audience listening to what children say and, in effect, answering. In fact, it is not clear whose voice children used when speaking in the town meeting. Neither is it clear what the audience heard, let alone was prepared to answer for.

Meeting

The town meeting is the culmination of a series of workshops held by COLAGE over the course of Family Week. In the workshops, children and teenagers are coached in making media presentations, effective public speaking, community organizing, and anger management—"for when your best friend outs you in public." The children who are selected to speak at the meeting have all completed the series of workshops and have demonstrated to a collection of their peers that they possess the ability to openly discuss a wide range of issues affecting the lives of children in LGBT families in a voice that is representative of an assumed collective and that is sympathetic to the larger political project put forward by COLAGE.

Sherry, a founding member of COLAGE and a professional advocate and activist for alternative families, explained the overtly political purpose of children speaking out at the meeting. According to Sherry, the children who take part in the town meeting are drawn to the opportunity to "sway the general public's negative opinion of same-sex families and achieve justice by speaking persuasively." The political persuasion comes from the children appearing "well adjusted, above average, and articulate enough to break down the image of families of choice as being radically different from your average normal American family." From Sherry, we learn that the town meeting is designed with the idea in mind that acts of public address possess the almost magical ability to change the wider and more general sense that LGBT families are abnormal, a condition defined by the rules of heteronormative kinship and the idea that the people with whom one belongs and who one is are matters of kinship.

The meeting room that August day filled beyond capacity, a clear indication of the importance of what was about to unfold. The event was held in a church, rather than one of the restaurants, cafés, hotel lobbies, and even bars that had served as venues for the other events of Family Week 2001. A recognized activist and advocate for children in LGBT families had been enlisted to act as a moderator, and a social worker had been recruited to ensure that the discussion remained productive for all involved and to mediate any overly intense or excessive emotional reactions children or parents might have in response to the proceedings.

Once the chairs had been filled, each child on the discussion panel made a brief autobiographical statement. Lisa described how a single mother had adopted her. Her mother later became involved with a woman who then performed a second-parent adoption so she could share guardianship of Lisa. Lisa's two mothers have since split, but they maintain joint custody of Lisa. Lisa now spends an equal amount of time with each of her mothers, who maintain separate households in the same city.

Tom described himself as a "consummated child," meaning he was conceived and born while his mother and father were still married. His father later came out, was divorced from Tom's mother, and now lives with another man. Tom's primary residence is with his father, a few blocks away from his mother.

Ned did not know who his father was. His two mothers had gone to a sperm bank when they decided to have a child and had selected an anonymous donor. Ned said that his mothers wanted the identity of the donor to remain unknown, that they were explicit in their desire to form a family without a man, to avoid any possibility of a paternal figure entering into their family life. Not having a father, even in name, secured the meaning of family in Ned's household.

Rachel explained that she had been conceived through a legally arranged surrogacy and that her two fathers had planned for her to maintain a relationship with her biological mother. She went on to say she was still in close contact with her birth mother—"getting two or three phone calls a month and a couple of visits each year"—but she didn't consider her "bio-mom" to be part of the family. She was "more of a friend than anything else."

The panelists' autobiographical accounts provide a sense of the broad spectrum of narratives about sexuality, the law, descent, and biological notions of relatedness that are available for rendering family relationships legible. Clearly, there is no single definition of kinship in same-sex families, and narratives of biological relatedness remain in circulation within the "kinscripts" of LGBT families (Carrington 1999; Stack & Burton 1994).

After the introductions, the forum was opened to questions from the floor. In the following excerpts, I have left the children's narratives largely unaltered, presenting their words as they were spoken and recorded during the meeting. The only changes I have made are intended to ensure readability. The language the speakers used in the town meeting seems almost predictable, even scripted, while remaining laden with affect.

> VOICE 1 (FEMALE): Hi. I'm a clinical social worker, and I just want to thank all of you for agreeing to take part in this meeting. I have a daughter who didn't want to come up off the beach this afternoon, but I wish she were here so she could hear all that you might have to say. She's been here before, but this year, well, who knows, what happened. This is our third year coming to Family Week, and my third year coming to this meeting. It's really a unique opportunity for all of us parents to hear from you kids and to get a sense of what you're really going through in your personal and emotional lives, and to really celebrate what goes on in our families. Now, my question is, how do you deal with the fact that your family is not necessarily like everybody else's when you're

out on the playground at school or hanging out with your friends at the movies, or the mall, or wherever you go on your own time? How do you deal with the fact that you don't go home to a family like all your friends do? I guess, more simply, how do you tell your friends about your family—and honestly—do other kids give you a hard time because your family is different?

NED (SIXTEEN, FROM NEW JERSEY): I guess I'll answer since I'm one of the older ones here and have been dealing with this sort of thing all my life. You know, if I'm getting a hard time from somebody about my family, then they really aren't my friend, so I just don't really hang around with them. It's really kind of basic. I'm not friends with people who can't accept me or who choose not to accept me for who I am and where I come from. There are plenty of other people out there to be friends with, and I just look for them to hang around with, and it always works out. Who wants to be friends with people who don't accept you for who you are? So, I don't really have to deal with being hassled so much at school, or wherever. I mean, what's the big deal? All families are different. I just happen to have two moms. And if you can't handle it and want to give someone a hard time about something like that, then you look like the jerk, not me. I just try to pass that message along whenever something like that happens and deal with it that way.

Ned's comments about the value and importance of accepting diversity generated exuberant applause from the audience. Once it quieted, the proceedings continued.

VOICE 1: What about telling your friends about going home to your moms? How do you handle that?

NED: I guess I kind of deal with not going home to what we are told is a normal family by knowing all families are different and that the Brady Bunch, or whatever model we have from television, doesn't really exist for anybody. [Light laughter fills the room.] I'm proud of my family and my two mothers, and it doesn't matter that we are different and that some people have a hard time understanding us. I know that I'm loved and that my mothers are doing everything to take care of me and that I can always go to them no matter what. [Applause.] And, you know, when I hear about my friends and their families, I think I've really got a better deal. I know I'm wanted and that both my mothers really love me because they had to work really hard to have me. I might joke that my father is a turkey baster, but it's really a better deal to have two moms. I know that they both really love me and want me . . . than to have a dad who just goes to work all the time and doesn't really care. [Laughter and applause fill the room.] I have two loving parents who are equally involved with my life and making sure that I have a safe place to go and come home to. You know I don't really go around broadcasting that I have two moms, but somehow just about everybody knows, so I don't even have to tell very many people anymore. And when I do, I usually wait until I know them pretty well before I say anything because I want to know how they're going to react before I say anything. So I guess I wait and see if I want to be friends with someone before I start telling them about my family, and after I know I want to be friends with them, it's just not a big deal. It just happens, and things seem to take care of themselves. [Applause again fills the room.]

VOICE 2 (MALE): Quickly, I was wondering if one of you might be able to say what's the best thing that your parents have done for you in terms of helping you cope with any problems that have come up at school.

RACHEL (FIFTEEN, FROM BOSTON): I think the best thing my parents have done was to get involved. I think I was in, like, sixth grade or something, and some of the kids in my class were really picking on me and giving me a hard time because they just didn't understand. So after I went to my teachers and told them I was having a hard time and needed help and nothing really happened, my fathers decided to talk to some of the people at school—like the guidance counselors and the principal— about what to do. It was really making me kind of miserable. So, it was decided that we'd have a family education day where everybody would come in and talk about their families, and we did. After that day, we organized to have a few different people's parents come in and talk to the class about their families. My dad came in and explained all about our family and how we're no different from anybody else's really, I just happen to have two dads. After that, everything was better. Everyone understood and everything just got better. Everybody just stopped picking on me. So I guess the best thing my dad has done is to be involved in my life and help me out at school. [Applause and encouraging shouts fill the room.]

VOICE 3 (MALE): Wow, that's a really compelling story. I'm so happy to hear that things like that actually work. I'm always worried that I'm just meddling in my kid's life and making things worse for my son, but I guess not. [Laughter.] I'm wondering about how important things like this are to you guys. [He makes a sweeping arm gesture to encompass the room.] What's it like coming here to Family Week, and what do you take away from something like this?

CLAIRE (SIXTEEN, FROM CALIFORNIA): Oh, man! This week is really important. It's so important because it's the only time, I feel, that we can really let down our barriers. I know the whole time I'm here, I can walk into a room and know everybody else around me has had the same experiences that I've had and that I don't have to continually explain myself. [Applause and shouts fill the room.] I've been coming here for like five years now, I guess, and every year it's like meeting up with my big extended family. I really feel like all these people here are my family, we're all really close. Every year I meet new kids and people who are only coming here for the first time, and it's great. You can just see it through the week as they loosen up and start feeling comfortable enough to let their feelings out. Sometimes it's really intense, full of crying and stuff, but it always ends up being so great. I think everybody laughs as much as they cry. [Applause.] And, I think we all really depend on coming here and being a part of this whole thing because this is where we can really be who we are without having to worry. The people I know and meet here every year are really family to me. [Applause and shouts of encouragement fill the room.]

NED: Yeah, I totally agree. When I'm not here I usually feel like I live in a double world, and that breaks down here. It feels like you just have a huge amount in common with everyone else here, and it's really important. It helps get you through the rest of the time, when things might be bad at school or something like that. [Applause.]

VOICE 2: Okay, just a quick follow-up to my other question. What's the worst thing we, as parents, do?

RACHEL: I think definitely the worst thing that happens is when parents get overly involved with their kids' lives outside the house. By far, the worst thing that's ever happened to me is when my parents get involved with my social life. There are places that you want to have your own life and not be interfered with. Sometimes you just want to be normal and forget about your family and just be yourself. And, when your parents are continually getting themselves involved, it becomes impossible. But whenever this starts to happen, I usually just sit down with my dads and talk to them. I just say, "Hey, you know I can work this out myself and I don't need your help right now." They always let me know that they're there for me and that they respect what I'm going through and that they are there to help as opposed to cause problems. After we sit and talk honestly about what's going on in my life, they usually back off, and I can get back to being normal and having a normal life at school with my friends. [Applause again fills the room.]

CLAIRE: Yeah, you know, the last thing you want is your parents making everything out to be a big deal and making you the center of attention all the time because your parents happen to be lesbian or gay or whatever. [Light applause.] We aren't any different from any other kid. Everything isn't about your parents all the time, and it's important you guys know that. Sometimes we're sad or angry because we failed a test at school or because we feel like a dork because we aren't wearing the right shoes, and that has nothing to do with the fact that my dad is gay, or my mom's a lesbian, or whatever. And you guys really need to hear that. [Shouts of encouragement and applause fill the room.]

As Ned joked about having a "turkey-baster dad," two boys sitting close to me in the audience started to become agitated and noisy. As the meeting progressed, they became increasingly annoyed and withdrawn from what was taking place onstage. One boy rocked and wiggled back and forth in his chair, and the other lifted the nose of his skateboard up with his foot and let it drop so the wheels bounced noisily against the floor. Eventually, the boys' father intervened, whispering very loudly, "Knock it off! I brought you two here so you might learn something. If you can't behave yourselves and listen, then go outside! Now behave, or leave!"

The two boys looked at each other—as if testing their courage against their father's resolve— reached for their skateboards, got up from their seats, and pushed through the crowd to the door. They soon reappeared, visible through the open window of the meeting hall, in the courtyard of the church and began riding their skateboards on the architectural contours of the courtyard's landscaping. Other children who had abandoned their places in the audience soon joined the boys. By the end of the meeting, the sounds of skateboard wheels grinding across the pavement and the voices of teenagers joking and laughing infiltrated the discussion taking place in the meeting room. It is tempting to imagine the scene in the courtyard as the authentic lifeworld of children in queer families, the one containing the secret truth of children's lives and meant to be shielded from view by institutional review boards.

Performing Choice

In the town meeting, the meaning of what are often considered precultural forms of relationship—kinship and family—is explicitly constructed through public debate. During the meeting, children actively negotiate the terms of their care by educating their parents about the place of sexuality in the making of their lives and relationships. The design of the town meeting marks a shift in the imagination of the child from an innocent recipient and inheritor of culture to a shrewd observer and orator whose voice is constitutive of culture itself (Reynolds 1991; Ross 2003). The observations and orations of the children reconfigure the questions anthropologists have traditionally asked about kinship, from "Who is a relative and why?" (Ginsburg & Rapp 1995; Morgan 1870; Rivers 1968; Schneider 1968, 1972) to "What does kinship do and how might its workings be adjusted?"

The shift is made possible by children and adults participating in what Warner (2002) calls "like forms of reading, opining, arguing, and bearing witness" about the place of sexuality in the making of children's lives. The capacity of children's words to affect change resides in the commonly held perception that discourse operates on collectivities and that public address has the power to transform thought. In the town meeting, the idea that collectivities can act and bring about change through words provides a sense that sovereignty can be embodied and then exercised to bring relations into being and to make lives. The sense of sovereignty as an embodied form of power is central in public narratives about LGBT family formation, in which children's lives are pictured as originating in independently undertaken and creative actions.

Drawing on Warner's insights, I understand the process of selection, or peer review, that determines which children will "speak out" at the meeting as instructional, with children learning to "body forth" sovereign forms of power by engaging in the public circulation of discourse. It is through this instructional process that what is universal about and common to children and their parents, and what is human about relationships, is explored. I understand both Brian's sense of amazement that the words of some "unbelievably well-spoken children" could transform his relationship with his son and the expulsion of the boys with skateboards as expressions of the power that infuses participation in the circulation of such discourse: Those who do not speak appropriately, or those whose experience exceeds the institutionalized vocabulary of life and relationships as originating in a choice, are disciplined into compliance or rendered marginal to the public task of constructing the meaning of LGBT kinship.

It is the supposed truth told by children about the place of their parents' sexed bodies in the making of their lives and relationships that enables this disciplining to occur. It is perhaps ironic that the effort of the HIRB to limit my exposure to children was guided by the sense that it is dangerous and harmful for children to explore the place of sex in the context of their family relations. This sense might reside in the fear that children who publicly discuss their parents' sexuality are no longer innocent recipients of their parents' gifts of kinship and of life (which includes an idealized notion of sex and the family as life-granting enterprises) but shrewd speculators capable of bargaining for unknown prospects in the wider publics brought about by discursive circulations.

Yet, the town meeting is clearly guided by an ethic of restraint, and children and parents do not say everything they might. I understand the restraint exercised by the children as indicating their recognition that adults and parents consent to participate in family, which, from the children's perspective, is not chosen at all. After all, speaking appropriately at the town meeting, it seems, means not saying too much about the place of parental sexuality in the making of children's lives and relationships. Claire's, Rachel's, and Ned's words display the power of such restraint when they position normality as the goal to be achieved by children bearing witness to families of choice. By evoking norms, and expressing the desire to be normal, Claire and Rachel limit narratives that continually position a parent's queer sexuality as the defining feature of difference in the lives of children in LGBT families. By tracing the deployment of norms in the dialogue of the town meeting, I hope to comment on the operation of the very rules of kinship that define LGBT families as exceptional.

Breaking the Rules

Claire's and Rachel's evocation of social norms initially seems to challenge the idea that children with LGBT parents are different and thus belong in community—both with each other and with their parents—as if by nature. Claire and Rachel limit the extension of the rule that "makes everything out to be a big deal because our parents happen to be gay" by pointing to the important place of contingencies—like wearing the wrong shoes and doing poorly on a test at school—in a child's milieu. As Rachel's and Claire's words make apparent, the intensities that accompany such contingencies are constitutive of children's lives, and the agency of historical material objects is equal in importance and power to one's parent's sexuality when it comes to rendering children's lives and relationships legible.

Perhaps Gilles Deleuze has most productively explored the philosophical implications of the affect evoked by Rachel's and Claire's words. According to Deleuze:

> It is wrong to think that children are limited before all else to their parents, and only have access to milieus afterward, by extension or derivation. The father and mother are not coordinates of everything that is invested by the unconscious. There is never a moment when children are not already plunged into an actual milieu in which they are moving about, and in which the parents as persons simply play the role of openers or closers of doors, guardians of thresholds, connectors or disconnectors of zones (1997:63).

For Deleuze, the irresolvable tension between the movement of children through the world and the restrictive modes of interpretation that continually turn to parental sexuality to gain insight and describe a child's milieu calls for a "schizoanalysis" in which what appear as lapses, parapraxes, and symptoms are reconfigured as potential lines of flight. Embracing a Deleuzian mode of "schizoanalysis" when it comes to children's lives entails identifying the trajectories of such often abruptly interrupted lines of flight to "see if they can serve as indicators of new universes of reference capable of acquiring a consistency sufficient for turning a situation upside down" (Deleuze 1997:64). In the town meeting, I claim, what might be turned upside down are the universes defined by the sets of rules that reduce the heterogeneity of children's lives to operations and expressions of parental sexuality.

Rachel, Claire, and Ned deploy the affect and agency associated with shoes and tests at school to challenge accepted thinking about kinship, its origins, and its forms of identification in hopes of blunting the normative force of the rules that position heterosexual reproduction as normal. Yet the trajectories Ned, Claire, and Rachel identify, those that might turn the universe of idealized heterosexual kinship upside down, seem to strike against the transparent limits—"like birds that strike their beaks against a window" (Deleuze 1997:63)—established by the very rules from which the children seek flight. Some scholars have interpreted the concussive force of striking against these limits, and the injuries that ensue, as condemning those whose lives and relationships do not mirror the heterosexual norm to the marginality of abjection, and even social death (see, for instance, Borneman 1996; Butler 2000).

Rather than argue that these strikes are breaking points that end flights toward ideal forms of relating, I suggest we follow Claire's, Rachel's, and

Ned's lead and examine what the reinscription of the rules of an idealized form of kinship *does*.

The Rules Return

In their descriptions of the worst things parents do when trying to ease the burdens of belonging in queer families, Rachel and Claire illuminate the presence of an alternative social life, one in which the nagging presence of their parents' sexed bodies does not define them as different. Claire and Rachel both express the desire to be left alone so they can "be normal" or unencumbered by their parents' queer bodies. For Rachel and Claire, being normal equates with inhabiting a social milieu in which their lives and relationships are not continually read as an index of their queer parents' sexuality. Rachel makes this clear when she says, "Sometimes you just want to be normal and forget about your family and just be yourself." Claire reiterates this point when she adds, "You guys really need to hear that we aren't any different from other kids just because our parents happen to be lesbian or gay or whatever."

In Rachel's and Claire's words, the imagination of a true self—a self that might come to life when one's life and relations are not continually defined by parental sexuality—asserts itself against the image of a false self brought into being by societal commitments to heteronormative kinship. Rachel imagines that she can live as her "true" self when the rules that define her current relations as an afterword to her parent's sexed bodies are suspended. It would be a mistake to say the existence of such an imaginary indexes a real set of kin relations, in which those who fall outside the scope of its rules are committed to false or unlivable lives. The intensities accompanying such contingencies as the wearing of shoes and the taking of tests at school positions the reality of such relations as an idealization or even a symptom of the rules of a less than stable norm.

Following Deleuze, I suggest Rachel's and Claire's words illuminate how the imaginary and the real can act as superimposable parts, dependent on and in pursuit of each other. At the center of the pursuit lie suffering and the effort to understand the various taboos and regimes of representation that render relationships in LGBT families illegitimate, exceptional, and subject to rejection. The goal for analysis, as undertaken by Rachel, Claire, and Ned, is to isolate the symptoms accompanying these rules so that creative flight might replace repetition. The isolation of these rules and their symptoms takes place through public forms of speaking and by revealing the suffering the rules inflict, so the pain generated by their operation can be addressed and thoughtfully corrected.

In these public forums, the heterogeneous forms of life and relationship described by the children, forms brought into being by nonhuman actants like shoes and tests at school, gain the creative capacity to sustain the lives of those brought into the world through unsanctioned means. Such a potential stands in marked contrast to the dominant idea that families and children are either the natural outgrowth of heterosexual encounters or the expression of a natural life force infinitely propagating itself. We might think of this contrast as calling for the alignment of social norms that erroneously picture the creation of life and relationships as the exclusive task of heterosexuality with the normativity of biosocial forms of modernity, in which the creation of life and relationships takes place through the application of cultural techniques (Rabinow 1996).

The stumbling point in achieving this alignment seems to be suffering and accounting for the excessive pain that continues to accompany the formation of family relations, even when elaborate techniques have been developed and deployed to alleviate it. I understand the return to the rules of heteronormative kinship in the town meeting (when thinking about the suffering of children and the conditions of possibility for belonging in community) as providing a means to name the "excessive pain," to borrow a phrase from Michael Herzfeld (2001), that society inflicts on its members as a cost of belonging. It is the presence of such suffering that Emily first alerted us to, when she described the dark side of forming families, and Ron and Adam learned to endure.

Claire brings the audience's attention to the transferability of the norms of heterosexual kinship and to the way such norms can transfigure the suffering associated with family relations into a symptom of identifiable forms of power when she tells the audience about the importance of Gay Family Week for the children of LGBT parents. It is only during Family Week, she says, that she feels she can fully and safely be who she is.

When Claire claims she does not have to explain herself during Family Week because all who attend have families with similar origins, the rule that defines lives and relationships that do not mirror the heterosexual norm as exceptional provides a basis for locating the suffering associated with founding LGBT families. Claire's sentiment is generalizable across a range of subject positions because of the assumption that lesbian, gay, bisexual, and transgender relationships are sterile and, thus, must produce life through the conscious use of known biosocial technologies or not at all.

In his description of friendship, Ned gives voice to the tension between the promise of a heterogeneous community formulated on the principle of choice and the return of the sexed body as the very condition for belonging in community. For Ned, "friendship" names a form of belonging that is unencumbered by the constraints of normative notions of sexuality and kinship. Yet the very possibility for Ned to enter into friendship remains linked to his disclosing the place of sexuality in the creation of his family relationships. Ned offers this disclosure by humorously referring to his father as a "turkey baster" and thereby situates the origin of his life and relationships in sovereign acts of choice in which known biological and social technologies were applied to bring a desired life and kinship into the world. The importance of disclosure, then, rests on whether the "facts" of how his life was brought into being, once revealed, will or will not provide a basis for his exclusion. While Ned proposes friendship as providing an alternative form of belonging to kinship, the possibility of such belonging remains tied to publicly disclosing the place of sexuality in the family.

In Ned's narrative, the standing threat that a parent's sexuality might foreclose the possibility of a child's social acceptance is mediated by knowledge that queer family relationships cannot be accidental. For Ned, knowing that his two mothers had to work very hard to bring him and his family relations into being assuages the anxiety that who he is, and where he belongs, might be radically contingent, uncertain, and unwanted. A picture of such uncertainty, and an image of its suffering, is found in the father/child relationship in the heterosexual nuclear family—a relationship known to be infused with the standing threat of skepticism (see Cavell 1996; Donzelot 1979; Foucault 2003).

In Ned's narrative, children in heterosexual families suffer from skepticism, or from the uncertainty of knowing if they are truly loved, because they are never sure if their birth was accidental and if the care they need and receive is burdensome to their parents. Such a possibility exists because heterosexual unions are pictured as excessively fertile and continually risk creating unwanted lives.[2] Biosocial technology intercedes in the heterosexual family by putting this excessive fertility in check. It is in this context that I understand the vocabulary of choice to intersect with biogenetic kinship and heteronormative notions of family.

For the child in a heterosexual family, the threat of rejection, or the burden of skepticism about one's welcome in the world, cannot be assuaged by holding factual knowledge of one's origins and one's kin. Instead, idealized biogenetic kinship positions the standing threat of rejection as arising with

---

[2] It is this almost mechanical aspect of biological kinship that configures kinship as uncanny for William and David, as well as for Jon and Tim.

conception. Because of this, being unable to know if one is loved, and if one thereby belongs, is something that must be endured (Povinelli 2009).

In his search for friendship, Ned encounters the limit of discursive circulations about choice, and we learn how a child's sense of belonging is not a matter of choosing at all. Ned is not simply choosing between one friend and another or deciding between one form of relationship and another. He is negotiating the violence of a rule that renders suffering the threat of rejection and of not belonging natural, since the rule and its violence are pictured as arising with and through the creation of life itself. Emily alerts us to the importance of one knowing that he or she is willing to take on the burdens of a child who will face such negotiations when she says that one must "talk, talk, talk, and talk some more" before acting on the desire to bring a child into one's life.

In the very condition of possibility that family might be chosen, the violence of a rule that configures the pain of social rejection as natural is carried forth, and Ned, Claire, and Rachel come to inherit the predicament of a biosocial modernity in which a life might be brought into being through deliberate choice but in forms not necessarily acknowledged as valuable (Butler 2004; Ginsburg 1998; Rapp 1999). We need to ask about the legacy of "choice" in the lives of those who identify as LGBT and their children, since it speaks to questions of heredity and the world children will inhabit and inherit from their parents. To address these questions, I turn to discussions that took place in support groups devoted to the needs of gay fathers.

Overachieving

Wannabe Dads is an informal support group sponsored by Center Kids in New York City. As the name implies, the group is designed for men who wish to become fathers and is run by a small collection of gay men who have recently brought children into their lives. Meetings are held once a month and are generally organized around topics such as the pros and cons of adopting a child through city-run social services and how to select a lawyer skilled at handling the details of an international adoption. The meetings usually include a brief presentation by an expert in one of the many professional fields that provide services to LGBT parents, and they typically draw twenty to twenty-five men who move through the process of becoming fathers as a type of cohort. The structured portion of the meetings is generally followed by an open discussion among those in attendance. During the open discussions, men often share biographical details and experiential accounts of bringing a child into their lives, counterposing their accounts to the expert knowledge previously presented.

The friendships established through participation in groups like Wannabe Dads often provide the basis for creating the playgroups and other social networks that become increasingly important for parents after the arrival of a child. Many participants utilize the group for building and maintaining social ties and continue to attend meetings well after they have become fathers.

I first learned of the anxiety that surrounds questions of violence and heredity in LGBT families while attending a Wannabe Dads meeting. A man contemplating adoption raised the issue through the following question to the group:

> VOICE 1: I just have a brief question that maybe somebody can answer quickly. I hear all of you and am so impressed by what you've achieved and what you're all doing . . . and have done. It's really great and exciting for me to hear all this. It's fabulous. I'm just beginning the whole process—I just got an 800 number [a toll-free telephone number that can be used by women interested in placing their yet-to-be or recently born child in another's care], a lawyer, and I'm working with a great agency. That's all fine and good, so far no problem. I guess my concern is with myself and what I know is a common problem with gay men, and I'm wondering how it works in your life as parents . . . or soon to be . . . or wannabe dads . . . or whatever. It's with overachieving and my continual sense of myself as an overachiever. I know, as a gay man living here in New York City, like a lot of people, I carry this crazy drive with me, all over the place and into practically everything I do, to be excellent. You all must know what I'm talking about. It's that, "I'm gay and have to be better than everyone else in the room" thing, to prove to whoever it is in our lives—whatever phantom—that being gay doesn't equal all those horrible things we were told it would. You know, that we are all losers, going to end up alone, sexual perverts, delinquent, socially awkward, etc. What I worry about is how this might affect my family life. I'm already worried I'm going to feel like I need to be this superdad all the time; and you know, if my kid falls down on the playground or if I let him slip in the bassinet—God forbid—or fail to change that diaper ten minutes before it even gets wet, something like that . . . I'll just lose it. Does anybody else worry about this? Or is it just me?

His question elicited the following comments:

> VOICE 2: I know exactly what you're talking about, but don't worry. It all goes away, it just disappears when you have a kid. Kids make such a demand

on your time and take up so much of your attention and energy that everything just becomes about getting through the day and getting yourself to bed so you can get enough sleep to get up and start all over again … being a superdad, even though you might start out with that idea, just goes away. The kids set the terms and all you can do is just try to keep up. I just wouldn't worry about it. You're always going to feel like you're trying to catch up and just struggling to keep a semblance of order.

VOICE 1: So you don't think I need to worry about passing any of this on to my kid or anything like that?

VOICE 3: No, I just wouldn't worry about it. You won't have time. You're going to be too busy worrying about all sorts of other things, like making breakfast and doing laundry, and figuring out when you can get to the store to buy diapers. It will just go away. Having kids is the great equalizer. Everyone with kids is just hanging on, trying to get by, and doing the best they can.

The man who posed the original question seemed relieved, but he nevertheless took detailed notes about what was being said in response to his query.

The next time I heard about "overachieving" and violence was during Family Week in Provincetown (2001), when I attended a similar session organized by Sherry, one of the COLAGE founders we met earlier. The meeting was coming to a close when a man in the group named Greg brought up the issue. Greg, unlike the man in New York, had already completed an adoption and was enjoying his first year with Nick, his baby boy.

GREG: One thing I really worry about, and maybe you can comment on this, is my continual sense of overachieving and personal need to be perfect. I compensate for being gay like this, and I always have. I'm worried I'm going to pass this terrible tendency on to Nick. It's almost a compulsion with me; I can't do anything half-assed or part way. I know I'm totally unbearable sometimes. Racquetball? Forget it! I turn into a monster. I just become totally unbearable. What can I do so Nick gets the idea that he can fail and the world isn't going to end? I can deal with myself—that's why I have a therapist—but it's him I'm worried about. I don't want all this stuff falling on his head. Any suggestions?

SHERRY: Obviously, you can't control everything in your child's life. Right? You have to recognize that that's a symptom of what you're actually talking about right there. It's the idea that you can be perfect and teach your child how to not be perfect that is the problem. I hear this all the time in the sessions I run. And, if you think about it logically, it just doesn't make sense. You can't teach your kid how to fail perfectly, its really kind of logical. What you need to let your child know is that it's okay for them to try something new and have it not come out as they planned, or as they imagined. That's the difference. I feel like I'm repeating myself, but the most important thing you can do for your kid, and here I'm speaking to all of you here, is to just be there for them. Love them unconditionally. Let them know that you're available and open to them and that you love them no matter what. They need to know that, at the end of the day, no matter what's happened to them at school, on the playground, or at swim practice—even if it has nothing to do with you as parents—that they can come to you and ask questions or tell you how they're feeling openly, no matter what's gone on that day. They need to know that you aren't judging them because their hair isn't right, or because their pants are too short, or because they didn't get an A on their spelling homework that day, or they dropped the ball at baseball practice, whatever it is. Every other kid in the world is already doing that for them. They need to feel that they have a safe home where, if they do fail at something, or something doesn't turn out quite right, it will be okay. Think of it as building a safe environment for experiments. Be there and open and let them know that home is a safe, nurturing place where they can be who they are and discover who they want to be. You have to make a home where it's safe for them to experiment.

What is striking to me about the preceding exchange is how the question of inheritance, or what the parent passes on to the child, leads to a discussion of violence, its repercussions, and the symptoms it produces in its wake. What is at stake is the possibility that a parent who has experienced violence might unknowingly pass the residue of this violence or its symptoms on to his or her child. The possibility produces anxiety because it illuminates how parents might unintentionally, despite their best intentions, cause their child to suffer unnecessarily. It thus becomes imperative to identify the kinds of violence at work in one's life and relations, as well as their symptoms, so they do not become the invisible source of another's pain. If such violence remains invisible, the suffering that parents inflict on their children goes unnamed and thus remains beyond the reach of corrective measure and altered practice. In these narratives, homophobia—which I have argued is underwritten by kinship—names the founding violence of the queer subject. It is the standing threat of such violence that instantiates the provision of security as a defining feature of parental love in gay families.

My intention in discussing "overachieving" is to shed light on the ways in which the threat of violence in kinship makes the difference between repetition and creativity indistinguishable. Here, I am not dealing with stunning instances of violence, such as the disruption of family relationships through direct punitive legal action or gratuitous physical acts. Instead, I am looking at the subtle and ingrained sense that, despite a parent's best intention, his or her children will experience pain, perhaps as an unintended consequence of the parent's own actions or because of who they are and what they might represent, and at how the suffering of violence becomes folded into narratives of kinship.

Daily Sufferings

In his discussion the violence of everyday life, Arthur Kleinman (1997; see also Kleinman & Kleinman 1996) describes how suffering becomes real, or gains meaning, through the articulation of its symptoms as personal experience. For Kleinman (1988), the act of establishing the meaning of suffering is an exercise in translation, in which complaints are transferred from one semiotic system, that of symptom, into the signs of another, that of cause and origin.

Kleinman goes on to describe how the meaning of suffering is explicitly tied to the narration of one's experience and to expression of the legitimacy of one's need to care and to be cared for. By transposing Kleinman's logic onto the above discussion of overachieving, we can see how the words spoken in the support groups point toward the folding of identifiable violence, as pathology, into the multiple layers and structures of care found in LGBT families. For instance, Sherry describes how parents must respond to the injuries their children might suffer by "always being there for them, no matter what" and by "creating an open environment of unconditional love" where children will feel "safe." According to Sherry, it is by paying constant attention to the standing threat of violence that a parent can ensure that "the stuff" of previous injury does not "fall on the child," to use Greg's words, and come to define experience for a child.

Sherry goes on to say that Greg has to suppress the symptoms of his experiences of homophobia in his daily routine of caring for Nick, but he cannot forget them. Greg's experience of violence is not to be erased but to be utilized to imagine an open environment in which Nick is free to flourish through experimentation. By freeing Nick to experiment with different ways of being in the world, Greg ensures that he has an alternative to his own life, one in which violence has defined experience and sense of self.

The trace of violence and its role in shaping Greg's everyday experience is not to be undone either by Greg or by a therapist's intervention. Rather, Greg has an obligation not to pass his suffering on to Nick by remaining attuned to the productive work of the violence he has suffered, in its most minute details, in the creation of subjectivity (his own and Nick's). According to Sherry, this attention provides Nick with the best shot at emerging from childhood unencumbered by the burdens of homophobic violence. In this scenario, the figure of the "normal" child becomes the index of having broken the repetition of traumatic experience.

The message delivered in the Wannabe Dads meeting was slightly different: the traces of violence found in the subjectivity of LGBT parents will recede in the process of tending to the needs of a growing child. In essence, performing the day-to-day labor of caring for a growing child causes the symptoms of trauma to dissipate, thereby breaking any repetitions brought about by suffering traumatic violence. Freedom from the symptoms and legacy of such historically situated violence is achieved through immersion in the daily work of maintaining family relationships. The labor needed to maintain a virtually normal family life, complete with its struggles and exhaustions, is said to end the repetitions brought about by traumatic violence. In other words, it is by investing in the ordinary, and creating a life that mirrors the norm, that a child is assured of a future free from the suffering that defines the parent's life.

Yet Sherry's advice to Greg alerts us to a far more vexing conundrum lying at the heart of understanding the place of violence in the formation of the subject and the difference between traumatic repetition and creativity. Sherry directs attention to the difficulty, if not outright impossibility, of intentionally breaking, through corrective reasoned actions, the repetition of suffering brought about through traumatic violence. The uncertainty of kinship assures this result. As Sherry asserts, to break the repetition of suffering inaugurated by kinship, Greg must make the switch from straining to achieve the image of the perfect father (an effort manifested in his desire to teach his child to fail perfectly) to creating a new space in which Nick is safe and free to experiment with different ways of being and becoming. Through Sherry's corrective, we learn how performing the routines of everyday life with perfection, or modeling one's life on perceived norms, is the very work of violence from which Greg seeks relief. The error of believing that one can be a perfect parent—manifested in the attempt to teach a child how to fail perfectly or how *not* to suffer—proves to be the very vehicle by which the pain of the parent is transmitted to the child.

The conundrum Sherry identifies rests on the embrace of a constructivist notion of kinship for creating family relations. After all, one can never objectively assess the outcome of one's actions as a parent when the meaning of family relations is something that emerges through doing (which includes searching for the very meaning of being related). I understand the men in the Wannabe Dads support group as imparting this insight. Such a notion of family stands in sharp distinction to cultural accounts of kinship, in which the origins of family and the meaning of such terms as "father" are pregiven and readily knowable through something outside relations themselves, like biology or the law. It also stands in opposition to constructivist notions in which one actively creates the very form and contents of such categories as "queer," "father," or "family" through negotiated democratic actions or choice. In the place of such certainty, instead, we find paradox.

The paradox is given voice in Sherry's effort to educate Greg about the erroneous assumption that one can teach a child to "fail perfectly." Unconditional love provides redress for the suffering that children experience, but the existence of unconditional love can only be known retrospectively, or after the fact of violence. Such "aspect blindness," to borrow from Stanley Cavell (see Das 2007 for an ethnographic application of the concept), configures parental knowledge of family relations as vulnerable to others' ability to read one's actions through a diagnostic lens that exceeds one's own (Kleinman 1997). As a result, parents must be educated about the effects of their own actions on their children by their children. The figure of the child as a truth teller is imagined as providing the best route to such an education.

Sharon, the now-adult child of two men who live in New Hampshire, expressed the difficulty of working through the paradoxical relationship between kinship and violence voiced by Sherry. Sharon shared her description of homophobia and its violence while we were conversing about the place of activist and support groups, in particular, COLAGE, in the lives of children with LGB or T parents. I asked how she understands the sexuality of her fathers to have affected her life as a child, and she replied,

I don't really remember when I became aware that my dads' sexuality was supposed to be a huge factor in my life. I didn't really put it all together until pretty late in the game, like high school or something, and I couldn't really make sense of it until actually after I'd been off at college for a couple of years. I guess I needed distance to begin sorting things through. It was really shocking and kind of drove me crazy for a while. I remember becoming aware of how I always worked really hard in high school and middle school to always be so normal because if I wasn't, I thought my dads would be judged. I couldn't just be me, being me, with my friends at school. I had to be that well-adjusted and above-average kid who got the lead in the school play and lettered in both volleyball and speech and debate, or else my dads were going to be judged. I think that's why I always tried to be so perfect, and did so well in school. I guess I did a really good job of it, because I look back at it and I was a totally normal, popular, and basically happy kid with a bunch of friends. I was just a little nervous. Now I don't really care so much, but then I guess I was really wrapped up in it at that time without really knowing it, but also knowing it all the same. Even now it's kind of hard to talk about because I feel like I need to protect my parents and convert anybody who might think same-sex parenting is bad, to the cause.

What is striking about Sharon's statement is how the meaning of sexuality in her family relations is tied to the passage of time, continued reflection, and the still-present need to protect her two fathers from judgment. We see this in her awareness of how hard she worked to be "perfect" in high school, lest her foibles be linked to her parents' sexuality and come to bear witness to the inability of nonheterosexuals to be parents. As Sharon said, she was mostly unaware of how she was protecting her parents as a child and a teenager. Her judgment that her fathers' sexuality may have made her "a little crazy" came at a later date, when she had gained the distance needed to reflect on her situation. It was only after being away at school, and after time had elapsed, that Sharon became conscious of how she had compensated for her fathers' sexuality. It was only then that the place of sexuality in her family relationship became tangible in her daily life, and her observation that she remains "just a little nervous" gained an etiology in someone else's choice. The inherent violence of kinship and its normative force makes the symptoms of violence described by Sharon common to many whose life and relations do not align with the norm.

The slight concern or nervous undertone Sharon identifies within herself and then links to her parent's sexuality echoes her earlier efforts to shield her fathers from the multiple, possibly punishing, readings her actions and existence are subjected to in the general public. Sharon's slight agitation and her constant self surveillance speaks to the different ways children take on and body forth the adult's imagination of the child by presenting themselves back to the world as the image of an ideal child (Taussig 2003). It is tempting to rest, and find solace in Sharon's formulation because it resonates with the voices of the children found in the town meeting who declare that the children of gay parents are essentially "all right" since they are actively crafting selves that are both capable and equipped to defend against the injuries inflicted by a world that is ambivalent, even hostile, towards their family relations. Yet, nervousness is not always quite so easy to contain.

Sherry expressed how self surveillance and searching for places where one's parents sexuality interrupts one's elaboration of self is neither enough nor up to the challenge of managing the threats found in a world that is ripe with the potential for violence toward queer subjects and their children. In response to my asking how and where she experiences the effects of her father's sexuality she said the following.

> You want to know how this affects me and other kids? Sure, sometimes everything really is like they say it is in the Town Meeting, all perfect and rosy and full of rainbows, and sometimes its not. Okay, let me give you an example, my mother and father might have been married when I was born, and I might have spent a lot of time as a child with my father in San Francisco after they got divorced and he came out, but I spent most of my life in a small town in the Midwest. Everyone in that town knows everything about me, my dad, my family, and everything that happened. So how does it work? I still live there. If my car breaks down and I take it to some mechanic, I don't know if that guy, somebody I probably went to high school with, hates gay people and decides to fuck with my brakes. I worry that I'm going to get killed because some shithead hates me and my family for no real reason except we exist and he knows us. That's the way it works. That's what I carry around with me.

In Sherry's statement, the spectacular image of adult children living in fear of a violently homophobic society seems to burst the ideal picture of the social field crafted by children in such overtly performative contexts as those found in the Town Meeting, or those, like Sharon's, derived through therapeutic narratives. Sherry's description of the affective circulations defining life of children in queer families seem unmediated and visceral, and it is tempting to imagine her words as voicing the true condition of these children. After all, Sherry's words convey a sense of the ingrained threat that surrounds queer families and the potential violence carried in the social field. Her words also express how the potential of a violent response to the presence of certain bodies is folded into the choice to bring a child into the world (Das 1995).

When mapping the potential risks that threaten to erupt in the everyday, Sherry leans on established notions of ordinary and exceptional bodies and presuppositions about the distinctions between homosexuality and hetero-sexuality, or the very distinctions and violent splits she not only seeks shelter from but comes to embody as the child of a gay man. It is the promise that institutions like kinship and sexuality, whether normative or not, might work as external braces for shoring up and stabilizing spaces that provide shelter from what Povinelli calls "the pain of being outside form" (Povinelli 2001). What allows one to forget that the social field is constituted as violent and threatening is the embrace and commitment to these very institutions themselves and the divisions they entail. The fierce power of Sherry's rage and the subtle force of Sharon's constraint, both of which express their mutual desire to shelter and protect themselves as well as others and their families, demonstrates the fundamental instability of institutions and how neither sexuality or kinship can account for or hold children's experience in place. As Povinelli has argued, heteronormativity allows the knowledge that comes from negotiating the fault lines and paradoxes of desire and survival to appear fractured, doubled, or lacking in cohesion (Povinelli 2001). It is the shattering effect of Sherry's rage and the incessant murmur of Sharon's anxiety that makes exercises in elaborating kinship and sexuality far more than a grammatical or textual exercise. It is about registering the risks, and giving an account of the costs and pleasures, of entry into human life, no matter its modality.

5

Precarious Kinship

It has taken me longer to complete this book than I originally anticipated. Over time, my relationship to the concepts deployed in the research have changed and the incremental pressures exerted on my thinking by the voices of those I have known and worked with have transfigured my initial impression of the family and kin relations of gay men and their children. I might have foreseen this change since uncertainty as to the existence and meaning of one's relations and the importance of remaining attuned to the subtle, and sometimes not so subtle, forces configuring the emergence of family and kinship is a recurrent theme expressed in the lives and narratives of those I came to know through this research. But it took time for me to understand the importance of remaining attuned to the work of time, of waiting and seeing, before attempting to make meaningful statements about the relations I encountered in the course of this project, including my own.

I remain convinced that the failure to consider the influence of dispersed agencies like time, of institutions like the law, and of affect in the making of kinship allows the shifting arrangement of actors and actants that give birth to family relations and their meaning to be easily dismissed or passed over. I hope my elaborations have demonstrated the significance of remaining attuned to the multiple alliances between things, persons, laws, and institutions that give birth to the spaces of intimacy and affection as well as to the kin relations of the men I came to know. I know the voices of the men I worked with have helped me to understand aspects of myself, my family relations, and my experience in ways I did not anticipate when setting out to conduct this research. I also hope that my efforts have demonstrated that making kinship and living in family relations is a far from certain or clear process in the Western world. Rather, living in kinship is an aspiration and an achievement that must be renewed continually, even when the relations are made in accordance with established norms, such as heterosexual reproductive sex and marriage.

If recent scholars of kinship have demonstrated one thing, it is that kinship and family relations in Europe and America are infused with uncertainties and that these forms of relating stand in need of verification and explanation. The making of kinship and family is neither self-explanatory nor transparent, not even to those most intimately involved in the process. The same holds true for those engaged in the study of such relatedness. Open-ended questions about the existence of a relation, the meaning of being a relative as well as about the origins and the status of a relation, permeate efforts to build and live in kinship. This is why I am hesitant to embrace Marshall Sahlins's (2013) recent figuration of kinship as a transpersonal mutuality of being. For Sahlins, kinfolk are "members of one another" or "persons who participate intrinsically in each other's existence" (ix). Relatives, according to Sahlins, "emotionally and symbolically live each others' lives and die each other's deaths" (ix). Such relations are culturally partic-ular, meaning kinship is delimited and differentiated from other forms of relatedness through language and culture according to specific criteria, such as "having the same name, eating from the same land, born from the same woman, and so on" (44) In the light of the men who shared their lives with me, glossing kinship in these terms misses the uncertainty found in kinship and the ways intimate worlds and the futures they hold recede and vanish when certain relations are nominated as kinship and others not.

The human animal is certainly relational. Claude Lévi-Strauss (1969) famously described how there is no such thing as a single, isolated, or non-social human being in the opening chapters of *The Elementary Structures of Kinship*. Such a condition could be contrived only through culture itself, and it is thus social. If there is one thing the anthropological archive bears out it is that the human's *being* is relational, and thus cultural, and Sahlins has argued this point in his earlier work (Lévi-Strauss 1969; Malinowski 1927, 1929; Sahlins 1960). When Sahlins suggests that kinship is best described by mutuality of being, and thus claims to lay to rest the 150-year old anthropo-logical question concerning what kinship is, he glosses over the uncertainty, skepticism, and latent violence that arises within and through nomination itself. Yet, it proves crucial that the distinction between who is and who is not a relative be made because lives and futures are at stake. As the lives of the men with whom I worked bear witness, the criteria by which one might distinguish a relative from a nonrelative prove elusive at best, while the importance of making the distinction remains crucial because it is mortal. Lives and futures are made and unmade in and through kinship. All one need do is remember the close relationship between kinship and survival in the time of HIV/AIDS articulated by David in the introduction to this text.[1]

---

[1] See also Jon Borneman's (1996) discussion of the centrality of marriage in anthropo-logical discourse and the way it occludes the deaths brought about by HIV/AIDS.

Uncertainties of these sorts gain expression in the political actions, legal acts, and forms of creativity that constitute family life in twenty-first-century America. In the preceding pages, I have tried to articulate some of the ways gay men with children address the uncertainties that arise in conjunction with their efforts to live in kinship by focusing on how and when they reach a sense of certainty about the status and meaning of being a relative.

My efforts have been partially oriented by the centrality of reasoned action, choice, and creativity in popular as well as scholarly portraits of kinship. The increasing availability and use of reproductive technologies, surrogacy, and adoption for making families and the widespread societal movement away from the nuclear household as the primary site for raising children have led scholars and others interested in contemporary forms of family to investigate the sets of choices entailed in making family and kin relations. In these "pictures of relatedness," the sovereignty and creativity of individual actors are often positioned as bringing kinship into being and as shaping family relations and their meaning. Within these pictures, choice, dialogue, and democratic process are often presented as the primary modalities of founding family relations, and creative design is understood as providing the means of overcoming the obstacles that prevent one from realizing one's desire for the happiness and the future promised by participation in familial kinship.

When the creative actions, dialogue, and choices of individuals are seen as the primary modalities for bringing family relations and kinship into being, it becomes easy to conclude that queer families embody a living critique of established norms—as if all gay men plan their families as a corrective response to existing social arrangements and the obstructions of existing sets of rules—and are examples of the triumph of reason and will over archaic and repressive cultural forms and norms. The heroic portrait of queer kinship that emerges from these conclusions covers over and erases the broadly experienced and quite familiar sense of mystery and loss of agency and reason associated with the desire to bring a child into one's life and to live in familial kinship. The heroic portrait also occludes the uncertainties and skepticism that accompany efforts to build and live in family relations. Doubt that the relations formed by a gay man and his child actually constitute a family or suspicion about the capability of two erotically involved men to father a child threaten to undo relations that have been actively and creatively fashioned. The questions generated by such doubt are, of course, not exclusive to the experience of gay men with children and their observers. The nagging presence of skepticism surrounding family and kin relations, especially biological paternity, unsettles easy accounts in which the family relations and kinship of gay men are understood to be exceptional.

When the uncertainties and skepticism that accompany kinship are understood as ordinary, or as constitutive of family relations and kinship whatever the context, the resonances between the experience of family for gay men and their children and that of, for example, those who make kinship with the assistance of reproductive technologies or through international adoption and surrogacy, can be sensed. When the resonances between these different experiences are considered, the families of gay men with children can be seen to align closely with other families that exist in tension with the norms of the state. I have in mind the families of those who live in the United States without legal residency, families formed across racial and ethnic divides, or those based in religious polygamy. When viewed in this comparative light, gay men's experience of building and living in families can be seen to articulate with long-standing discussions in anthropology and political philosophy about the place of sexuality in the social order, of the family in the production of sociable citizens, and of kinship in the reproduction of society. More specifically, the public, political, and scholarly interest in queer families can be understood as part of a much longer set of discussions and debates about the place of sex in the public sphere and the place of paternity and the paternal relation in the social order.

In the preceding pages, I have tried to demonstrate how the family relations of gay men and their children offer entry into these long-standing public and political discussions by unsettling established ideas about the origins and meaning of paternity and the fixity of sexual categories. The fervent public and political debates currently taking place around questions of citizenship, marriage, and abortion in the United States demonstrate how interest in these topics extends far beyond the specificities of gay parenting. It is through conversations about such things as gay marriage and the public and political sanction of gay adoption and parenthood that the salience of kinship to the state's administration of life and death becomes apparent.

I have tried to show how the everyday tasks that accompany the maintenance of kin relations clearly unfold within milieus established and determined by the state and its institutional administrative procedures, but in ways that exceed and unsettle institutional portraits of the relationship between biology and kinship, sexuality and paternity, and the family and the law. The same holds true for the relation between the attitudes and affects defining kinship and the grammatical rules defining the relations between kin terms. Even in settings that appear the most normative, such as nuclear families created through marriage, anatomical conception, and birth, everyday events carry the capacity to dislodge established norms and accepted categories and evoke affects and actions that challenge established legal definitions of what constitutes a good parent and the modes of recognition that allow one to lay claim to a kin relation. It is the incongruence of lived relations with societal norms, and the need for all parents to address this gap, that challenges conceptions of queer parenting as being ruled by the logic of the exception.

While many gay men with children are overtly critical of the social and political sanction of biological relations, the men I worked with actively drew from established conventions and repertoires of familial kinship and parenting when building family lives and kin relations with children. The forms of intimacy found within these men's kin relations may be incongruent with the sexual norms associated with biological kinship, but this does not mean the men were driven to dramatically alter the accepted forms of care and structures of domesticity associated with established and idealized notions of the family. The families with whom I worked were striving to achieve recognizable and sanctioned forms of familial kinship, and to project them into a stable and livable future, as opposed to making families that fell outside established structures and grammars, as would be the case, for example, if one's kinship aspirations were oriented toward building families composed of three, four, or five erotically involved parents who were collectively raising multiple children. Given this aim, the men I knew sought out and utilized the law and the services of state agencies, medicine, and other available "helping professionals," which thus became the material from which family relations were born. I have tried to demonstrate how building family relations in accordance with state discourses and the law does not solidify the meaning of being a relative. The signing of legal documents and the public performance of care might make one a father in certain contexts, but in others these actions and these documents mean little or nothing.

The investment in building and living in recognized forms of familial kinship demonstrates how scholarly discussions of queer forms of kinship address a series of issues beyond the easy critique of established sexual norms and forms of intimacy found in biological figurations of kinship. I have proposed that the efforts extended by gay men to live in families with children and the work of maintaining these relations speak to an ethics in which an educative process is undertaken for the purpose of transforming and building a specific form of self. Such a figuration rests on the idea that kinship is a form of becoming that takes place through the commitment to an ongoing education about the possible meanings of being related to another, as, say, one senses a father to be related to his child. It is the open-ended quality of the education and necessary ongoing effort to become either a gay father or the progeny of a gay man, and thus a domestic citizen in a queer household, that challenges the easy figuration of family formation as coming about through a process of rational choice, reasoned action, or design. The open-ended quality of becoming kin challenges the idea that achieving state sanction and legal backing for one's kin relations, call it recognition, might solidify the meaning of words and relations in such a way that one is provided shelter and protection from uncertainty and rendered less vulnerable to another's words and claims.

I have difficulty embracing such a "hypermodern" notion of queer family life and its formation, in which democratic principles, communication, and reasoned action are positioned as bringing family relations into being, because such configurations fail to illuminate the unfinished quality of kinship, as the meaning of being related to another is continually (re)discovered, (re)learned, and (re)achieved time and time again. When paternity is seen as an aspiration, as opposed to an achievement, the work and costs associated with striving toward kinship emerge as crucial aspects of coming to understand family and kin relations themselves. I have focused my analysis on trying to understand how the vulnerabilities and suffering accompanying kin relations operate as modalities through which both relations and knowledge of these relations emerge, rather than as disruptive forces that place kin relations at risk. When anthropologists and other social scientists fail to acknowledge the ways suffering works agentially to bring both kinship and its meaning into being, they risk casting the families forged by gay men with children in the overly simplistic and reduced terms of what might be thought of as a hypermodernism. Here, reason, creative action, and individual choice are pictured as providing a means of overcoming, perhaps even heroically triumphing over, antiquated and adversarial cultural forms that oppress and oppose the capacity of gay men to form and live in viable kin relations. The cost of committing to such a hypermodern picture of queer kinship is ignoring the complex constellation of social arrangements and desires that establish the conditions of possibility for building and living in kinship in the twenty-first-century United States.

When the frame of analysis is shifted so queer families are not presumed to be ruled by the logic of the exception, as defined in relation to assumed sexual norms and the rules of biological kinship, the dispersed agencies and forms of knowledge that give rise to the capacity to claim the existence of a familial relation, such as paternity, emerge as crucial components that shape and define efforts to elaborate family relations. When these dispersed agencies and claims of knowledge are considered, the congruencies and alignments between queer families and those made through heterosexual reproduction, the law, or with reproductive technologies come into view, constituting one site among many at which the uncertainties and forms of skepticism surrounding kin relations are contested and negotiated. I hope I have documented the uncertainties that accompany efforts to live in familial kinship in the West alongside the forms of addressing such skepticism that emerge through the daily task of caring and being cared for in families of gay men with children.

It is the way queer families manifest the tensions and uncertainties that accompany building family relations in the West that challenges the easy figuration of gay families as the embodiment of a critically new form of relating. While it may seem that heterosexual kinship is secure and thus provides a position from which to establish the new or determine innovation, the anthropological archive and the debates in political philosophy demonstrate the opposite. It is precisely because the law and other institutions attempt to ground paternity and kinship in such objective criteria as biology, reproductive sexuality, and birth that kin relations are vulnerable to skepticism in Euro-America whether or not they originate in the law, heterosexual conception and birth, or the public performance of care. The accompanying cost is the capacity to claim with certainty how and if sexuality figures into the creation of paternity and family relations, whether they arise through heterosexual reproduction or otherwise. It is not that sexuality does not matter in the creation of kin relations and family or in their dissolution. It clearly does, but not because sexuality provides an anchor for securing kin relations. Rather, it is precisely because the law and institutions continually turn to biological conception and birth to secure life to the social order, and belonging to kinship, that certainty slips away. As a result, there can be no secure and stable place against which the new or the innovative might be established. It is not that there is no original model, but it just happens to be plastic and thus resists the rigid imposition of the objective criteria of the law and its grammars.

I have tried to demonstrate how making and building kin relations is akin to an ethics in which the self, both consciously and not, undergoes different forms of training and instruction and is transformed in such a way that it comes to embody particular relational structures (Faubion 2001b; Foucault 1997). Echoing Foucault, kinship is akin to sexuality and is thus not to be understood as a form of desire with paternity and paternal authority as its expression. Rather, it is something desirable whose work is about becoming as opposed to recognition and communication. Undertaking such training and cultivating such a way of life as well as a relation to the self and to others, I claim, have little or nothing to do with choice but, rather, with undergoing an open, educative process that transforms the self into a relative. It is the willingness to endure the instruction necessary to being a relative and, in so doing, become the subject of surveillance and discipline that complicates the readily available image of kinship as born from creative action. In the place of consciously undertaken creative action, I find a type of doing that is akin to what William Connolly (2010) has called "blindsight": a way of seeing what one does not have, a recognized capacity to be aware of doing something without necessarily knowing what is being done. From the men I came to know in my research, I learned about the experience of doing and being in kinship without necessarily knowing to whom one is related and how, and about the everyday forms of negotiating and addressing such uncertainty. Ideas about the human, states of nature, freedom, constraint, and the arrangement of different orders of being that can and do emerge through the kinds of obligations and entanglements found in familial kinship are at stake, as the lives of these men and their children demonstrate.

While I was writing the preliminary results of this research, my father returned to the United States to receive treatment for a metastatic disease after living abroad for twenty-three years. Three months after his return, on Thanksgiving Day, he told me he was gay while we were walking my sister's dog in the woods. The surprise, at the time—which returns, often amplified—is that, somehow, I already knew, but I could not tell. He died shortly after I earned my doctorate.

The men whose lives I entered and the work their words compelled allow me to make partial sense of what my father said on that blustery day. I wish he were still here so he could tell me more.

Bibliography

Abelove, H., & Barale, M. A. (1993). *The Lesbian and Gay Studies Reader.* Hove, UK: Psychology Press.

Agamben, G. (1998). *Homo Sacer* (Translated by D. Heller-Roazen). Stanford: Stanford University Press.

Agamben, G. (2000). *Means Without End: Notes on Politics.* Minneapolis: University of Minnesota Press.

Agamben, G. (2002). *Remnants of Auschwitz: The Witness and the Archive.* New York: Zone Books.

Asad, T. (1993). *Genealogies of Religion: Discipline and Reasons of Power in Christianity and Islam.* Baltimore: Johns Hopkins University Press.

Asad, T. (2003). *Formations of the Secular: Christianity, Islam, Modernity.* Stanford, CA: Stanford University Press.

Austin, J. L. (1975). *How to Do Things with Words.* Cambridge, MA: Harvard University Press.

Bachofen, J. J. (1967 [1861]). *Myth, Religion, and Mother Right.* Princeton: Princeton University Press.

Beattie, J. (1968). *Other Cultures: Aims, Methods and Achievements in Social Anthropology.* New York: Free Press.

Bennett, J. (2009). *Vibrant Matter: A Political Ecology of Things.* Durham, NC: Duke University Press.

Berlant, L., & Warner, M. (1998). Sex in Public. *Critical Inquiry, 24*(2): 547–566.

Bersani, L. (1995). *Loving Men.* New York: Routledge.

Bersani, L. (1996). *Homos.* Cambridge, MA: Harvard University Press.

Bersani, L., & Phillips, A. (2008). *Intimacies.* Chicago: University of Chicago Press.

Biehl, J. (2004). Life of the Mind: The Interface of Psycho-Pharmaceuticals, Domestic Economies, and Social Abandonment. *American Ethnologist, 31*(4): 475–496.

Biehl, J. (2005). *Vita: Life in a Zone of Social Abandonment.* Berkeley: University of California Press.

Biehl, J., Coutinho, D., & Outeiro, A. L. (2001). Technology and Affect: HIV/AIDS Testing in Brazil. *Culture, Medicine, and Psychiatry, 25*(1): 87–129.

Bluebond-Langner, M. (1980). *The Private World of Dying Children.* Princeton: Princeton University Press.

Borneman, J. (1996). Until Death Do Us Part: Marriage/Death in Anthropological Discourse. *American Ethnologist, 23*(2): 215–235.

Borneman, J. (1997). Caring and Being Cared For: Displacing Marriage, Kinship, Gender and Sexuality. *International Social Science Journal, 49*(154): 573–584.

Borneman, J. (2013). Intimacy, Disclosure and Marital Normativity. In *Intimacies: A New World of Relational Life*, edited by A. Frank, P. T. Clough, & S. Seidman, pp. 117–129. New York: Routledge.

Butler, J. (1990). *Gender Trouble: Feminism and the Subversion of Identity.* New York: Routledge.

Butler, J. (1993). *Bodies That Matter: On the Discursive Limits of "Sex."* New York: Routledge.

Butler, J. (2000). *Antigone's Claim: Kinship Between Life & Death.* New York: Columbia University Press.

Butler, J. (2002). Is Kinship Always Already Heterosexual? *Differences, 13*(1): 14–44.

Butler, J. (2004). *Undoing Gender.* New York: Routledge.

Butler, J. (2005). *Giving an Account of Oneself.* New York: Fordham University Press.

Butler, J. (2006). *Precarious Life: The Powers of Mourning and Violence.* New York: Verso Books.

Canguilhem, G. (1989). *The Normal and the Pathological.* New York: Zone Books.

Carp, E. W. (2000). *Family Matters: Secrecy and Disclosure in the History of Adoption.* Cambridge, MA: Harvard University Press.

Carrington, C. (1999). *No Place Like Home: Relationships and Family Life among Lesbians and Gay Men.* Chicago: University of Chicago Press.

Carsten, J. (2000a). *Cultures of Relatedness: New Approaches to the Study of Kinship.* Cambridge; Cambridge University Press.

Carsten, J. (2000b). "Knowing Where You've Come From": Ruptures and Continuities of Time and Kinship in Narratives of Adoption Reunions. *Journal of the Royal Anthropological Institute, 6*(4): 687–703.

Carsten, J. (2004). *After Kinship* (2). Cambridge: Cambridge University Press.

Carsten, J. (2007). *Ghosts of Memory: Essays on Remembrance and Relatedness.* Oxford: Wiley-Blackwell.

Cavell, S. (1987). *Disowning Knowledge in Six Plays of Shakespeare.* Cambridge: Cambridge University Press.

Cavell, S. (1994). *In Quest of the Ordinary: Lines of Skepticism and Romanticism.* Chicago: University of Chicago Press.

Cavell, S. (1996). *Contesting Tears: The Hollywood Melodrama of the Unknown Woman.* Chicago: University of Chicago Press.

Cavell, S. (2005). *Cities of Words: Pedagogical Letters on a Register of the Moral Life.* Cambridge, MA: Belknap Press of Harvard University Press.

Cavell, S. (2006). *Philosophy the Day after Tomorrow.* Cambridge, MA: Belknap Press of Harvard University Press.

Chambers, S. A. (2009). *The Queer Politics of Television*. New York: Palgrave Macmillan.

Chatterji, R., Chattoo, S., & Das, V. (1998). The Death of the Clinic? Normality and Pathology in Recrafting Old Bodies. In *Vital Signs: Feminist Reconfigurations of the Bio/logical Body*, edited by M. Shidrick & J. Price, pp. 171–191. Edinburgh: Edinburgh University Press.

Chauncey, G. (1994). *Gay New York: Gender, Urban Culture, and the Making of the Gay Male World 1890–1940*. New York: Basic Books.

Clifford, J., & Marcus, G. E. (1986). *Writing Culture: The Poetics and Politics of Ethnography*. Berkeley: University of California Press.

Collier, J., & Yanagisako, S. (1987). *Gender and Kinship: Essays Towards a Unified Analysis of Gender and Kinship*. Stanford: Stanford University Press.

Connolly, W. E. (2010). *A World of Becoming*. Durham, NC: Duke University Press.

Crapanzano, V. (1980). *Tuhami: Portrait of a Moroccan*. Chicago: University of Chicago Press.

Das, V. (1990). Our Work Is to Cry: Your Work to Listen. In *Mirrors of Violence: Communities, Riots and Survivors in South Asia*, edited by V. Das, pp. 345–398. New Delhi: Oxford University Press.

Das, V. (1995). Voice as Birth of Culture. *Ethnos*, *60*(3): 159–179.

Das, V. (2000). The Act of Witnessing: Violence, Poisonous Knowledge, and Subjectivity. In *Violence and Subjectivity*, edited by V. Das et al., pp. 205–225. Berkeley: University of California Press.

Das, V. (2006). Secularism and the Argument from Nature. In *Powers of the Secular Modern: Talal Asad and His Interlocutors*, edited by C. H. David Scott, pp. 93–112. Stanford: Stanford University Press.

Das, V. (2007). *Life and Words: Violence and the Descent into the Ordinary*. Berkeley: University of California Press.

Das, V., & Poole, D. (2004). *Anthropology in the Margins of the State*. Santa Fe: School of American Research Press.

Das, V., & Reynolds, P. (2003). The Child on the Wing: Children Negotiating the Everyday Geography of Violence. Johns Hopkins University. www.jhu.edu /child/documents/CHILD%20WEB% 20DRAFT% 20ESSAY.pdf, April 21, 2009.

Das, V., Kleinman, A., Ramphele, M., & Reynolds, P. (2000). *Violence and Subjectivity*. Berkeley: University of California Press.

Day, S. E. (2007a). *On the Game: Women and Sex Work*. London: Pluto Press.

Day, S. E. (2007b). Threading Time in the Biographies of London Sex Workers. In *Ghosts of Memory: Essays on Remembrance and Relatedness*, edited by J. Carsten, pp. 172–193. Oxford: Wiley-Blackwell.

Dean, T. (2009). *Unlimited Intimacy: Reflections on the Subculture of Barebacking*. Chicago: University of Chicago Press.

De Lauretis, T. (1987). *Technologies of Gender: Essays on Theory, Film, and Fiction*. Bloomington: Indiana University Press.

Deleuze, G. (1997). *Essays Critical and Clinical*. Minneapolis: University of Minnesota Press.

Deleuze, G., & Guattari, F. (1987). *A Thousand Plateaus: Capitalism and Schizophrenia* (Translated by Brian Massumi). Minneapolis: University of Minnesota Press.

Derrida, J. (1992). Force of Law: The Mystical Foundation of Authority. In *Deconstruction and the Possibility of Justice*, edited by D. Cornell, M. Rosenfeld, & D. G. Carlson, pp. 3–67. New York: Routledge.

Desjarlais, R. (2003). *Sensory Biographies: Lives and Deaths Among Nepal's Yolmo Buddhists*. Berkeley: University of California Press.

Donzelot, J. (1979). *Policing the Family*. Baltimore: Johns Hopkins University Press.

Edelman, L. (2004). *No Future: Queer Theory and the Death Drive*. Durham, NC: Duke University Press.

Elshtain, J. B. (1982). *The Family in Political Thought*. Amherst: University of Massachusetts Press.

Eng, D. L. (2010). *The Feeling of Kinship: Queer Liberalism and the Racialization of Intimacy*. Durham, NC: Duke University Press.

Engels, F. (1942). *The Origin of the Family*. London: Penguin Classics.

Fassin, D., Rechtman, R., & Gomme, R. (2009). *The Empire of Trauma: An Inquiry into the Condition of Victimhood*. Princeton: Princeton University Press.

Fassin, E. (2001). Same Sex, Different Politics: "Gay Marriage" Debates in France and the United States. *Public Culture, 13*(2): 215–232.

Fassin, E. (2006). The Rise and Fall of Sexual Politics in the Public Sphere: A Transatlantic Contrast. *Public Culture, 18*(1): 79–92.

Faubion, J. D. (1996). Kinship Is Dead. Long Live Kinship. A Review Article. *Comparative Studies in Society and History, 38*(1): 67–91.

Faubion, J. D. (2001a). Introduction: Toward an Anthropology of the Ethics of Kinship. In *The Ethics of Kinship: Ethnographic Inquiries*, edited by J. D. Faubion, pp. 1–28. Lanham, MD: Rowman and Littlefield.

Faubion, J. D. (2001b). Toward an Anthropology of Ethics: Foucault and the Pedagogies of Autopoiesis. *Representations, 74*: 83–104.

Filmer, R. (1991). *Patriarcha and Other Writings* (Edited by J. P. Sommerville). Cambridge: Cambridge University Press.

Firth, R. (1956). *Two Studies of Kinship in London*. London: Athlone Press.

Firth, R. (1969). *Essays on Social Organization and Values*. London: Berg.

Firth, R., Hubert, J., & Forge, A. (1970). *Families and Their Relatives*. London: Routledge.

Fischer, M. M. J. (2003). *Emergent Forms of Life and the Anthropological Voice*. Durham, NC: Duke University Press.

Fortes, M. (1957). *The Web of Kinship Among the Tallensi: The Second Part of an Analysis of the Social Structure of a Trans-Volta Tribe*. Oxford: Oxford University Press.

Fortes, M. (1970). *Kinship and the Social Order: The Legacy of Lewis Henry Morgan*. London: Routledge.

Foucault, M. (1978). *The History of Sexuality*. New York: Pantheon Books.

Foucault, M. (1983). Interview with James O'Higgins. *Salmagundi*, Fall 1982– Winter 1983: 58–59.

Foucault, M. (1997). *Ethics: Subjectivity and Truth (Essential Works of Foucault, 1954–1984, Vol. 1)*. New York: New Press.

Foucault, M. (2003). *Abnormal: Lectures at the Collège de France, 1974–1975* (A. S. V. Marchetti and A. I. Davidson, trans.). New York: Picador.

Foucault, M. (2009). *Security, Territory, Population: Lectures at the Collège de France 1977–1978*. New York: Picador USA.

Foucault, M. (2010). *The Birth of Biopolitics: Lectures at the Collège de France, 1978–1979* (Edited by A. I. Davidson, translated by G. Burchell). New York: Picador.

Fox, R. (1983). *Kinship and Marriage: An Anthropological Perspective*. Cambridge: Cambridge University Press.

Franklin, S. (2001). Biologization Revisited: Kinship Theory in the Context of the New Biologies. *Relative Values: Reconfiguring Kinship Studies*, edited by S. Franklin & S. McKinnon, pp. 302–322. Durham, NC: Duke University Press.

Franklin, S. (2003). Ethical Biocapital: New Strategies of Cell Culture. *Remaking Life and Death: Towards and Anthropology of the Biosciences*, edited by S. Franklin & M. Lock. Santa Fe: School of American Research Press.

Franklin, S. (2013). *Biological Relatives: IVF, Stem Cells, and the Future of Kinship*. Durham, NC: Duke University Press.

Franklin, S., & McKinnon, S. (2001). *Relative Values: Reconfiguring Kinship Studies*. Durham, NC: Duke University Press.

Franklin, S., & Roberts, C. (2006). *Born and Made: An Ethnography of Preimplantation Genetic Diagnosis*. Princeton, NJ: Princeton University Press.

Freud, S. (1919). The "Uncanny." *The Standard Edition of the Complete Psychological Works of Sigmund Freud, Volume XVII (1917–1919): An Infantile Neurosis and Other Works*, 217–256. New York: Norton.

Freud, S. (1922). Beyond the Pleasure Principle. *The Standard Edition of the Complete Psychological Works of Sigmund Freud, Volume XVIII (1920–1922): Beyond the Pleasure Principle, Group Psychology, and Other Works*, 3–23. New York: Norton.

Galluccio, M., & Gallucio, J. (2001). *An American Family*. New York: St. Martin's Press.

Geertz, C. (1976). *The Religion of Java*. Chicago: University of Chicago Press.

Geertz, C. (1983). *Local Knowledge: Further Essays in Interpretive Anthropology*. New York: Basic Books.

Giddens, A. (1992). *The Transformation of Intimacy: Sexuality, Love, and Eroticism in Modern Societies*. Stanford: Stanford University Press.

Ginsburg, F. D. (1998). *Contested Lives: The Abortion Debate in an American Community*. Berkeley: University of California Press.

Ginsburg, F. D., & Rapp, R. (1995). *Conceiving the New World Order: The Global Politics of Reproduction*. Berkeley: University of California Press.

Goffman, E. (1963). *Stigma: Notes on the Management of Spoiled Identity*. New York: Prentice-Hall.

Good, M.-J. D., Brodwin, P. E., Good, B. J., & Kleinman, A. (1994). *Pain as Human Experience: An Anthropological Perspective*. Berkeley: University of California Press.

Goodenough, W. H. (1965). Yankee Kinship Terminology: A Problem of Componential Analysis. *American Anthropologist, 67*(5): 259–287.

Goodrich, P., & Carlson, D. (1998). *Law and the Postmodern Mind: Essays on Psychoanalysis and Jurisprudence*. Ann Arbor: University of Michigan Press.

Green, J. (2000). *The Velveteen Father: An Unexpected Journey to Parenthood*. New York: Ballantine Books.

Haraway, D. (1991). *Simians, Cyborgs, and Women: The Reinvention of Nature*. New York: Routledge.

Haraway, D. (1994). A Manifesto for Cyborgs: Science, Technology, and Socialist Feminism in the 1980s. In *The Postmodern Turn: New Perspectives on Social Theory*, edited by S. Seidman, pp. 82–118. Cambridge: Cambridge University Press.

Haraway, D. J. (2003). *The Companion Species Manifesto: Dogs, People, and Significant Otherness*. Chicago: Prickly Paradigm Press.

Harding, S. G. (1986). *The Science Question in Feminism*. Ithaca, NY: Cornell University Press.

Hegel, G. F. W. (2008 [1821]). *Philosophy of Right*. New York: Cosimo Classics.

Helmreich, S. (2008). Species of Biocapital. *Science as Culture, 17*(4), 463–478.

Herzfeld, M. (2001). *Anthropology: Theoretical Practice in Culture and Society*. Malden, MA: Wiley-Blackwell.

Hobbes, T. (1998 [1651]). *Leviathan*. Oxford: Oxford University Press.

Howell, S., & Marre, D. (2006). To Kin a Transnationally Adopted Child in Norway and Spain: The Achievement of Resemblances and Belonging. *Ethnos, 71*(3): 293–316.

Humphrey, C. 2008. Reassembling Individual Subjects: Events and Decisions in Troubled Times. *Anthropological Theory, 8*(4): 357–380.

Kaeser, G., & Gillespie, P. (1999). *Love Makes a Family: Portraits of Lesbian, Gay, Bisexual, and Transgender Parents and Their Families*. Amherst: University of Massachusetts Press.

Kant, I. (2002 [1821]). *Critique of Practical Reason*. Indianapolis: Hackett.

Kleinman, A. (1988). *The Illness Narratives: Suffering, Healing, and the Human Condition*. New York: Basic Books.

Kleinman, A. (1997). *Writing at the Margin: Discourse between Anthropology and Medicine*. Berkeley: University of California Press.

Kleinman, A., & Kleinman, J. (1996). The Appeal of Experience; the Dismay of Images: Cultural Appropriations of Suffering in Our Times. *Daedalus, 125*(1): 1–23.

Kuper, A. (1988). *The Invention of Primitive Society: Transformations of an Illusion.* New York: Routledge.

Laplanche, J., & Mehlman, J. (1976). *Life and Death in Psychoanalysis.* Baltimore: Johns Hopkins University Press.

Leach, E. R. (1966a). *Rethinking Anthropology.* London: Berg.

Leach, E. R. (1966b). Virgin Birth. *Proceedings of the Royal Anthropological Institute of Great Britain and Ireland,* 1966: 39–49.

Legendre, P. (1997). *Law and the Unconscious: A Legendre Reader* (Edited by P. Goodrich). New York: St. Martin's Press.

Lehr, V. (1999). *Queer Family Values: Debunking the Myth of the Nuclear Family.* Philadelphia: Temple University Press.

Lerner, R., Nagai, A. K., & Ethics and Public Policy Center. (2001). *No Basis: What the Studies Don't Tell Us about Same-Sex Parenting.* Washington, DC: Marriage Law Project.

Lévi-Strauss, C. (1958). *Structural Anthropology.* London: Basic Books.

Lévi-Strauss, C. (1963). *Structural Anthropology.* New York: Basic Books.

Lévi-Strauss, C. (1969). *The Elementary Structures of Kinship.* Boston: Beacon Press.

Lewin, E. (1993). *Lesbian Mothers: Accounts of Gender in American Culture.* Ithaca, NY: Cornell University Press.

Lewin, E. (2009). *Gay Fatherhood: Narratives of Family and Citizenship in America.* Chicago: University of Chicago Press.

Leys, R. (2000). *Trauma: A Genealogy.* Chicago: University of Chicago Press.

Lingis, A. (2000). *Dangerous Emotions.* Berkeley: University of California Press.

Lingis, A. (2011). *Violence and Splendor (Studies in Phenomenology and Existential Philosophy).* Evanston, IL: Northwestern University Press.

Lock, M. (2003). On Making Up the Good-as-Dead in a Utilitarian World. *Remaking Life and Death: Towards and Anthropology of the Biosciences,* edited by S. Franklin & M. Lock. Santa Fe: School of American Research Press.

Locke, J. (1982 [1690]). *The Second Treatise of Government: An Essay Concerning the True Original, Extent and End of Civil Government.* London: Basil Blackwell.

Maine, H. S. (1861). *Ancient Law: Its Connection with the Early History of Society and Its Relations to Modern Ideas.* New York: Charles Scribner.

Malinowski, B. (1927). *Sex and Repression in Savage Society.* London: Kegan, Paul, Trench, Trubner & Co.

Malinowski, B. (1929). *The Sexual Life of Savages in North-Western Melanesia.* New York: Eugenics Publishing.

Marcus, G. E., & Fischer, M. M. J. (1986). *Anthropology as Cultural Critique: An Experimental Moment in the Human Sciences.* Chicago: University of Chicago Press.

Martin, A. (1993). *The Lesbian and Gay Parenting Handbook: Creating and Raising Our Families.* New York: Harper Perennial.

Marx, K. (2011 [1906]). *Capital, Volume I: A Critique of Political Economy.* New York: Modern Library.

McKinnon, S. (1994). American Kinship/American Incest: Asymmetries in a Scientific Discourse. In *Naturalizing Power: Essays in Feminist Cultural Analysis,* edited by C. Delaney & S. Yanagisako, pp. 25–46. New York: Routledge.

McLennan, J. F. (1885). *The Patriarchal Theory: Based on the Papers of the Late John Ferguson McLennan.* London: Crystal Palace Press.

Mehta, U. S. (1999). *Liberalism and Empire: A Study in Nineteenth-Century British Liberal Thought.* Chicago: University of Chicago Press.

Mintz, S. (1960). *Worker in the Cane: A Puerto Rican Life History.* New Haven: Yale University Press.

Moon, M. (2013). *Darger's Resources.* Durham, NC: Duke University Press.

Morgan, L. H. (1870). *Systems of Consanguinity and Affinity of the Human Family.* Lincoln: University of Nebraska Press.

Morgan, L. H. (1877). *Ancient Society; Or, Researches in the Lines of Human Progress From Savagery, Through Barbarism to Civilization.* New York: H. Holt.

Morgen, K. B. (1995). *Getting Simon: Two Gay Doctors' Journey to Fatherhood.* Putney, VT: Bramble Books.

Needham, R. (1971). *Rethinking Kinship and Marriage.* London: Routledge.

Newton, E. (1995). *Cherry Grove, Fire Island.* Boston: Beacon Press.

Pateman, C. (1988). *The Sexual Contract.* Stanford: Stanford University Press.

Patterson, C. J. (2005). Lesbian and Gay Parents and their Children: Summary of Research Findings. In American Psychological Association, *Lesbian and Gay Parenting,* pp. 5–22. Washington, DC: American Psychological Association.

Peletz, M. G. (1995). Kinship Studies in Late Twentieth-Century Anthropology. *Annual Review of Anthropology, 24:* 343–372.

Peletz, M. G. (2001). Ambivalence in Kinship. In *Relative Values: Reconfiguring Kinship Studies,* edited by S. Franklin & S. McKinnon, pp. 413–444. Durham, NC: Duke University Press.

Povinelli, E. A. (2001). Sexuality At Risk: Psychoanalysis Metapragmatically. In *Homosexuality and Psychoanalysis,* edited by T. Dean & C. Lane, pp. 387–411. Chicago: University of Chicago Press.

Povinelli, E. A. (2002a). *The Cunning of Recognition: Indigenous Alterities and the Making of Australian Multiculturalism.* Durham, NC: Duke University Press.

Povinelli, E. A. (2002b). Notes on Gridlock: Genealogy, Intimacy, Sexuality. *Public Culture, 14*(1): 215–238.

Povinelli, E. A. (2006). *The Empire of Love: Toward a Theory of Intimacy, Genealogy, and Carnality.* Durham, NC: Duke University Press.

Povinelli, E. A. (2009). The Child in the Broom Closet: States of Killing and Letting Die. In *States of Violence: War, Capital Punishment and Letting Die*, edited by A. Sarat & J. L. Culbert, pp. 169–191. New York: Cambridge University Press.

Rabinow, P. (1996). *Essays on the Anthropology of Reason*. Princeton: Princeton University Press.

Radcliffe-Brown, A. R. (1965). *Structure and Function in Primitive Society: Essays and Addresses*. London: Taylor & Francis.

Ragoné, H. (1994). *Surrogate Motherhood: Conception in the Heart*. Boulder, CO: Westview Press.

Rajan, K. (2006). *Bio-Capital: The Constitution of Postgenomic Life*. Durham, NC: Duke University Press.

Rapp, R. (1978). Family and Class in Contemporary America: Notes Toward an Understanding of Ideology. *Science & Society, 42*(3): 278–300.

Rapp, R. (1999). *Testing Women, Testing the Fetus: The Social Impact of Amniocentesis in America*. New York: Routledge.

Rapp, R., & Ginsburg, F. D. (2001). Enabling Disability, Rewriting Kinship, Reimagining Citizenship. *Public Culture, 13*(3): 533–556.

Reiter, R. (1975). *Towards an Anthropology of Women*. New York: Monthly Review Press.

Republican National Committee. (2012). *Resolution for Marriage and Children*. Washington, DC: Republican National Committee.

Reynolds, P. (1991). *Dance Civet Cat: Child Labor in the Zambezi Valley*. Athens: Ohio University Press.

Reynolds, P. (2000). The Ground of All Making: State Violence, the Family, and Political Activists. In *Violence and Subjectivity*, edited by V. Das et al., pp. 141–170. Berkeley: University of California Press.

Reynolds, P. (2012). *War in Worcester: Youth and the Apartheid State*. New York: Fordham University Press.

Richman, K. (2010). *Courting Change: Queer Parents, Judges, and the Transformation of American Family Law*. New York: New York University Press.

Rivers, W. H. R. (1900). A Genealogical Method of Collecting Social and Vital Statistics. *Journal of the Anthropological Institute of Great Britain and Ireland, 30*: 74–82.

Rivers, W. H. R. (1968). *Social Organization* (Edited by W. J. Perry). London: Dawsons.

Rivers, W. H. R., Seligman, C. G., Myers, C. S., McDougall, W., Ray, S. H., & Wilkin, A. (1912). *Reports of the Cambridge Anthropological Expedition to Torres Straits*. Cambridge: Cambridge University Press.

Robson, R. (1998). *Sappho Goes to Law School: Fragments in Lesbian Legal Theory*. New York: Columbia University Press.

Rosaldo, M. (1980). The Use and Abuse of Anthropology: Reflections on

Feminism and Cross-Cultural Understanding. *Signs: Journal of Women in Culture and Society* 5(3): 389–417.

Rosaldo, M., & Lamphere, L. (1974). *Women, Culture, and Society*. Stanford: Stanford University Press.

Rose, N., & Miller, P. (2008). *Governing the Present: Administering Economic, Social, and Personal Life*. Cambridge, UK: Polity Press.

Ross, F. C. (2003). On Having Voice and Being Heard. *Anthropological Theory*, 3(3): 325–341.

Rousseau, J. J. (2002 [1762]). *The Social Contract: And, the First and Second Discourses* (Edited by S. Dunn). New Haven: Yale University Press.

Rubin, G. (1975). The Traffic in Women: Notes on the "Political Economy" of Sex. In *Toward an Anthropology of Women*, edited by R. Reiter, pp. 157–210. New York: Monthly Review Press.

Sahlins, M. (1960). *Evolution and Culture*. Ann Arbor: University of Michigan Press

Sahlins, M. (2013). *What Kinship Is—And Is Not*. Chicago: University of Chicago Press.

Sarat, A., & Kearns, T. R. (1995). *Law in Everyday Life*. Ann Arbor: University of Michigan Press.

Savage, D. (2000). *The Kid: What Happened after My Boyfriend and I Decided to Go Get Pregnant*. New York: Penguin Books.

Schneider, D. M. (1968). *American Kinship: A Cultural Account*. Chicago: University of Chicago Press.

Schneider, D. M. (1972). What Is Kinship All About? In *Kinship Studies in the Morgan Centennial Year*, edited by P. Reining, pp. 32–63. Washington, DC: Anthropological Society of Washington.

Schneider, D. M. (1984). *A Critique of the Study of Kinship*. Ann Arbor: University of Michigan Press.

Schneider, D. M. (1997). The Power of Culture: Notes on Some Aspects of Gay and Lesbian Kinship in America Today. *Cultural Anthropology*, 12(2): 270–274.

Schneider, D. M., & Homans, G. C. (1955). Kinship Terminology and the American Kinship System. *American Anthropologist*, 57(6):1194–1208.

Sedgwick, E. K. (1993). *Tendencies*. Durham, NC: Duke University Press.

Sedgwick, E. K., & Frank, A. (2003). *Touching Feeling: Affect, Pedagogy, Performativity*. Durham, NC: Duke University Press.

Seremetakis, C. N. (1996). *The Senses Still: Perception and Memory as Material Culture in Modernity*. Chicago: University of Chicago Press.

Silverstein, M. (1976). Shifters, Linguistic Categories, and Cultural Description. In *Meaning in Anthropology*, edited by K. H. Basso & H. A. Selby, pp. 11–56. Albuquerque: University of New Mexico Press.

Silverstein, M. (1979). The Elements: A Parasession on Linguistic Units and Levels. In *Papers from the Conference on Non-Slavic Languages of the U.S.S.R.* Chicago: Chicago Linguistic Society.

Silverstein, M., & Urban, G. (1996). *The Natural History of Discourse*. Chicago: University of Chicago Press.

Stacey, J. (1998). *Brave New Families: Stories of Domestic Upheaval in Late-Twentieth-Century America*. Berkeley: University of California Press.

Stacey, J., & Thorne, B. (1985). The Missing Feminist Revolution in Sociology. *Social Problems, 32*(4): 301–316.

Stack, C., & Burton, L. M. (1994). *Kinscripts: Reflections on Family, Generation, and Culture. Mothering: Ideology, Experience, and Agency*, edited by E. N. Glenn & G. Chang, pp. 33–44. New York: Routledge.

Strathern, M. (1987). An Awkward Relationship: The Case of Feminism and Anthropology. *Signs: Journal of Women and Society, 12*(2): 276–292.

Strathern, M. (1992a). *After Nature: English Kinship in the Late Twentieth Century*. Cambridge: Cambridge University Press.

Strathern, M. (1992b). *Reproducing the Future: Anthropology, Kinship, and the New Reproductive Technologies*. New York: Routledge.

Strathern, M. (1996). Cutting the Network. *Journal of the Royal Anthropological Institute, 2*(3): 517–535.

Strathern, M. (2005). *Kinship, Law, and the Unexpected: Relatives Are Always a Surprise*. Cambridge: Cambridge University Press.

Strong, T. (2002). Kinship Between Judith Butler and Anthropology? *Ethnos, 67*(3): 401–418.

Stychin, C. F. (1995). *Law's Desire: Sexuality and the Limits of Justice*. London: Burns & Oates.

Sullivan, A. (1996). *Virtually Normal: An Argument About Homosexuality*. New York: Macmillan.

Sullivan, M. (2004). *The Family of Woman: Lesbian Mothers, Their Children, and the Undoing of Gender*. Berkeley: University of California Press.

Taussig, M. T. (1993). *Mimesis and Alterity: A Particular History of the Senses*. New York: Routledge.

Taussig, M. T. (2003). The Adult's Imagination of the Child's Imagination. In *Aesthetic Subjects*, edited by P. R. Matthews & D. McWhirter, pp. 449–468. Minneapolis: University of Minnesota Press.

Tylor, E. B. (1871). *Primitive Culture, vol. 1*. London: John Murray.

Viefhues-Bailey, L. H. (2010). *Between a Man and a Woman? Why Conservatives Oppose Same-Sex Marriage*. New York: Columbia University Press.

Warner, M. (2002). Publics and Counter Publics. *Public Culture, 14*(1): 49–90.

Weeks, J., Heaphy, B., & Donovan, C. (2001). *Same Sex Intimacies: Families of Choice and Other Life Experiments*. New York: Routledge.

Weston, K. (1991). *Families We Choose: Lesbians, Gays, Kinship*. New York: Columbia University Press.

Weston, K. (1993). Lesbian and Gay Studies in the House of Anthropology. *Annual Review of Anthropology, 22*: 339–367.

Weston, K. (1999). Introduction: Capturing More Than the Moment—

Lesbian/Gay Families in the Making. In *Love Makes a Family: Portraits of Lesbian, Gay, Bisexual, and Transgender Parents and Their Families,* edited by P. Gillespie, pp. 3–10. Amherst: University of Massachusetts.

Yanagisako, S., & Collier, J. (1994). Gender and Kinship Reconsidered: Toward a Unified Analysis. In *Assessing Cultural Anthropology,* edited by R. Borofsky, pp. 190–203. New York: McGraw-Hill.

Yanagisako, S., & Delaney, C. (1995). *Naturalizing Power: Essays in Feminist Cultural Analysis.* New York: Routledge.

Young, A. (1995). *The Harmony of Illusions: Inventing Post-Traumatic Stress Disorder.* Princeton: Princeton University Press.

Index

administrative discourse, 59
adoption: gay men's experiences of,
    9–16, 23, 26–27, 70–71, 91–93, 100,
    106; law and, 11–12, 23, 26, 91–93;
    role of gay men's sexuality in, 10–11,
    13–14, 91–93, 100, 106
affect/affection: role in kinship, 73–77,
    80–89; role in paternity, 37–40
AIDS. *See* HIV/AIDS
anthropology: marginalization of
    queer kinship, 80–82; perspectives
    on kin terms, 55–57; place of pater-
    nity in, 3; reflections on encounters
    between gay fathers and, 51–54
"antisocial" critique, 43n2
artificial insemination: metadiscourse
    involving, 71–76; reflections on
    biological kinship and paternity in
    relation to, 44–45, 67–70, 76–80

belonging: children and, 133–135,
    146–149; gay men and alternative
    forms of, 35–37
Bersani, Leo, 48–49n5
biocapital, 44n3
biogenetic kinship. *See* biological
    kinship
biological kinship: attitudes toward,
    71; configured by gender, 68–70;
    gay sociality counterposed to,
    35–37; machine-like quality of, 53;
    reflections on paternity and, 44–45,
    67–70, 76–80; relationship between
    kin terms and, 45–46, 50–51, 55–58,
    76–77
birth announcements, 50–51
birth mothers, 50–51, 138

blindsight, 166
Bogus, Terry, 127
Borneman, John, 39, 81–82
Brian, 134–135

Cavell, Stanley, 19–20, 69
Center Kids symposium, 127–132
children: belonging and, 133–135,
    146–149; gay parents on desire for,
    4–8, 40–43, 129–130; inheritance
    of suffering and violence, 13–15,
    150–158; institutional maintenance
    of privacy around lives of, 125–127;
    milieu of, 145; reflections on impact
    of parental sexuality, 132–149,
    155–158; usage of kin terms by,
    82–89
Children of Lesbians and Gays Every-
    where (COLAGE), 132–133
choice: configured by biological
    kinship and gender, 68–70; role in
    queer kinship, 113–114, 127–132,
    143–144, 161, 164
citizenship: characterized by presence
    of public institutions in family life,
    11–12; role of familial kinship in,
    21–22, 43
civil unions, 9, 61
Claire, 141, 142, 144–146, 147
clinical discourse, 9–10
COLAGE. *See* Children of Lesbians and
    Gays Everywhere
commitment ceremonies, 8
Connolly, William, 166
consent: role in kinship, 115–116; role
    in paternal authority, 121–123
counterpublics, 135